International Humanitarian Law and Justice

In the last decade, there has been a turn to history in international humanitarian law and its accompanying fields. To examine this historization and to expand the current scope of scholarship, this book brings together scholars from various fields, including law, history, sociology, and international relations. Human rights law, international criminal law, and the law on the use of force are all explored across the text's four main themes: historiographies of selected fields of international law; evolution of specific international humanitarian law rules in the context of legal gaps and fault lines; emotions as a factor in international law; and how actors can influence history. This work will enhance and broaden readers' knowledge of the field and serve as an excellent starting point for further research.

Mats Deland is Associate Professor in history and temporary lecturer at Mittuniversitet, Sundsvall, Sweden. His publications include *Purgatorium* (vol. 1, 2010, vol. 2, 2017) and he has expertise in Holocaust studies and Genocide studies, Urban history, Right-Wing Extremism, and the History of International Law.

Dr. Mark Klamberg (Jur. Dr. Stockholm University, LL.M. Raoul Wallenberg Institute and Jur. Kand. Lund University) is Associate Professor in international law at Stockholm University. He is the author of several publications on international criminal law, surveillance, privacy, and other fields of international law, including *Evidence in International Criminal Trials: Confronting Legal Gaps and the Reconstruction of Disputed Events* (Martinus Nijhoff Publishers, 2013) and *Power and Law in the International Society – International Relations as the Sociology of International Law* (Routledge, 2015). He is the chief editor of the *Commentary on the Law of the ICC* (CLICC).

Pål Wrange (PhD, LL.M.) is Professor in public international law at Stockholm University and the Director of the Stockholm Center for International Law and Justice. He is a former principal legal advisor at the Swedish Ministry for Foreign Affairs. He has published widely on international law, international relations and theory, and he has worked and consulted for the European Union, governments, and NGOs. He is currently working on a book on non-state actors, right authority, and the right to use military violence.

International Humanitarian Law and Justice

Historical and Sociological Perspectives

Edited by Mats Deland, Mark Klamberg and Pål Wrange

Routledge
Taylor & Francis Group
LONDON AND NEW YORK

First published 2019 by Routledge

2 Park Square, Milton Park, Abingdon, Oxfordshire OX14 4RN
52 Vanderbilt Avenue, New York, NY 10017

Routledge is an imprint of the Taylor & Francis Group, an informa business

First issued in paperback 2020

British Library Cataloguing-in-Publication Data
A catalogue record for this book is available from the British Library

Library of Congress Cataloging-in-Publication Data
Names: Deland, Mats, editor. | Klamberg, Mark, editor. | Wrange, Pål, editor.
Title: International humanitarian law and justice: historical and sociological perspectives / Edited by Mats Deland, Mark Klamberg, and Pål Wrange.
Description: New York, NY: Routledge, 2019. |
Includes bibliographical references and index.
Identifiers: LCCN 2018024838 | ISBN 9781138477551 (hbk) | ISBN 9781351104432 (web pdf) | ISBN 9781351104425 (epub) | ISBN 9781351104418 (mobipocket)
Subjects: LCSH: Humanitarian law–History. | International law–Sociological aspects. | Sociological jurisprudence.
Classification: LCC KZ6471 .I585 2018 | DDC 341.6/7–dc2
LC record available at https://lccn.loc.gov/2018024838

ISBN: 978-1-138-47755-1 (hbk)
ISBN: 978-0-367-49856-6 (pbk)

Typeset in Galliard
by codeMantra

Contents

Contributors

Mats Deland is Associate Professor in history and temporary lecturer at Mittuniversitet, Sundsvall, Sweden. His publications include *Purgatorium* (vol. 1, 2010, vol. 2, 2017) and he has expertise in Holocaust studies and Genocide studies, Urban history, Right-Wing Extremism, and the History of International Law. Email: mats.deland@gmail.com

Anna Evangelidi is a PhD candidate and Graduate Teaching Assistant at The City Law School, City, University of London, United Kingdom. Email: anna.evangelidi.1@city.ac.uk

Alexandra Hofer is a PhD candidate in Public International Law at Ghent University. She has a Master's in International Relations, Peace, Conflict, and Security and a LL.M. in Public International Law from the Université libre de Bruxelles. Prior to joining Ghent in Summer 2015, Alexandra completed an internship within the Trial Division of the International Criminal Court. Email: alexandra.hofer@ugent.be

Dr. Mark Klamberg (Jur. Dr. Stockholm University, LL.M. Raoul Wallenberg Institute and Jur. Kand. Lund University) is Associate Professor in international law at Stockholm University. He is the author of several publications on international criminal law, surveillance, privacy, and other fields of international law, including *Evidence in International Criminal Trials: Confronting Legal Gaps and the Reconstruction of Disputed Events* (Martinus Nijhoff Publishers, 2013) and *Power and Law in the International Society – International Relations as the Sociology of International Law* (Routledge, 2015). He is the chief editor of the *Commentary on the Law of the ICC* (CLICC). Email: Mark.Klamberg@juridicum.su.se

Mark Lewis is an Associate Professor of European History at the College of Staten Island and at the Graduate Center (City University of New York). He received a BA from Stanford University and an MA and PhD from the University of California, Los Angeles. He is the co-author of *Himmler's Jewish Tailor: The Story of Holocaust Survivor Jacob Frank* (Syracuse University Press, 2000) and the author of *The Birth of the New Justice: The Internationalization of Crime and Punishment, 1919–1950* (Oxford University Press, 2014)

The latter won the Fraenkel Prize from the Wiener Library (2013) and the inaugural Bronisław Geremek Prize from the College of Europe and the Geremek Foundation (2015). Email: Mark.lewis@csi.cuny.edu

Mateusz Piątkowski is a PhD Candidate at the University of Lodz, Poland. Attorney at law in District Bar Association in Lodz, Poland. He is a Researcher in international humanitarian law and the law of aerial warfare. Email: piatkowskimat@gmail.com

Damien Rogers is Senior Lecturer at Massey University's Centre for Defence and Security Studies, New Zealand. Holding a PhD in Political Science and International Relations from the Australian National university and a PhD in Law from the University of Waikato, Rogers is author of two monographs: *Postinternationalism and Small Arms Control: Theory, Politics, Security* (Ashgate, Surry, 2009; and reproduced by Routledge, New York, 2016) and *Law, Politics and the Limits of Prosecuting Mass Atrocity* (Palgrave Macmillan, New York, 2017). Email: D.R.Rogers@massey.ac.nz

Daniel Marc Segesser is Director of undergraduate studies (Studienleiter) and Adjunct Professor (Privatdozent) at the Department of History of the University of Bern in Switzerland. His current research focuses on the history of international law in the period between 1872 and 1945 as well as on aspects of transnational, environmental, and global history of the First World War. His major publications are *Recht statt Rache oder Rache durch Recht: Kriegsverbrechen in der internationalen wissenschaftlichen Debatte 1872–1945* (Paderborn 2010), *Der Erste Weltkrieg in globaler Perspektive* (Wiesbaden 2010, 4th edition 2014) and *Empire und Totaler Krieg: Australien 1905–1918* (Paderborn 2002). Email: daniel.segesser@hist.unibe.ch

Sebastian M. Spitra holds degrees in law and philosophy from the University of Vienna. Currently, he is a research fellow at the Institute for legal and constitutional history at the Viennese law faculty. He teaches and conducts research in constitutional history, theory, and history of international law. Since 2016, he is a fellow of the Vienna Doctoral Academy and received a research scholarship of the Heinrich-Graf-Hardegg'sche Stiftung. In January and February 2018, he was granted a fellowship at the Max Planck Institute for Comparative Public Law and International Law. He is Grotius Fellow of the University of Michigan Law School 2018–2019. Email: sebastian.spitra@univie.ac.at

Rebecca Sutton is a PhD Candidate in the Department of Law at the London School of Economics (LSE) in the UK. Her doctoral research, which focuses on the civilian status of international humanitarian actors under International Humanitarian Law, is funded by scholarships from the Pierre Elliot Trudeau Foundation and the Social Science and Humanities Research Council of Canada (SSHRC). Rebecca is qualified as a Barrister and Solicitor, called to the Ontario Bar in Canada. She holds a Juris Doctor from the University of Toronto and an MSc in Violence, Conflict and Development from SOAS.

Rebecca previously worked in the humanitarian field, serving as Country Director for War Child Canada in Darfur, Sudan from 2009 to 2011. Her research has been published in the *National Journal of Constitutional Law*, *Criminal Law Quarterly*, *Citizenship Studies*, *Refuge*, and the *Canadian Graduate Journal of Sociology and Criminology*.

Nele Verlinden is a PhD fellow at the Leuven Centre for Global Governance Studies. Her research focuses on state support to parties to armed conflict and the consequences thereof under *jus in bello*, *jus ad bellum*, and neutrality law. Previously, Nele was a legal adviser in the arms unit of the International Committee of the Red Cross (ICRC), where her work mainly dealt with the Arms Trade Treaty. She also worked as a consultant for the customary law database of the ICRC and as a legal attaché in the ICRC's legal division. Nele obtained a Master of Laws degree from the KU Leuven in 2011 and an LL.M. in International Humanitarian Law and Human Rights Law from the Geneva Academy of International Humanitarian Law and Human Rights. She has been a visiting researcher at the Max Planck Institute for Comparative and Public International Law (Heidelberg), at the Grotius Centre for International Legal Studies (Leiden Law School) and within the Laureate Program on International Law at Melbourne Law School. Since October 2014, she is co-editor of the Digest of State Practice for the *Journal on the Use of Force and International Law*. Her research is supported by the Research Foundation Flanders (FWO). Email: nele.verlinden@kuleuven.be

Pål Wrange (PhD, LL.M.) is Professor of public international law at Stockholm University, the Director of the Stockholm Center for International Law and Justice and the Vice-Dean for Research Affairs. He is also a former principal legal advisor at the Swedish Ministry for Foreign Affairs. Professor Wrange has published widely on international law, international relations and theory, and he has worked and consulted for the European Union, governments, and NGOs. He is currently working on a book on non-state actors, right authority, and the right to use military violence. Email: Pal.Wrange@juridicum.su.se

Ka Lok Yip holds a PhD in international law, summa cum laude, from the Graduate Institute of International and Development Studies, Geneva, Switzerland. Email: kalok.yip@gmail.com

Introduction

Mats Deland, Mark Klamberg, and Pål Wrange

This volume has its origins in a conference held in Uppsala, Sweden, in October 2016.[1] About 80 scholars from four continents came together to discuss a subject that has attracted increasing interest during the last few years – the history of international law and justice. Although we are still far from an institutionalized cooperation over the faculty limits, what the Swiss historian Daniel Segesser calls *integrale Rechtsgeschichte*, scholars from both "camps" do meet from time to time in what may be a common field.

The three conference conveners, two from a law faculty and one historian, approached the project with different kinds of experiences. Mark Klamberg has analysed procedural questions of evidence in international courts and how international law and its institutions influence international trade, environmental protection, human rights, international criminal justice and the use of force.[2] Pål Wrange has among other things, in his dissertation, done a comprehensive investigation of the legal concept of neutrality with the help of Reinhart Koselleck's method of conceptual history.[3] Mats Deland has investigated Sweden's war crimes policy after the Second World War.[4] These subjects are all connected to the broadened interest in international law, and particularly the laws of war that started in the 1990s and developed through the 2000s.

While international lawyers have always had a professional interest in the history of their discipline, few scholars have been devoted to the topic. Wilhelm Grewe's monumental *Epochen der Völkerrechtsgeschichte* from 1984, translated into English in 2004, was one of few exceptions, as was, Stephen Neff, who has pursued a consistent interest in the history of the law of war since the 1980s. A sign of the growing interest was the founding of the *Journal of the History*

1 The conference, "Historicising International Law – Could we? Should we?" was held October 6–8, 2016 at the Uppsala university. It was convened by the Hugo Valentin Center, Department of History, Uppsala University and the Stockholm Center for International Law and Justice, Stockholm University. The conference was partly financed by a grant from the Swedish Research Council.

2 Klamberg, 2013; 2015.

3 Wrange, 2007.

4 Deland, 2012.

of International Law in 1999, but the singularly most influential event was the publication of Martti Koskenniemi's the *Gentle Civilizer of Nations* in 2002.

Three years later, Tony Anghie's *Imperialism, sovereignty, and the making of international* law was published, as a signpost of a post-colonial turn in the field, and critique of Eurocentrism has been one of the long-term results of the "historical turn" within the study of international law. In their introduction to the *Oxford handbook of the history of international law*, Bardo Fassbender and Anne Peters emphasize that they want to change the direction of how this history is written by avoiding the previous Eurocentrist bias.

However, at the same time, Fassbender and Peters stay within a largely developmentalist frame by "focusing on… a 'living bond' between the past and the present."[5] There is a lot that speaks for such an approach. It is an empirical fact that the extent of international law has increased both in volume and spatial coverage over the years and that certain ways of legal understanding, with their origin in Europe, have been privileged in a nearly universalizing way. Although legal concepts have changed meaning over the years in a way that makes it difficult to say that it is the "same" laws that have persisted, and although contributions from other parts than Europa have been unacknowledged and partly still remain to be discovered by research, and furthermore that abandoned or scrapped parts of law are just as important to understand what was happening and what has happened since, there still remains a temptation to see the contemporary law as a result of history in a way that suggests an (evolutionary) direction or a (teleological) meaning – or both. This may be a factor that makes the history of law harder to write than histories of other subjects. Laws can be changed or even abandoned, but law itself remains and holds its grip in a more tangible way than most other objects. The fact that lawyers have a habit – or a duty – of using history in their daily practice, to understand, interpret and adjudicate according to existing laws, further adds to this difficulty.

But maybe an even bigger problem is on the side of the historians. Few historians have taken a full lawyer's education, including court service. This is not only an issue of competence. While research training is largely the same within most fields, and differs mainly by the methods employed, legal training also contains an ethical component that can be compared with what is an important part of medical and psychological education. Like a doctor, a lawyer generally learns to believe in her trade. A historian is also the subject of ethical commitments, but not in the same way. Without a full training in law, she will write history of law in a different way than the lawyer. She will probably see other things, important things, but she will not understand law in the same way.

There is also an objective side to this. Mirjan R. Damaška points out, in a discussion of the role of international courts, that the legal concept of truth is narrower than the truth that results from a historical study. While the aim of a court is to individualize guilt and to present facts that help in reaching a verdict,

5 Fassbender and Peters, 2012, p. 2.

the scope of relevant facts is much broader in a historical study, which may result in a more nuanced and equivocal view of what took place.[6] That is why there basically exist two sorts of history of law – the one written at the law faculty, and the one written in the faculty of the humanities. For the time being, the best we can do is to bring them together to dialogue and to share experiences. That was the aim of our conference.

In the organizing of the conference, we made a conscious effort to broaden the participation beyond the usual Anglo-Saxon realm. For instance, Emiliano Buis of the university of Buenos Aires took it upon himself to organize one of our seminars (on law and emotions) while we also had papers on subjects as diverse the contribution of the Maya native Americans to international law in the 16th century and recent attempts to create an equivalent to the Responsibility to Protect doctrine for countries that are haunted by recurrent (and partly climate-induced) natural disasters. This diversity is not fully reflected in this book.

The conference made it clear that there are very different conceptions of what history is. In relation to law, the important thing is that law is contextualized, with the help of other theories or other kinds of analytical tools, rather than just chronologized. We changed the title of the book accordingly, and our experience is also that the history of law is best served with a living dialogue not only between historians and lawyers but also with colleagues from political science, economics, sociology and other disciplines, and we believe that the sample of articles included here shows that this is the case.

The book is not about international law in general, but about the laws of war or, as it has often been called since the 1970s, international humanitarian law (IHL). It soon become apparent for us when editing the volume that this concept was too narrow. We added the word "justice" to account for research that addresses legal practice rather than the actual drafting and interpretation of law.

The laws of war is perhaps the most well-researched subfield in the history of international law, and perhaps also the most politicized. It could be argued that it was pioneered already in the 1860s, with the investigation of predecessors to the ideas contained in the first Geneva Convention, commissioned by the Prussian foreign office.[7] In the following decades, juridical treatises and proposals for amendments of the first codifications were often followed by some kind of historical enquiry.[8] The first, and still impressing standard work from a historian – the English 19th-century specialist Geoffrey Best – was however not published until 1980. Explicitly referring to the philosopher Michael Walzer's *Just and unjust wars* (1977) as the kind of book he had *not* been trying to write, the book nonetheless was read as a part of the increased interest in IHL after the Vietnam War (and the additional protocols of the Geneva conventions in 1977).[9] That interest was further spurred in the 1990s, after the war in Yugoslavia and

6 Damaška, 2008, p. 338, cf the discussion in Klamberg, 2013, p. 500.

7 Final version: Gurlt, 1873. Gurlt was a medical doctor.

8 Cf e g Lueder, 1876.

9 Best, 1980; 1994.

genocides in Rwanda and Srebrenica. Legal scholars Ingrid Detter, Theodor Meron and William A. Schabas and many others have provided important works where existing law is presented against a historical background.[10] On their part, historians such as Alex Gillespie, Karma Nabulsi and James Q. Whitman have done their best to narrow the distance to the legal expertise and deepen our understanding.[11] The literature is now vast, particularly on the legal side. What is still largely missing, but slowly developing, is the interdisciplinary dialogue that is the subject of this collection.

The ways in which international humanitarian law can be told are basically the same as for international law generally: it can be told as a story of doctrines, or with the focus on either the persons or the social context that they are involved in or how it is understood or used or changed at any period of time. Another way to understand this is to speak about its internal and its external development, where internal development has its focus on traits that are inherent to legal doctrine while external is a common name for all other influences. It goes without saying that a study can be a combination between any of these approaches and that the distinctions between them are analytical rather than real. At the same time, however, it is in these distinctions that the interesting developments take place, for instance, when a historian goes into a detailed discussion of legal doctrine or a lawyer tries to understand the personal circumstances behind legal institutional developments.[12]

This book is divided into four themes that will discuss different aspects of how law and justice relate to society and its history.

In the introduction to the first part, "Historiographies," Wrange discusses the importance and value of historicizing international law in general. The historization of international law may contextualise legal ideologies and concepts, get it out of Eurocentrism and contribute to a "social history of international law." This first part contains texts on international criminal law as part of the modernist project (Rogers), the colonial roots of the international rules for the protection of cultural heritage (Spitra), how the police organization of the Austro-Hungarian empire became the blueprint for the cooperation of the European police forces after the First world war, and for the dissemination of information and cooperation with the military (Lewis), and if *jus in bello* in non-international armed conflict may undermine the rules on jus ad bellum (Wrange).

The second part is called "Navigating through legal gaps and fault lines" and concerns specific rules and concepts in the IHL field. The introduction presents different ways of theorizing, observing and analysing changes in IHL. This includes internal and external modes of theorizing, the tension between structure and agency, theories of evolution and how change can be understood in the context of legal gaps and fault lines. This part contains three texts: how

10 Detter, 1987; Meron, 1998; Schabas, 2000; 2012.

11 Gillespie, 2011; Nabulsi, 1999; Whitman, 2012.

12 For instance, Segesser, 2010; Koskenniemi, 2010.

international actors struggle over the principle of distinction (Sutton), restraint *in bello* (Evangelidi) and aerial operations in the beginning of the Second World War (Piatkowski).

The third part "Emotions and identities as factors in international law" is introduced by Deland who argues that the issue of law and emotions is basically a way to acknowledge the limits of analytical abstractions and rational choice models. This part contains three texts examining different aspects of the relation between emotions and the law, including propaganda, deactivation of emotions among soldiers and emotional stress among civilians in war zones (Verlinden), how the influence of cognitive structures and agency on the use of force influences the design of regulations for the conduct of armed hostilities (Lok Yip) and the influence of hostile national identities on the understanding and practice of IHL rules (Hofer).

The fourth and last part, "How personalities can influence history," sets out to describe the difference between how legal historians approach general history compared to how general historians take account of legal history. It reconnects to the structure versus agency debate in acknowledging that while legal history as an academic discipline initially had a structural focus, general history was well into the 20th century more focused on individual (male) actors. The two fields have during the 20th century moved closer to each other, open to take into account agency as well as structure. The section contains one text about how the international lawyer Raphaël Lemkin tried to connect the protection of ethnic minorities with the protection of their cultural heritage in the process leading up to the Genocide convention (Klamberg); how the chair of the ICRC Gustave Moynier presented the first and ultimately aborted proposal for an international criminal court in the aftermath of the French-German war 1870–1871 (Segesser); and how the Swedish branch of the Red Cross movement was created as part of a feminist campaign for equal access to higher education (Deland).

***

The conference was organized mainly by Mats Deland. The book has been edited by the three editors jointly, but Mats had the main responsibility and carried the heaviest burden.

The editors wish to thank Stiftelsen Juridisk Fakultetslitteratur for its crucial support for the editing. We also want to thank the Swedish Research Council, for its contribution to the financing of the conference.

It has been a pleasure to work with Chloe James at Routledge.

Mats Deland Mark Klamberg Pål Wrange

References

Antony Anghie, *Imperialism, Sovereignty, and the Making of International*, Cambridge University Press, Cambridge, 2005.

Geoffrey Best, *Humanity in Warfare. The Modern History of the International Law of Armed Conflicts*, Weidenfeld & Nicolson, London, 1980.

Geoffrey Best, *War & Law since 1945*, Clarendon Press, London, 1994.

Mirjan R. Damaška, "What is the Point of International Criminal Justice?", *Chicago-Kent Law Review*, vol. 83, no. 1, 2008, pp. 329–365.

Mats Deland, "Ausgebliebene Bestrafung: Schwedens Untätigkeit gegenüber den baltischen Kriegsverbrechern", in Sebastian Lehmann, Robert Bohn and Uwe Danker (Eds.), *Reichskommissariat Ostland: Tatort und Erinnerungsobjekt*, Ferdinand Schöningh Verlag, Paderborn, 2012, pp. 251–268.

Ingrid Detter, *The Law of War*, Cambridge University Press, Cambridge, 1987.

Bardo Fassbender and Anne Peters, "Introduction: Towards a Global History of International Law", in Bardo Fassbender and Anne Peters (Eds.), *The Oxford Handbook of the History of International Law*, Oxford University Press, Oxford, 2012, pp. 1–24.

Alex Gillespie, *A History of the Laws of War, Vols 1–3*, Harts Publishing, Haywarts Heath, 2011.

Wilhelm G. Grewe, *Epochen der Völkerrechtsgeschichte*, Nomos, Baden-Baden, 1984.

Ernst Julius Gurlt, *Zur Geschichte der internationalen und freiwilligen Krankenpflege im Kriege*, Verlag F. C. W. Vogel, Leipzig, 1873.

Mark Klamberg, *Evidence in International Criminal Trials. Confronting Legal Gaps and the Reconstruction of Disputed Events*, Brill, Leiden, 2013.

Mark Klamberg, *Power and Law in International Society. International Relations as the Sociology of International Law*, Routledge, London, 2015.

Martti Koskenniemi, *The Gentle Civilizer of Nations. The Rise and Fall of International Law 1870–1960*, Cambridge University Press, Cambridge, 2010.

Carl Lueder, *Die Genfer Convention; historisch und kritisch-dogmatisch mit Vorschlägen zu ihrer Verbesserung, unter Darlegung und Prüfung der mit ihr gemachten Erfahrungen und unter Benutzung der amtlichen, theilweise ungedruckten Quellen bearb.*, Besold, Erlangen, 1876.

Theodor Meron, *War Crimes Law Comes of Age: Essays*, Oxford University Press, Oxford, 1998.

Karma Nabulsi, *Traditions of War. Occupation, Resistance and the Law*, Oxford University Press, Oxford, 1999.

Daniel Marc Segesser, *Recht statt Rache oder Rache durch Recht? Die Ahndung von Kriegsverbrechen in der internationalen fachwissenschaftlichen Debatte 1872–1945*, Ferdinand Schöningh, Paderborn, 2010.

William A. Schabas, *Genocide in International Law. The Crime of Crimes*, Cambridge University Press, Cambridge, 2000.

William A. Schabas, *Unimaginable Atrocities. Justice, Politics, and Rights at the War Crimes Tribunals*, Oxford University Press, Oxford, 2012.

James Q. Whitman, *The Verdict of Battle: The Law of Victory in the Making of Modern War*, Harvard University Press, Cambridge, MA, 2012.

Pål Wrange, *Impartial or Uninvolved? The Anatomy of 20th Century Doctrine on the Law of Neutrality*, Department of Law, Stockholm University, 2007.

Part I

1 Introduction

Historicizing international humanitarian law[1]

Pål Wrange

> There is no set of maxims more important for an historian than this: that the actual causes of a thing's origin and its eventual uses, the manner of its incorporation into a system of purposes, are worlds apart; that everything that exists, no matter what its origin, is periodically reinterpreted by those in power in terms of fresh intentions; that all processes in the organic world are processes of outstripping and overcoming, and that, in turn, all outstripping and overcoming means reinterpretation, rearrangement, in the course of which the earlier meaning and purpose are necessarily either obscured or lost.[2]
>
> Friedrich Nietzsche

1.1 Introduction

In 2005, the International Committee of the Red Cross (ICRC) published its monumental study "Customary International Humanitarian Law." In three volumes of over 5,000 pages, 161 rules are derived and explained.[3] In 2015, the US Department of Defense published another monumental work, a "Law of War Manual," comprising some 1,200 pages of rules. By looking at the covers and perusing the tables of contents of these two works, one notices that they to a large extent cover the same types of rules but do so under different names – "international humanitarian law" versus "the law of war." One further notices that the law of war manual refers to both the just war tradition and chivalry, as well as provides mini-histories of a number of rules – on 14 occasions going back as far as antiquity. By contrast, while the ICRC volume briefly acknowledges the

1 I would like to thank participants at the Stockholm Centre for International Law and Justice Thursday brown bag lunch seminars (Mats Deland, Nikola Hajdin, Mark Klamberg, Said Mahmoudi, and Martin Ratcovich) for their helpful comments. Mistakes are mine. This chapter builds partly on Chapter 2 in my *Impartial or Uninvolved? The Anatomy of 20th Century Doctrine on the Law of Neutrality,* Dokumaten, Visby, 2007.

2 Nietzsche, 1956, p. 209. The quotation continues thus, "No matter how well we understand the utility of a certain physiological organ (or of a legal institution, a custom, a political convention, an artistic genre, a cultic trait) we do not thereby understand anything of its origin. I realize that this truth must distress the traditionalist, for, from time immemorial, the demonstrable purpose of a thing has been considered its *causa fiendi* – the eye is made for seeing, the hand for grasping."

3 Henckaerts and Doswald-Beck, 2005.

old customary practices, it was "Henry Dunant who was the true pioneer of contemporary international humanitarian law" and its "driving force" has been the ICRC.[4] These seemingly superficial linguistic and historiographical differences are not only interesting but also of legal and political significance.[5] The histories of a legal regime help determine the pedigree, the identity, and the content of its norms.

1.2 Why history of international (humanitarian) law?

Historiography has some general benefits: For instance, it can point out that both the world and our perceptions of it are contingent: What was once different from now can again be different.

But there are also specific gains to be made. The most obvious interest for a lawyer is to understand and assess concrete arguments about what the law is. As David Kennedy notes,

> an argument about a rule or principle … is almost always an argument about history – that the particular norm proffered has a provenance as law rather than politics, has become general rather than specific, has come through history to stand outside history.[6]

In legal argument, the use of history is determined by legal doctrines: doctrines of sources (which ones count?) and doctrines of interpretation (the original intention, subsequent practice, the textual context, etc.). If meaning is dependent upon the intention of the author (the judge, the legislator, the commentator) or on what the recipient thought, we want to know who the relevant author or recipient was. So doctrine and history collude to assign authority, to determine whose meaning of the law it is that governs us, here and now.[7]

International law as we know it cannot be thought of without history: In fact, "international law is … a field of practice whose meaning and significance is constantly organised around, and through the medium of, a discourse that links present to past."[8] As Craven says, it was after "… the turn to history at the end of the 18th Century" that "international law was to acquire its specifiable and discrete (disciplinary) content through the articulation of historical accounts of its emergence."[9]

4 Henckaerts and Doswald-Beck, 2005, vol. I, pp. xv, xxxi, xxxi. See also ICRC, 2010: "Efforts to regulate warfare … [in] history … remained temporary, local arrangements, until the middle of the 19th century when the newly created ICRC encouraged the adoption of the first Geneva Convention."

5 Alexander, 2015.

6 Kennedy, 1999. See also Skouteris, 2017, p. 1.

7 This follows from many textbooks on law. For the purpose of this debate, it has been developed in Orford, 2013, pp. 171–174. For a more general but still very pertinent discussion, see Walker, 2015, p. 152.

8 Craven, 2016, p. 34.

9 Craven, 2016, p. 32.

While law is indeterminate in the sense that one cannot settle the outcome of a legal argument by logic, it is not the case that anything can happen in real life. Regimes of legal argument constrain the way an issue is talked about and law takes place in a discursive community.[10] A historical review can explain how these regimes have developed and how that community has been created.

As identified by Koskenniemi, at least three types of critical research questions pertaining to history can be identified. First, "to contextualise the legal ideologies or concepts within the intellectual, social, and political environment in which they have operated." Second, to get out of Eurocentrism by providing stories about the influence of people from and events in other parts of the world and third to write a "social history of international law," like studies of the relation between normative systems and "types of international society" or "macro-level economic and social developments."[11]

This leads us to wider sets of questions about the procedural and substantive legitimacy of the law.[12] Has it come about in a fair manner? Whose interests has it served?[13] And such questions can lead to policy questions like the ones that Tony Anghie asks, namely if "the postcolonial world [can] deploy for its own purposes the law which had enabled its suppressions in the first place?"[14] Or, in slightly more optimistic terms, how to rethink "current strategies directed at harnessing the political potential of international law."[15]

To sum up, I quote Allot's magnificent opening essay in the first issue of the *Journal of the History of International Law*:

> The writing of the intrinsic history of international law – the history of the law itself – will re-form our consciousness of the identity, the functioning, and the potentiality of international law as law. The writing of the extrinsic history of international law – its relationship to the history of other social phenomena – will reform our consciousness of the role of international law in the forming, re-forming, and re-making of international society. In particular, it will re-make international law's idea-of-itself...[16]

1.3 Contextualization in history

How, then, should historical research be carried out? Lesaffer complains that to many writers, "[t]he past is only the mine where facts and figures are to be

10 Cf. Kratochwil, 1989, p. 132 and MacIntyre, 1984, p. 10.

11 Koskenniemi, 2004. For a critique of how historiography is actually carried out at present – not entirely in line with the program set out in the body text – see Katz Cogan, 2014, p. 375.

12 Skouteris notes the "significance of the field's historical consciousness for its legitimacy." Skouteris, 2017.

13 Cf. Kingsbury and Straumann, 2010, p. 51.

14 Anghie, 2005, p. 8.

15 Pahuja, 2011, p. 5.

16 Allott, 1999, p. 20.

found to sustain and corroborate existing theories."[17] Much of this debate has centered around concerns brought to the fore by the so-called Cambridge school of intellectual history, which has attacked, *inter alia*, anachronism, prolapses (reading a future meaning into a word or a text), and teleology (the assumption that there is a meaning to history).[18] Their standard call has been for contextualizing: "to understand texts for the specific speech acts that they are, we need to understand the historical context in which they were uttered."[19]

This is not a straightforward matter, however. As Brett notes, it is important to keep in mind that "there may be plural contexts for any one text, and these contexts may themselves overlap or be related in certain ways."[20] "'[C]ontext' can be multidimensional: a specific political situation, a social or cultural milieu, an institutional context like a courtroom ... what other people were saying at the time and the conventions governing that saying."[21] Lawyers would point out that legal and other arguments made by governments have to be explained (also) in terms of the prevailing legal views at the time, so a treaty has to be assessed and understood in the context of its contemporary legal universe.[22]

Furthermore, whatever context one considers, the question what a statement means is crucial. "Meaning" can be taken as either the "objective" meaning, what the words say, or the "subjective" meaning, what the author really meant, and neither is a simple matter. Pocock says, "What we have called paradigms are linguistic constructs recognized as carrying increasingly complex loads of biases, but at the same time carrying loads in excess of what can be predicted or controlled at a given moment."[23] Consequently, "what evokes a certain cluster of factual assertions, and value judgments concerning them, to one set of hearers will simultaneously evoke another cluster and recommend another resolution of conduct in the ears of another set."[24] So, there are meanings that are beyond the control of the author or the grasp of the reader.

17 Lesaffer, 2007, p. 35. See also Kennedy, 1999, p. 89. Even dedicated historical research by trained international lawyers has been criticized along these lines: Hunter, 2013. For a discussion of this critique, see Orford, 2015.

18 Bourke, 2016, p. 1. See also the seminal Skinner, 1969.

19 Brett, 2002, p. 116.

20 Brett, 2002, p. 123.

21 Brett, 2002, p. 116.

22 As Tony Carty (2012) says,

> It is impossible not only to interpret state practice but even to determine what is relevant state practice and how it forms, or does not form, international law, without a prior decision about what is international law, and such answers cannot be provided by states. ... It is therefore difficult – I would say impossible – to write a history of international law in all its aspects without including doctrine, or, in other terms, the internal perspective.
>
> (p. 973)

23 Pocock, 1971, p. 287.

24 Pocock, 1971, p. 17.

At any rate, it seems to be the contemporaneous conditions of meaning which are the object of Pocock's analysis.[25] Nevertheless, total contextualization is impossible because that would presuppose that we can understand the past as the people of those days did.[26] And that is impossible because even if we could reconstruct the discursive universe of, say, Grotius, we could never eradicate our own. That is, we would have to forget a good deal of what we now know, and Grotius did not know. And if we could do that, how would we then communicate our findings to present readers, who have not gone through the same process? Therefore, any historiography must be treated as an act of intervention rather than one of discovery.[27]

1.4 Approaches to the history of international (humanitarian) law

International law scholars who engage in serious work in legal history generally recognize that contextualization is necessary.[28] But they also recognize that this need is determined by "the chosen approach and the historical problem to be solved."[29] As Orford points out, "a legal reading differs from a historical reading, in that it is not concerned with the past as history but with the past as law."[30] As already mentioned, the international lawyer's historical interest is usually based on a concern for the present and the future rather than the past as such. In other words, it is about what has been passed down rather than about presenting the past "as it really was." But because of the great legitimacy of that "passed down," there is struggle over what it is. "The past, far from being gone, is constantly being retrieved as a source or rationalisation of present obligation,"[31] and must therefore be subjected to critical assessments.

For an "internal" history of international law, a number of approaches are possible in addition to those of the Cambridge school.[32] In my own work, I have used conceptual history, as developed by Reinhart Koselleck. I wanted to know the role of concepts, such as neutrality, sovereignty, international, war, peace – how they affect one another, how they have been talked about, and how they function in international legal discourse.[33] Moreover, I have tried to describe the discursive production of concepts in texts. By "describe," I mean

25 Cf. "[T]here must be reasons of a contemporary nature that render it plausible that their thought should have been so conditioned." Pocock, 1971, p. 33. Cf. also Binder and Weisberg, 2000, p. 359.

26 This discussion owes a bit to the Harlan-Hollinger debate, in Harlan, 1989, p. 581 and in Hollinger, 1989, p. 610.

27 I have borrowed and extended the scope of these words from Craven, p. 34.

28 Peters and Fassbender, 2012, p. 13.

29 Peters and Fassbender, 2012, p. 1.

30 Orford, 2013, p. 177.

31 Orford, 2013, p. 175

32 See also Peters and Fassbender, 2012, p. 13.

33 See, for instance, Koselleck, 1985. For a very interesting discussion on historical and philosophical analyses of concepts, see Bartelson, 2007.

not merely to show how it has happened but, to quote Foucault, one could also "seek the immediate reason for them … in the discursive system and in the possibilities or impossibilities of utterance which it provides."[34] Another useful approach, in particular to enrich the Cambridge approach, is to use reception history (*Rezeptionsgeschichte*), pioneered by German scholar Hans Robert Jauss. Yet another approach, suggested by David D'Avray, is to use Niklas Luhmann's system theory, to describe the relation between various systems of thought.[35] One could also eschew monolithic rigor and engage in thick description or – conversely – try to find historic causation between the law and the world. Or perhaps one would like to do both and then add some or all of the other approaches mentioned, and more, all the time admitting that the most interesting facts are often the ones that are the least possible to prove.

In this chapter, Sebastian Spitra discusses different historiographies of the protection of cultural heritage, which provides quite different perspectives and delimitations of this body of law, and finds that most or all of them contain important silences, or gaps, which inhibit a broader understanding of the legal treatment of such property. Damian Rogers analyses some crucial instances of the rise of international criminal law from propitious politico-strategic circumstances in the deeper and more profound context of the politico-cultural project of modernity. Mark Lewis writes a fascinating pre-history of current international police cooperation, showing the growth of an administrative practice of trans-border cooperation during the First World War in that very place that shortly thereafter came to be the home of what is now Interpol. In my own text, I trace different understandings of the issue of so-called combatant privilege (to kill in war) for non-state actors and I find that a conditional combatant privilege has been introduced through humanitarian and international criminal justice discourses. These four pieces display different approaches to the history of international law but they all contribute to a deeper and more critical understanding of their subject matters.

References

Amanda Alexander, "A Short History of International Humanitarian Law", *European Journal of International Law*, vol. 26, no. 1, 2015, pp. 109–138.

Philip Allott, "International Law and the Idea of History", *Journal of the History of International Law*, vol. 1, no. 1, 1999, pp. 1–21.

Antony Anghie, *Sovereignty, Imperialism and the Making of International Law*, Cambridge University Press, Cambridge, 2005.

Jens Bartelson, "Philosophy and History in the Study of Political Thought", *Journal of the Philosophy of History*, vol. 1, no 1, 2007, pp. 101–124.

Guyora Binder and Robert Weisberg, *Literary Criticisms of Law*, Princeton University Press, Princeton, NJ, 2000.

34 Foucault, 1972.

35 International lawyers may be more familiar with Luhmann's followers, Günther Teubner and Andreas Fischer-Lescano.

Richard Bourke, "The Cambridge School", paper, Queen Mary University [2016], available at: www.qmul.ac.uk/history/media/ph/news/The-Cambridge-School.pdf (accessed 15 January 2018).

Annabel Brett, "What is Intellectual History Now?", in David Cannadine (Ed.), *What is History Now?*, Palgrave Macmillan, London, 2002, pp. 113–131.

Carty, "Doctrine Versus State Practice", in Fassbender, B., Peters, A., Peter, S., and Högger, D. (Eds.), *The Oxford Handbook of the History of International Law*, Oxford University Press, Oxford, 2012.

Anthony Carty, "Doctrine versus State Practice", Bardo Fassbender and Anne Peters (Eds.), *The Oxford Handbook of the History of International Law*, Oxford University Press, Oxford, 2012, pp. 972–996.

Matt Craven, "Theorising the Turn to History in International Law", in Anne Orford and Florian Hoffman (Eds.), *The Oxford Handbook of the Theory of International Law. Oxford University Press*, Oxford University Press, Oxford, 2016, pp. 21–37.

Bardo Fassbender and Anne Peters, "Introduction: Towards a Global History of International Law", in Bardo Fassbender and Anne Peters (Eds.), *The Oxford Handbook of the History of International Law*, Oxford University Press, Oxford, 2012.

Michel Foucault, *The archaeology of knowledge* (A. M. Sheridan Smith, transl.), Pantheon Books, New York, 1972.

David Harlan, "Intellectual History and the Return of Literature", *The American Historical Review*, vol. 94, no. 3, 1989, pp. 581–609.

David Harlan, "Reply to David Hollinger", *The American Historical Review*, vol. 94, no. 3, 1989, pp. 622–626.

Jean-Marie Henckaerts and Louise Doswald-Beck, *Customary International Humanitarian Law*, vols. 1 & 2, Cambridge University Press, Cambridge, 2005.

David Hollinger, "The Return of the Prodigal: The Persistence of Historical Knowing", *The American Historical Review*, vol. 94, no. 3, 1989, pp. 610–621.

Ian Hunter, "The Figure of Man and the Territorialisation of Justice in 'Enlightenment' Natural Law: Pufendorf and Vattel", *Intellectual History Review*, vol. 23, no. 3, 2013, pp. 289–307.

ICRC, "Development of modern international humanitarian law", 2010, available at: www.icrc.org/eng/who-we-are/history/since-1945/history-ihl/overview-development-modern-international-humanitarian-law.htm (accessed 15 April 2018).

Jacob Katz Cogan, "Review of Bardo Fassbender and Anne Peters eds., The Oxford Handbook of the History of International Law", *American Journal of International Law*, vol. 108, 2014, p. 371.

David Kennedy, "The Disciplines of International Law and Policy", *Leiden Journal of International Law*, vol. 12, no. 1, 1999, pp. 9–133.

Benedict Kingsbury and Benjamin Straumann, "State of Nature versus Commercial Sociability as the Basis of International Law: Reflections on the Roman Foundations and Current Interpretations of the International Political and Legal Thought of Grotius, Hobbes and Pufendorf", in Samantha Besson and John Tasioulas (Eds.), *The Philosophy of International Law*, Oxford University Press, Oxford, 2010, pp. 33–52.

Reinhart Koselleck, *Futures Past: On the Semantics of Historical Time* (Keith Tribe transl.), MIT Press, Cambridge, MA, 1985.

Martti Koskenniemi, "The History of International Law Today", *Rechtsgeschichte*, vol. 4, 2004, pp. 61–66.

Friedrich V. Kratochwil, *Rules, Norms, and Decision: On the Conditions of Practical and Legal Reasoning in International Relations and Domestic Affairs*, Cambridge University Press, Cambridge, 1989.

Randal Lesaffer, "International Law and its History: The Story of an Unrequited Love", in Matthew Craven, Malgosia Fitzmaurice and Maria Vogiatzi (Eds.), *Time, History and International Law*, Martinus Nijhoff, Leiden, 2007, pp. 27–42.

Alisdair MacIntyre, *After Virtue: A Study in Moral Theory* (2nd ed.), University of Notre Dame Press, Notre Dame, OK, 1984.

Friedrich Nietzsche, *The Genealogy of Morals 1887* (Francis Golffing, transl.), Doubleday Press, New York, 1956.

Anne Orford, "International Law and the Limits of History", in Wouter Werner, Marieke de Hoon and Alexis Galán (Eds.), *The Law of International Lawyers: Reading Martti Koskenniemi*, Cambridge University Press, Cambridge, 2015, pp. 297–320.

Anne Orford, "On International Legal Method", *London Review of International Law*, vol. 1, no. 1, 2013, pp. 166–197.

Sundhya Pahuja, *Decolonising International Law: Development, Economic Growth and the Politics of Universality*, Cambridge University Press, Cambridge, 2011.

John Greville Agard Pocock, *Politics, Language, and Time: Essays on Political Thought and History*, University of Chicago Press, Chicago, IL, 1971.

Quentin Skinner, "Meaning and Understanding", *History and Theory*, vol. 8, no. 1, 1969, pp. 3–53.

Thomas Skouteris, "The Turn to History in International Law", Oxford Bibliographies, 2017, DOI: 10.1093/OBO/9780199796953-0154 (accessed 19 April 2018).

Neil Walker, *Intimations of Global Law*, Cambridge University Press, Cambridge, 2015.

Pål Wrange, *Impartial or Uninvolved? The Anatomy of 20th Century Doctrine on the Law of Neutrality*, Dokumaten, Visby, 2007.

2 Historicising international criminal trials within the modernist project

Damien Rogers

2.1 Introduction

Much of the legal scholarship concerned with international criminal law (ICL) – an evolving body of rules which prohibits the commission of war crimes, crimes against humanity and crimes of genocide as well as crimes against peace and, more recently, crimes of aggression – examines major institutions applying those rules to particular cases. Academic textbooks produced by highly reputable publishing presses focus on "the crimes that are dealt with by international courts and tribunals as well as the procedures that police the investigation and prosecution of these crimes."[1] Efforts are made to offer "a coherent theoretical framework to the patchwork of disparate rules, principles, concepts, and legal constructs that at present make up international criminal law."[2] While such textbooks include cursory descriptions of the establishment of various ICL institutions, few mainstream accounts appear genuinely concerned with the complex circumstances giving rise to international criminal trials. Critical scholarship does, however, take these circumstances seriously by recognising that, despite "a surge in scholarship of ICL, in institutions, and in the public debate, [...] the structures constructing international criminal law remain largely unchecked and unquestioned."[3]

Taking its cue from mainstream accounts and critical scholarship, this chapter argues that propitious politico-strategic circumstances are necessary but, on their own, insufficient factors to fully explain the rise of the International Military Tribunal (IMT) for the Trial of German War Criminals, the International Military Tribunal for the Far East (IMTFE), the International Criminal Tribunal for the former Yugoslavia (ICTY), the International Criminal Tribunal for Rwanda (ICTR) and the International Criminal Court (ICC). It begins by illuminating the relationship between shifting politico-strategic circumstances and the design of those institutions before signalling the important politico-economic dimension of international criminal trials. This chapter then

1 Cryer et al., 2011, back flap.
2 Cassese, 2008, p. xiii.
3 Schwöbel, 2014, p. 2.

goes further, highlighting a politico-cultural dimension by situating those trials in the deeper and more profound context of modernity. By modernity, I mean the politico-cultural project which, emerging from 17th-century Europe, currently prevails in contemporary world affairs.[4] As a project, modernity is engaged in "deep" global politics through which humans control life on this planet and includes specific sub-cultures with potential to generate civilisations of global proportions. As humans seek to obtain power over others to have their specific conception of culture prevail not only do they illuminate the context for modernist world affairs but they also constitute the dynamics of world affairs itself.[5] Notwithstanding many ambiguities surrounding the concept of modernity, there is an underlying consensus that rests upon a shared assumption concerning the role of rationalism in the development and spread of new ways of thinking about nature and human society.[6]

The cultural-wide commitment to rationalism is evident in this chapter's critique. Rather than offering constructive criticism helping ensure ICL's smoother enforcement, this critique reveals that international criminal trials are never detached from underlying configurations of material and ideational power.[7] In so doing, this chapter forms part of a broader episteme and shares the rationalising habits of the modernist mind that are also subjected here to criticism. Yet, this highly rationalist epistemological approach, in which international criminal trials and the attendant scholarship are reified through distal cogitation, is also a limited way of knowing. These limitations warrant acknowledgement because, even though objectifying world affairs through the rational gaze reflects and re-inscribes our Enlightenment heritage, the light of the mind that illuminates those world affairs can also blind us to what occurs, curtailing what we might know.[8] A rationalist epistemology cannot, for example, help scholars to feel, to understand and then to explain what it is like to be a victim of serious international crime, to be on trial as an accused or to carry out the responsibilities associated with being a prosecutor or a member of the bench.

2.2 Mainstream accounts and the politico-strategic dimension

Most mainstream accounts describing the rise of ICL institutions focus, somewhat myopically, on a politico-strategic dimension best characterised by a set of state-making practices with "statesmen and stateswomen doing the business of the 'state' [...] It features diplomatic initiatives and armed force."[9] These accounts acknowledge the IMTs as the first successful international attempts to

4 Giddens, 1990, p. 1.
5 Pettman, 2001, pp. 42, 46.
6 Toulmin, 1990, p. 9.
7 Cox, 1981, p. 129.
8 Pettman, 2001, p. 8.
9 Pettman, 2001, p. 25.

prosecute war criminals, describing the IMT and the IMTFE as creations of a war-fighting coalition of great powers – namely, the United States, United Kingdom, France, the Soviet Union and China – that emerged victorious from the Second World War.[10] Coalition members' foreign policies are shown to inform the design of both tribunals as, firstly, the benches and prosecution teams were composed only of persons belonging to those victorious nations and, secondly, the jurisdictional reach shielded victors from charges of crimes they may have committed during the hostilities and "from the criminal liability for the racist, colonialist, and repressive policies of their own regimes."[11] While this may have compromised the tribunals' impartiality, leading some scholars to label it victors' justice,[12] both tribunals are understood by others as a continuation of war by judicial means.[13] Wishing to maintain their military superiority over potential rivals, these tribunals sent a powerful deterrent to any would-be revisionists of this new post-conflict settlement. Recourse to the rule of international law further insulated the states-based system of international affairs from alternative ways of organising world affairs because states, as subjects of international law, entrench their primacy through any application of international law even where the objects of that law are individuals and groups. While the law enforced at the tribunals was innovative, this novelty served the coalition's immediate security interests.[14]

Mainstream accounts almost always describe the establishment of the ad hoc international criminal tribunals in politico-strategic terms too.[15] Attention is usually paid to a new set of circumstances emerging within the United Nations Security Council following the USSR's demise though the Council's five permanent members are essentially the victorious coalition fostered some 50 years earlier.[16] Even though the P-5 did not always support these tribunals in equal measure, under a more active phase, the Council forged a consensus establishing the ICTY and the ICTR, creating benches and prosecutorial teams that were more international than those of the IMTs. The ad hoc tribunals' nomenclature, which included "criminal" rather than "military," indicates that the institutions' designers perceived themselves less as victorious occupiers and more as hegemons designing and enforcing rules for international affairs. For some scholars, the international criminal tribunals were a continuation of politics, rather than war, by judicial means.[17]

Mainstream accounts usually situate the ICC's creation within that same set of politico-strategic circumstances, though, of course, negotiations occurring

10 See, for instance: Cryer et al., 2011, pp. 111–119; Cassese, 2008, pp. 319–322; and Goldstone and Smith, 2009, pp. 40–64.
11 Schabas, 2012, p. 75.
12 Minear, 1971, pp. 80, 93.
13 Reydams and Wouters, 2012, p. 29.
14 Sellars, 2013, p. 118.
15 Cryer, 2011, pp. 122–124; Cassese, 2008, pp. 324–328; Goldstone and Smith, 2009, pp. 97–100.
16 Schabas, 2012, p. 77.
17 Reydams and Wouters, 2012, p. 29.

in Rome were less constrained than those occurring earlier within the UN Security Council.[18] These accounts describe how negotiations gave rise to three major groups, the largest of which was the so-called like-minded group of states which included Canada, Australia and the UK; these states believed they could design a global architecture for the pursuit of international criminal justice that would be considered fair and legitimate by the international community because they lacked great power status.[19] A second major group comprising the United States, Russian Federation and the People's Republic of China (PRC) also emerged during negotiations, dissolving the consensus established half a century earlier when they voted against France and the UK.[20] The third major group emerging at Rome was a non-aligned movement that comprised many of those smaller, developing states which, having achieved independence after the Second World War, were numerically dominant in this forum. Also receiving attention in these mainstream accounts was the impact on diplomatic negotiations of various non-governmental organisations (NGOs) represented in large numbers at Rome: officially accredited NGOs outnumbered states by a figure of 236 to 160.[21] NGOs advocated for their various objectives by presenting papers and lobbying delegations, both from within delegations and from the meeting's margins, helping foster a sense of purpose among, and a set of expectations of, the group of like-minded states.

Some mainstream accounts reveal the significance of politico-strategic circumstances to prosecutorial conduct during trial. Suspects named in the IMT indictment draw attention to Germany's state-making efforts of policy formulation, administration, law enforcement and military affairs.[22] Most of the accused featuring in the IMTFE indictment emerged from within the elite of Japanese policy-making organs, specifically the Cabinet, diplomatic corps and military, and held positions of authority in, or influence over, their government's war-making effort.[23] Most of the individuals indicted by the ICTY were either in positions of authority within local or national governance structures or involved with the armed forces that constabulary or guarding prisons. At the ICTR, many of those indicted were ministers or senior officials in the Hutu-led government, held the position of *Bourgemestre* or *préfét* or counsellor, were members of the Rwandan armed forces and constabulary or belonged to the *Interahamwe*.[24] As some accounts of the ICC indicate, an apparent prosecutorial bias – which targets only leaders of rebel non-state armed groups in those situations referred to the Court by state-parties, only senior members of the so-called outlaw states in those situations referred to the Court by the Security

18 Cryer, 2011, pp. 144–149; Cassese, 2008, pp. 328–330; Goldstone and Smith, 2009, pp. 110–114.
19 Bosco, 2014, p. 39.
20 Reydams and Wouters, 2012, pp. 75–76.
21 Reydams and Wouters, 2012, pp. 72–75; see also Bosco, 2014, p. 46.
22 Taylor, 1992, pp. 78–115.
23 Boister and Cryer, 2008, pp. 54–60.
24 de Vlaming, 2012, pp. 547–570.

Council and only those who use force to subvert the democratic process investigated under the prosecutors own *proprio motu* powers[25] – reflects and reinforces the authority of sovereignty-bound state-makers.

Few mainstream accounts, however, contextualise international criminal trials alongside various state reconstruction efforts. This is somewhat surprising given that the first set of trials accompanied major efforts to reconstruct the West German and Japanese militarist states as peace-loving democracies. The denazification policy, which sought to deny active Nazi supporters access to all important official Offices and cause the demise of the Nazi Party as a force to be reckoned with within Germany's domestic politics, was nothing short of a "political cleansing" of post-war Germany that attempted "to create a democratic phoenix out of the ashes of defeated fascism."[26] The intention to establish democracy in Japan featured in the Potsdam Declaration, which signalled the coalition's intentions to occupy Japan in order to ensure its full de-militarisation, the surrender of its armed forces, the dismantling of its military industries and the removal of the militaristic clique responsible for Japan's aggression. In addition to encouraging the rise of political parties, members of the coalition also codified a new Constitution, reformed local government, separated the judiciary from the executive, encouraged the rise of unionism and introduced significant land reform.[27] The second and third sets of trials, furthermore, also occurred alongside post-conflict state-making practices during the 1990s. While democratisation following Yugoslavian balkanisation took various forms, depending on the territory in question, the shift towards democratisation in Rwanda began with the Belgian colonial administration in the 1960s when, as a UN Trust territory, the country began to grow some of its key democratic institutions.[28] ICC trials occur alongside efforts to reconstruct certain states after mass atrocities as the UN Security Council authorised peacekeeping operations not only to support the work of the ICC Prosecutor[29] but also to strengthen democratic institutions and electoral processes in several African countries.[30]

2.3 Critical scholarship and the politico-economic dimension

While the politico-strategic dimension is undoubtedly important in describing the establishment and design of ICL institutions, critical scholarship also discerns a significant politico-economic dimension epitomised not by "diplomats

25 Hoile, 2014, pp. 245, 270, 275–276, 353, 372.

26 Artz, 1995, pp. 717–719.

27 See Beasley, 1975, pp. 279–284.

28 Paris, 2004, pp. 69–78, 97–111.

29 UN Security Council Resolution 2164 (2014).

30 UN Security Council Resolution 1925 (2010); UN Security Council Resolution 2149 (2014); UN Security Council Resolution 1528 (2004) and UN Security Council Resolution 2164 (2014).

and military personnel but entrepreneurs and investors […] producers and consumers, traders and investors, managers and workers, doing the business of 'the market.'"[31] Some critical scholarship, for example, gives focus to the economic restructuring that can precede outbreaks of armed conflict and mass atrocity.[32] Other scholars explain that the mix of democracy and economic liberalisation not only fails to resolve major issues, including systemic poverty and woefully inadequate access to basic human needs, but also increases the likelihood of violent confrontation within societies.[33] In so doing, these more critically minded scholars offer contending, yet expansive, frames for understanding the immediate circumstances giving rise to international criminal trials.

The reconstruction of national economies as bastions of free-market enterprise that accompanies international criminal trials also receive attention within this scholarship.[34] The trial of German war criminals, for example, took place as the Morgenthau Plan attempted to resuscitate the German economy as a much-needed foreign market for US exports. The international criminals trials of the 1990s occurred, as both the former Yugoslavia and Rwanda were subjected to "the most ambitious and concerted international effort to rehabilitate war-shattered states since the Allied post-war reconstruction of Germany and Japan."[35] Driven by the so-called Washington Consensus, the reconstruction of these economies involved extensive deregulation and privatisation.[36] Similar politico-economic transitions are underway in those African countries forming part of the ICC's caseload, despite the dominant neoliberal paradigm casting a large shadow over the various economic causes of Africa's conflicts and atrocities.[37]

The conduct of the trials themselves receives attention too, especially when the "hidden histories" of those industrials, and other economic actors, involved in conducting atrocities during the Second World War are recovered and brought into the light of day.[38] The indictment of these industrials undoubtedly formed part of the victorious coalition's desire to discipline the German economy. The lack of economic actors featuring in the ICTY and ICTR indictments issued during the 1990s reveals a reluctance to highlight any complicity between prevailing neoliberal orthodoxies and the conditions giving rise to armed conflict and mass atrocity. It also recognises that local entrepreneurs and business owners would prove important to the success of any post-conflict reconstruction efforts.[39]

Critical scholarship also reveals the ways in which members of the victorious coalition reshaped the international system in their own interests. When their delegations met in London to negotiate the guiding principles for prosecuting

31 Pettman, 2001, p. 25.
32 Krever, 2014, p. 130
33 Salih, 2009, p. 134.
34 Baars, 2013, p. 174.
35 Paris, 2004, p. 4.
36 Paris, 2004, p. 29.
37 Salih, 2009, p. 155.
38 Baars, 2013, pp. 163–192.
39 Rogers, 2017, pp. 146–147.

war criminals, the United Nations Charter was signed at the San Francisco Conference, which created an intergovernmental organisation that legitimised the distribution of power within politico-strategic affairs in the coalition's longer-term security interests.[40] At about the same time, an international economic system was created through the so-called Bretton Woods Institutions – the International Bank for Reconstruction and Development (now the World Bank) and the International Monetary Fund (IMF) – which the United States in particular used to ensure international commerce furthered their own economic needs. US Treasury's chief economist, Harry Dexter White, was appointed the IMF's first director and the IMF and the World Bank were both located in Washington, D.C.[41] As US foreign policymakers began building the foundations for a hub-and-spokes model of international trade, with the US economy at its centre, the IMTs "served to simultaneously legitimize and showcase the US's role as the rising hegemon of the 'free world,'"[42] and would facilitate "international criminal law's effective deployment in the service of capitalism's victor's justice."[43] The establishment of the ICC adds a new institution to the post-Second World War architecture of global governance. Sitting alongside the UN and its Security Council as the summit of politico-strategic affairs, and the World Bank, IMF and World Trade Organization (WTO) as the pinnacle of politico-economic affairs, the ICC completes the tripartite system. While the precise impact of the ICC's workload remains to be seen, its ongoing existence will no doubt contribute to the making of global legal culture based on a notion of neo-individualism or, put in another way, cosmopolitanism. The groups and networks that control these institutions have a powerful say over the conduct of contemporary world affairs. However, it is not necessarily state leaders that call the shots, but rather, representatives of a certain modernist utopian project that uses violence as a means of remaking a perfected version of society.[44]

2.4 Critique and the politico-cultural dimension

Both mainstream accounts and critical scholarship appear blind to the deeper context in which these trials occur. Put simply, the politico-cultural project of modernity – including the ongoing contest among its subsidiary movements that coalesce around particular utopian variegations of politico-strategic, politico-economic and politico-social preferences – is neglected. The significance of this underlying context is, however, discerned though a critique of prosecutorial opening statements showing the international criminal trial "is an investigation of, and accusation directed against, the political project of the accused."[45]

40 Zolo, 2009, pp. 13–18.
41 Baars, 2013, p. 176.
42 Baars, 2013, p. 164.
43 Baars, 2013, p. 187.
44 Gray, 2007, pp. 15–28.
45 Gerry 2007, p. 13. See also Rogers, 2017, pp. 325–350.

It also shows that this prosecutorial conduct helps naturalise the capitalist economies sustaining the hegemons.[46]

Justice Jackson's opening statement at the IMT valorised democracies and free markets while condemning Nazi atrocities as "abnormal and inhuman,"[47] "a campaign of arrogance, brutality, and annihilation"[48] that passed "in magnitude and savagery any limits of what is tolerable by modern civilization."[49] Jackson characterised the Nazis as "a ring of evil men,"[50] "without whose evil architecture the world would not have been for so long scourged with the violence and lawlessness, and wracked with the agonies and convulsions, of this terrible war."[51] Similarly, Joseph Keenan used his opening statement at the IMTFE to extol the virtues of democracies and free markets as he denounced the Shinto-Imperialists as insane and "willing to bring the world to a premature end in their mad ambition for domination"[52] for "they declared war on civilization" and this was a "mad scheme for domination and control of Eastern Asia, and as they advanced, ultimately the entire world."[53] These evil and mad acts were deemed repugnant because they function as the antithesis of a rational modernity. Such denunciations of the Nazis as evil and the Shinto-Imperialists as insane serve no obvious legal purpose within the trial, focusing as they do on the character of the accused rather than their guilt. The explicit condemnation does, however, sharpen the focus on the threatening nature of their utopian projects and underscores the need for those projects to be destroyed. When nationalism is based on racial supremacy, it becomes repugnant and its proponents forfeit their place among the human community. Nazis and Shinto-Imperialists were an anathema to the modern civilised world and represented a practical threat to it – as borne out by the destruction wrought by the Second World War.

Grant Niemann, the first prosecutor to deliver an opening statement at the ICTY, gave focus to the way in which the accused, Duško Tadić, underwent a metamorphosis from appearing "to get on well with the Muslim population and [who counted] among his close associates one Emir Karabasic"[54] to someone capable of committing serious international crimes. The transformation is signalled by Tadić's increasing involvement in the Serb Nationalist Party as civil war approached. Yakob Haile-Mariam, the first prosecutor to deliver an opening statement at the ICTR, took an approach similar to Niemann's, saying that

46 Koskenniemi, 2011, pp. 129–130.

47 International Military Tribunal, *Trial of the Major War Criminals before the International Military Tribunal*, II, Proceedings, Nuremberg, Germany, 1947, 14 November–30 November 1945, p. 102.

48 IMT, 1947, p. 100.

49 IMT, 1947, p. 127.

50 IMT, 1947, p. 112.

51 IMT, 1947, p. 105.

52 Keenan, *Opening Statement of the Prosecution*, Northcroft Archive (Prosecution's Documents file), 4 June 1946, Macmillan Brown Library, University of Canterbury, New Zealand, p. 1.

53 Keenan, 946, p. 2.

54 *Prosecutor v. Tadić* (Case No. IT-94-1), ICTY Transcript, 7 May 1996, p. 26.

Jean-Paul Akayesu "was seen as a gentle and amiable person, who drank beer with the local boys and played football with the local boys"[55] until the Prime Minister made a speech in which senior members of the Government made it clear that officials either side with them and support the killing or lose their positions of authority, after which "Akayesu succumbed and followed the avenue of killing, and ordering killings."[56] Rather than disqualifying the accused from humanity's ranks by describing them as evil or insane, these prosecutors demonstrate a more complex and nuanced understanding of the relationship between the accused's acts and the immediate circumstances underlying the two differing situations of internal armed conflict. Although the capacity to commit atrocities is understood to be an intrinsic part of the accused's character, unleashed only under certain conditions, this behaviour still had to be condemned by the prosecutors. Again, denouncing the accused at the start of a trial serves no obvious legal purpose within international criminal trial processes though it sharpened focus on the utopian projects of the accused; in this case when nationalism is fused with ethnic supremacy, it becomes intolerable. Less dangerous than those who initiate international armed conflicts only to lose them, these troublemakers and their utopian projects destroyed through "highly discretionary legal and political violence of the hegemon"[57] because their mere existence is an affront to those who enjoy positions of power and influence over modernist world affairs.

Moreno-Ocampo used his first opening statement at the ICC to show that the accused was less shaped by material circumstances and more shaped those circumstances for his own ends.[58] The opening statement describes Thomas Lubanga's insatiable hunger for power and influence, which involved illegitimate political violence.[59] It was Lubanga's custom to deal with opponents violently.[60] He deliberately misled the international community by issuing orders to demobilise child solders before re-recruiting most of them and ordering them into combat roles.[61] Moreno-Ocampo does not characterise Lubunga as either evil or insane, nor is the political project of the accused demonised. Rather, Moreno-Ocampo omits all but a bare mention of the political group to which Lubanga belongs, possibly as a way to "de-politicize" the trial proceedings. The type of group to which Lubunga belongs is, however, denounced a rebel "army of children."[62] This armed group is an anathema to Moreno-Ocampo because of its deplorable treatment of minors, which it consumed as it grew. It was not only a direct threat to the state but was also parasitic on society and an affront to the values of the civilised international community. The ICC Prosecutor deploys the language of the War on Terror. Observe its frequent use: "They cannot forget

55 *Prosecutor v. Akayesu* (Case No. ICTR-94-4), ICTR Transcript, 9 January 1997, p. 33.
56 *Akayesu*, ICTR T, pp. 37–38.
57 Simpson, 2007, p. 161.
58 *Prosecutor v. Lubanga* (Case No. ICC-01/04-01/06), Transcript, 26 January 2009, p. 27.
59 *Lubanga*, ICC T, pp. 24–25.
60 *Lubanga*, ICC T, p. 27.
61 *Lubanga*, ICC T, pp. 30–31.
62 *Lubanga*, ICC T, p. 16.

the terror they felt and *the terror* they inflicted"[63]; "The environment *of terror* that Lubanga's men created in the camps"[64]; "The children were *terrorized*"[65] and "It is difficult to imagine the suffering or *the terror* of the men and the women and children who were burned alive, hacked to death, or chased from their homes by armed youths".[66] This language, which paints the accused as a terrorist of sorts, thereby placing him beyond the protection of law, is nothing short of belligerent. There is not even a need to denigrate the utopian project of the accused. The single word, "terror," is a loaded gun in the prosecutor's hand.

Invoking symbolic expulsion and excommunication and spoken alongside efforts to reconstruct war-torn states and economies, these opening statements embody a rhetoric of war. But it is war not in the sense that it calls for waging of international or non-international armed conflict through a clash, or a series of clashes, of arms in battle as Clausewitz would have it.[67] Nor is it global civil war in the Schmittian sense where the world's territory is divided into states and spheres of influences, which become objects over which battles are fought within a self-enclosed states-based system.[68] It is the silent war that Michel Foucault described as the politics that follows armed conflict and re-inscribes the unequal distribution of military power in international organisations, instruments of international law, and the practices and norms of international society.[69] In other words, it is a politico-cultural civil war waged as a war of pacification by those who seek to maintain control over the architecture for governing the conduct of international affairs and, beyond that, the modernist project. In this sense, war rhetoric calls for, and normalises, the ongoing politico-cultural civil war fought through, firstly, the reconstruction of conflict-affected countries and, secondly, the enforcement of ICL in the aftermath of mass atrocity. It reflects, reinforces and reproduces the power enjoyed by those in positions of superior authority within zones of privilege and prosperity. The enforcement of ICL operates here like some covert fifth column as modernity is remaking itself in terms determined by those in positions of power and influence in world affairs and it is done as a means of reflecting their values and serving their interest. Given that the utopian project of economic liberalisation reigns supreme within modernist world affairs, all other rivals are automatically deemed inauthentic, fraudulent and illegitimate.

2.5 Conclusion

Drawing on mainstream accounts of ICL institutions, this chapter has shown that there is a discernable relationship between a shifting set of politico-strategic

63 *Lubanga*, ICC T, pp. 4–5.
64 *Lubanga*, ICC T, p. 6.
65 *Lubanga*, ICC T, p. 7.
66 *Lubanga*, ICC T, p. 14.
67 von Clausewitz, 1974.
68 Schmitt, 2006, p. 352.
69 Foucault, 2003, pp. 15–16.

circumstances and the design, composition and jurisdictional reach of these tribunals. Although awareness of these propitious politico-strategic circumstances proves necessary to explaining the significance of international criminal trials, these circumstances are, on their own, insufficient. Drawing on critical scholarship, this chapter has also shown that international criminal trials operate as a site where liberal proponents seek to legitimise their efforts to reconstruct politico-strategic and politico-economic institutions in the aftermath of armed conflict. Their liberal aspirations and efforts do not stop there, however, because they have designed and then managed architecture for governing the politico-strategic and politico-economic dimensions of international life. While mainstream accounts of ICL institutions seldom reflect on the complicity between existing configurations of power and their own pious reproduction of official truths, critical scholarship reveals the large extent to which scholarly knowledge about ICL, even that which offers constructive criticism, serves the capitalist status quo[70] and that ICL is "inextricably bound up in the logic of neoliberalism – as evidenced in its markets and marketing culture."[71]

By undertaking a very brief critique, this chapter demonstrates that an awareness of the modernist context also proves important to explaining international criminal trials. As a new form of politics emerging as a continuation of the Second World War by other means, this transition to peace and the ensuing establishment of the international tribunals and courts provided a new front in a politico-cultural civil war fought by proponents of economic liberalisation for control over the modernist project. It is a hitherto unseen and rarely acknowledged war over the states, economies and societies of their defeated enemies and the trials themselves form an important element of the peace following victory by force of arms. While critical scholars broaden their notion of the political to cover both the politico-strategic and politico-economic dimensions, this chapter has shown that bifurcating those immediate circumstances from their deeper politico-cultural context does better justice to the rise of ICL institutions. "We are always writing the history of the same war," Foucault reminds us, "even when we are writing the history of peace and its institutions."[72]

References

Donna E. Artz, "Nuremberg, Denazification and Democracy: The Hate Speech Problem at the International Military Tribunal", *New York Law School Journal of Human Rights*, vol. 12, no. 3, 1995, pp. 689–758.

Grietje Baars, "Capitalism's Victor's Justice? The Hidden Stories Behind the Prosecution of Industrialists Post-WWII", in Kevin Jon Heller and Gerry Simpson (Eds.), *The Hidden Histories of War Crimes Trials*, Oxford University Press, Oxford, 2013, pp. 163–192.

70 Baars, 2014, p. 197.
71 Schwöbel, 2014, p. 265.
72 Foucault, 2003, p. 16.

Grietje Baars, "Making ICL History: On the Need to Move Beyond Pre-Fab Critiques of ICL", in Christine Schwöbel (Ed.), *Critical Approaches to International Criminal Law: An Introduction*, Routledge, New York, 2014, pp. 196–218.
William G. Beasley, *The Modern History of Japan*, Weidenfeld and Nicolson, London, 1975.
Neil Boister and Robert Cryer, *The Tokyo International Military Tribunal: A Reappraisal*, Oxford University Press, Oxford, 2008.
David Bosco, *Rough Justice: The International Criminal Court in a World of Power Politics*, Oxford University Press, Oxford, 2014.
Antonio Cassese, *International Criminal Law*, Oxford University Press, Oxford, 2008.
Carl von Clausewitz, *On War* (1832, transl. 1873 John Graham), Viking-Penguin, Auckland, 1974.
Robert W. Cox, "Social Forces, States and World Orders: Beyond International Relations Theory", *Millennium—Journal of International Studies*, vol. 10, no. 2, 1981, pp. 439–456.
Robert Cryer, Håkan Friman, Darryl Robinson and Elizabeth Wilmshurst, *An Introduction to International Criminal Law and Procedure*, Cambridge University Press, Cambridge, 2011.
Michael Foucault, *"Society Must Be Defended": Lectures at the College De France, 1975–76*, Picador, New York, 2003.
Anthony Giddens, *The Consequences of Modernity*, Stanford University Press, Stanford, CA, 1990.
Richard J. Goldstone and Adam M. Smith, *International Judicial Institutions: The Architecture of International Justice at Home and Abroad*, Routledge, New York, 2009, pp. 40–64.
John Gray, *Black Mass: Apocalyptic Religion and the Death of Utopia*, Penguin, New York, 2007.
David Hoile, *Justice Denied: The Reality of the International Criminal Court*, Africa Research Centre, London, 2014.
Martti Koskennemi, *The Politics of International Law*, Hart Publish, Oxford, 2011.
Tor Krever, "Unveiling (and Veiling) Politics in International Criminal Trials", in Christine Schwöbel (Ed.), *Critical Approaches to International Criminal Law: An Introduction*, Routledge, New York, 2014, pp. 117–137.
Richard H. Minear, *Victors' Justice: The Tokyo War Crimes Trial*, Princeton University Press, Princeton, NJ, 1971.
Roland Paris, *At War's End: Building Peace after Civil Conflict*, Cambridge University Press, Cambridge, 2004.
Ralph Pettman, *World Politics: Rationalism and Beyond*, Palgrave Macmillan, New York, 2001.
Luc Reydams and Jan Wouters, "The Politics of Establishing International Criminal Tribunals", in Luc Reydams, Jan Wouters and Cedric Ryngaert (Eds.), *International Prosecutors*, Oxford University Press, Oxford, 2012, pp. 81–112.
Damien Rogers, "Prosecutors Opening Statements: The Rhetoric of Law, Politics, and Silent War", in Nabou Hayashi and Cecilia Bailliet (Eds.), *The Legitimacy of International Criminal Tribunals*, Cambridge University Press, Cambridge, 2017, pp. 325–350.
Damien Rogers, *Law, Politics and the Limits of Prosecuting Mass Atrocity*, Palgrave Macmillan, New York, 2017.

M. A. Mohamed Salih, "A Critique of the Political Economy of the Liberal Peace: Elements of an African experience", in Edward Newman, Roland Paris and Oliver P. Richmond (Eds.), *New Perspectives on Liberal Peacebuilding*, United Nations University Press, Tokyo, New York, Paris, 2009, pp. 133–159.

William Schabas, *Unimaginable Atrocities: Justice, Politics, and Rights at the War Crimes Tribunals*, Oxford University Press, Oxford, 2012.

Carl Schmitt, *The Nomos of the Earth in the International Law of Jus Publicum Europaem*, Telos Press, New York, 2006.

Christine Schwöbel, "The Market and Marketing Culture of International Criminal Law", in Christine Schwöbel (Ed.), *Critical Approaches to International Criminal Law: An Introduction*, Routledge, New York, 2014, pp. 264–280.

Christine Schwöbel, *Critical Approaches to International Criminal Law: An Introduction*, Routledge, New York, 2014.

Kristen Sellars, *'Crimes against Peace' and International Law*, Cambridge University Press, Cambridge, 2013.

Gerry Simpson, *Law, War and Crime: War Crimes Trials and the Reinvention of International Law*, Polity, Cambridge, 2007.

Telford Taylor, *The Anatomy of the Nuremberg Trials: A Personal Memoir*, Skyhorse Publishing, New York, 1992.

Stephen Toulmin, *Cosmopolis: The Hidden Agenda of Modernity*, University of Chicago Press, Chicago, IL, 1990.

Frederiek de Vlaming, "Selection of Defendants" in Luc Reydams et al. (Eds.), *International Prosecutors*, Oxford University Press, Oxford, 2012, pp. 542–571.

Danilo Zolo, *Victors' Justice: From Nuremberg to Baghdad*, Verso, London and New York, 2009.

Official material and similar

International Military Tribunal, *Trial of the Major War Criminals before the International Military Tribunal*, II, Proceedings, Nuremberg, Germany, 1947, 14 November–30 November 1945.

Keenan, Joseph B., *Opening Statement of the Prosecution*, Northcroft Archive (Prosecution's Documents file), 4 June 1946, Macmillan Brown Library, University of Canterbury, New Zealand.

Prosecutor v. Akayesu, (Case No. ICTR-94-4), ICTR Transcript, 9 January 1997, p. 33.

Prosecutor v. Lubanga, (Case No. ICC-01/04-01/06), Transcript, 26 January 2009, p. 27.

Prosecutor v. Tadić, (Case No. IT-94-1), ICTY Transcript, 7 May 1996, p. 26.

UN Security Council Resolution 1528 (2004).

UN Security Council Resolution 1925 (2010).

UN Security Council Resolution 2149 (2014).

UN Security Council Resolution 2164 (2014).

UN Security Council Resolution 2164 (2014).

3 Engaging history in the legal protection of cultural heritage in war and peace

Sebastian M. Spitra

3.1 Introduction: confronting the history of cultural heritage in international law with its Apocrypha

In September 2016, the International Criminal Court (ICC) judgment on Al-Mahdi about the destruction of UNESCO world heritage sites in Timbuktu showed that issues of cultural heritage concern wide fields of international law today. While most legal histories on this complex topic repeat a certain canon of narratives and sources to tell the story of that subject, the current "historical turn" in international law creates new opportunities for writing a history of this field.

This text analyses the current historiography of cultural heritage protection. The emphasis is placed on the protection in times of war since the wartime aspects took the center stage in earlier international legal scholarship. However, the focus on peacetime has increased in commentaries. In consequence, I will contrast the wartime narratives of this field with the peacetime histories of cultural heritage protection in order to provide a broader spectrum of the often neglected or ignored topics of that area of international humanitarian law.

My contribution has two purposes. First, I want to discuss the shortcomings of previous approaches to the history of this subject in the light of the historical turn in international law. Second, I will offer an outlook for a potential new narrative of the legal histories of cultural heritage administration and protection. To begin with, a short sketch of current perspectives of legal history and of historicizing law in a multipolar world shall be given.

3.2 Current perspectives to historicize the law in a multipolar world

3.2.1 Reorienting Europe and the West: some tasks for a legal history today

The European understanding of law and the European legal history were for a long time the paradigms for defining law and therefore also what the subject of a legal history essentially had to be. In public law, civil law, or international law, the narrative of the history of law has been a purely European project. But, this

Eurocentric focus has shifted under the influence of global history and postcolonial studies toward a legal history of Europe in a global perspective.[1] Therefore, a "Universal History of Legal Thought" as Roberto Unger puts it, would be the current challenge in historicizing the law.[2]

This corresponds to the most important task of European legal history set out in a recent text by the director of the Max Planck Institute for European legal history, Thomas Duve.[3] He suggests that the key assignment of historicizing the law is to engage global perspectives on Europe.[4] By these means, Duve wants to establish a precondition for a global dialog on (historical) justice.

This is closely connected to Martti Koskenniemi's thoughts under the heading "Dealing with Eurocentrism."[5] Koskenniemi sees the three main tasks of history of international law in writing intellectual histories, in focusing on the West and its "Others," and in a history of sociology of international law.[6] All these approaches contest the common assumptions of international lawyers about history.[7] Such attitudes are being increasingly criticized after the turn to history in international law.

3.2.2 Contesting common assumptions of "mainstream" legal history

Four of these main common assumptions which international lawyers have been acting on toward history were described and criticized by the Greek-Dutch scholar Thomas Skouteris.[8] With his specific approach to the history of international law, he identifies common shortcomings in the use of history in the legal writings:

1 *International legal history is about the search for the truth.* This conviction sees the historical empirical facts that are reported in history as objective and free from subjective or ideological influence. In particular, pretentions of having established the single valid truth should be avoided.
2 *Using historical knowledge is different from writing histories.* Repeating unquestioned and common everyday legal histories like the progress of international law legitimates and naturalizes certain conceptions of international law.
3 *Law has a definite relationship to a social context.* It is often assumed that legal events are responses to wider social contexts. So, a simple cause-and-effect pattern is employed for describing the evolving legal regulations.

1 Duve, 2012, pp. 18–71.
2 Unger, 2015, p. 53.
3 Duve, 2014, p. 30.
4 A project that has its important forerunners in other disciplines, such as Chakrabarty, 2000.
5 Koskenniemi, 2011, pp. 152–177.
6 Koskenniemi, 2004, pp. 61–66.
7 For an overview of current research on the history of international law, see Dhont, 2016, pp. 313–334.
8 Skouteris, 2012, pp. 99–121.

4 *Humanity's path is evolutionary and international law is an agent of social progress.* International law is regarded as progressing in a linear fashion. Even disastrous events are seen as forces that confirm this teleology.[9] However, we cannot escape teleological thinking or speaking, if we reflect such issues from a historical perspective.[10] Reassessing the progress narrative of international law is only possible if we have a new benchmark or criteria that allow us to reconsider the traditional notion of progress.

Skouteris' crucial point is that history should be employed as a technique of criticism rather than used for searching the truth. Some of the exemplified common assumptions can be found in narratives about the legal administration and protection of cultural heritage, such as in three recent examples of studies to which I now turn.

3.3 Approaching the Canon: problems of traditional histories of cultural property protection

The history of the protection of cultural heritage in international law has been treated in various legal fields in recent years. Public international law, comparative law, and international relations are only some but probably the most influential areas of research that have been concerned with the history of this subject. Therefore, the following authors are taken as paradigm to discuss the treatment of the history protecting cultural heritage in each of these disciplines.

3.3.1 History as a prelude and "mainstream history"

Kerstin Odendahl, who is currently professor of public international law in Kiel (Germany), wrote her habilitation thesis on the subject of the protection of cultural heritage. Her approach brings together the different developments in the legal system of safeguarding these objects on the national, European, and international levels. She examines history to find common doctrines, principles, and developments in public law, public international law, and European law.[11] Her vital aim is to describe a coherent normative system of rules regarding cultural heritage that incorporates the national, European, and international levels.[12] So, like many other scholars, she approaches history primarily as the antecedent of contemporary law.[13] I took her work as an example because it appears to be the most elaborated and all-encompassing study on this subject.

9 Craven, 2007, pp. 27–42.
10 Koskenniemi, 2007, pp. 122–148.
11 Odendahl, 2005, p. 5.
12 Odendahl, 2005, p. 2.
13 For just a few further examples, see Wolfrum, 2012; Greenwood, 2013, pp. 1–44; O'Keefe, 2006; Carducci, 2000, pp. 289–392; Toman, 1996; von Schorlemer, 2016.

Odendahl focuses, in her thoughtful and carefully structured historical survey, on the intellectual attitudes toward cultural property as well as on the juridification of these rules. But she reflects both aspects separately from each other and just in the context of domestic law of Germany and not for the European or the international level. When she discusses the European and international levels, she concentrates on the legal codification projects and misses to state the intellectual background governing the conduct with cultural property.

Such a norm-centered history of cultural property leaves especially the international legal doctrine aside. Although Odendahl refers, in a short paragraph, to international customary law that developed at the beginning of the 19th century,[14] a closer survey of doctrine would have provided her study with deeper insights as I will point out later.

3.3.2 Inscribed teleology in writing history

Wayne Sandholtz has written a book with the title *Prohibiting Plunder* that investigates the emergence of norms of protection for cultural heritage from an international relations perspective.[15] Sandholtz has a chair for international relations at the University of Southern California. His study is actually a piece of historiography that starts – after a prelude on international relations theory about norm change – with Hugo Grotius and ends with the Bagdad Museum case in 2003 and a glimpse on the dynamic of norm change.

Sandholtz describes the norm change as an evolution from the *ius gentium* right of the victor to the movable enemy's property (war booty) to the protection regimes of cultural property that are now safeguarding those items. His international relations approach explains this change in the norms of international law as outcomes of normative arguments, which may be supported by great power structures. In contrast to Kerstin Odendahl, he delves into the normative debates and arguments on the rules in their historical settings.

But, the shortcoming of his approach appears as a by-product of his international relations perspective. Sandholtz pins down the discourse on the subject of safeguarding cultural heritage in international law in a system of norm cycles. In every phase in which a norm change occurs, he applies such a scheme of norm cycle to provide a full explanation of the development.[16] For example, when he discusses the Napoleonic plunder around 1800, Sandholtz argues that the norm cycle consists of four parts: (1) the norm context before the norm change, (2) the action that leads to the norm, (3) the arguments, and finally (4) the results, namely the rule change.[17]

This conception leaves at least two questions open. The first question concerns the "arguments" that Sandholtz mentions. They represent what I want to

14 Odendahl, 2005, p. 124.
15 Sandholtz, 2007.
16 See, for example, Sandholtz, 2007, pp. 9, 48, 102, 128, 168, 192, 213, 231, 242, 261.
17 Sandholtz, 2007, p. 47.

call polemically a hegemonic discourse, which silences many different voices in the debates. This results from the inherent teleology of his approach that analyses the arguments only from the perspective of their outcome, which means the new rule.

This brings up the second question: what does "rule" mean in this context? Is it just the designation of the principle according to which one behaves? Does the post-Napoleonic restitution of substantial parts of the Louvre that were war booty amount to the restitution rule in international law? That would evoke an understanding of rules and norms exclusively based on social behavior and ignore that international law is a legal normative system. But that is what Sandholtz's international relations approach implies. He also distinguishes different degrees of normativity in his concept which further suggests such a behavioral view on normativity.

3.3.3 Narratives of dichotomy: the national and international gap

John Henry Merryman was a Stanford Professor and one of the most influential academics in the field of art and law.[18] He theorized the history and present of cultural heritage norms in international law as a dichotomy of nationalism and internationalism. In his 1986 and 2005 published historical accounts of the development of legal protection of cultural property in international law, Merryman draws a straight line between the first codification of the laws of war in the Instructions for the Government of Armies of the United States in the Field, General Order No. 100 of 1863 (the so-called Lieber Code) and the Hague Convention for the Protection of Cultural Property in the Event of Armed Conflict of 1954. They represent for Merryman the keystone of cultural heritage internationalism. He organizes the history of the legal regimes safeguarding cultural heritage as reflecting a difference between internationalism and nationalism.[19] As an example of nationalism, Merryman lists some draft conventions of the League of Nations as well as the UNESCO Convention on the Means of Prohibiting and Preventing the Illicit Export, Import and Transfer of Ownership of Cultural Property of 1970.

As a proponent of internationalism, Merryman argued that the state should withdraw from cultural property matters and let the free-market bring the cultural assets in circulation among the different nations.[20] National borders should be open to trade in cultural property and legal conjunction of these items to the nation should be as loose as possible to ensure their free exchange.

Merryman also distinguishes between market countries of cultural property, which are often Western countries without an own large stock of cultural

18 On his legacy, see Shapiro, 2014, pp. 237–242; Feldman, 2014, pp. 243–250.
19 Merryman, 1986, p. 833.
20 Merryman, 2005, pp. 11–39.

assets, and source countries with huge amounts of items within their borders.[21] Merryman sees this situation similarly to an oversupply situation that needs some balance for allowing the demand for cultural property to fulfill its course. Merryman identifies the cultural property nationalism as more common in source countries, whereas the internationalists can be mostly found among market countries that rely on the exchange of cultural items. From this setting, Merryman draws his historical conclusions and interprets history through the lenses of this dichotomy. Eventually, he applies a teleological frame that represents certain interests when he considers cultural property nationalism and internationalism in the historical development. By these means, he ignores histories of the colonial and imperialistic appropriation of cultural treasures in the past.

3.4 "The West is the best?": writing new histories

The three discussed approaches face different limits that are inherent in their methods. In this part, I want to characterize the different limitations and provide suggestions with regard to the methods of modern history of international law.

3.4.1 "Tell me what the papers say": omitted investigations in doctrine

Kerstin Odendahl writes what one could call a "realist" history according to Martti Koskenniemi and therefore she misses a valuable addition for her history of the rules on cultural heritage protection. With her focuses on the legal codifications, she loses sight of the rich international legal doctrine in that field.[22] This point also applies to Merryman's texts. Sandholtz, by contrast, takes a look on doctrinal issues in his book. And there are other works as well that engage doctrine for their histories about the legal protection of cultural heritage. But instead of giving an accurate synopsis of doctrinal opinions on this topic, Sandholtz analyses the debates and arguments only teleologically in the light of the norm change as outcome. Another striking fact with regard to other works in this field is that the analyzed writers and doctrines seem to have canonized in the legal historiography during the 19th century.

Most of international law scholars during the 19th century made reference to lawyers like Emer de Vattel,[23] Henry Wagner Halleck,[24] or Johann Caspar Bluntschli[25] when they dealt with cultural heritage issues. Each of them is being evoked to stress certain arguments or demonstrate specific conclusions. These

21 This distinction is also being adopted by many other scholars today, e.g., Hoffman, 2006.

22 Martti Koskenniemi stressed the importance of combining both the "realist" and the "idealist" approaches to history: Koskenniemi, 2011, p. 161.

23 de Vattel, 1758, p. 139.

24 Halleck, 1861, pp. 451–455; Halleck, 1866, p. 208.

25 Bluntschli, 1866, p. 27; Bluntschli, 1868, p. 348–352.

references can also be found in modern historical portraits of the development of the legal protection regime. So the discussions of the 19th century are being reproduced and thus canonized in the current debates about the history of cultural heritage protection.

For example, when discussing the prohibition of destroying cultural monuments, many contemporary authors have cited Emer de Vattel's statements.[26] In the 19th century, hardly any scholar doubted the existence of this norm in international law and the reference to the Swiss Vattel gives the evidence to that certitude. A more debated subject was the restitution of cultural heritage. In this context, reference is often made to the American army officer and international lawyer Halleck.[27] His arguments are widely used to demonstrate the pros and especially the cons of the restitution of cultural heritage that has been seized during the course of war. Lastly, the influence of the codification projects dealing with the rules of war on international legal doctrine is foremost argued with quoting Bluntschli.[28]

Besides these canonical authors and arguments, there were a lot of other international lawyers who considered these topics in their treatises. Therefore, an investigation in further textbooks would illuminate the broad spectrum of opinions that were reflected in that matter and reveal that most of the recent historical sketches are just discussing the tip of the iceberg.

3.4.2 "That's what the papers say": discontinuities not progress

In my own work, I survey international law textbooks of the 19th century from different countries and regions, such as Germany, Austria, Switzerland, Italy, France, the United States, Great Britain, Spain, Portugal, and Latin America.[29] This research adds many new perspectives to the common assumptions about the development of the protection of cultural property in international law. That opens potential for revising old narratives and constructing potential new ones. A new narrative to frame the international legal discourse in the 19th century might be one of nationality that looks closely on the different viewpoints, developments, and attitudes among various nations. In order to demonstrate the different evolutions in various European countries, I will present a short extract of my findings from 19th-century doctrine in Germany and Great Britain.

The first international jurists that wrote about cultural heritage with regard to the protection from seizure in the course of war came from Germany. These discussions started in German language textbooks right in the aftermath of

26 See, e.g., Toman, 2008, pp. 121–153; Merryman, 2005, pp. 11–39; Genius-Devime, 1996, p. 180.

27 See, e.g., Sandholtz, 2007; Vrdoljak, 2006, p. 28.

28 See e.g., Vrdoljak, 2007, p. 65; Carducci, 2000, p. 299; Toman, 1996, p. 7; Genius-Devime, 1996, p. 182.

29 The starting point of my research was Macalister-Smith and Schwietzke, 2001, pp. 75–142.

Napoleon's defeat. The conversations on this legal level were triggered by the restitution of art that was plundered during the Napoleonic wars.

Johann Ludwig Klüber[30] and Georg Friedrich von Martens[31] were the first prominent scholars that raised the topic in their treatises. Both legitimated the legal rule that prohibits the abduction of cultural items in times of war with reference to Johann Jakob Moser,[32] one of the most famous 18th century's publicists of the Holy Roman Empire.[33] So, Klüber and Martens legitimized the norm with this historic account of Moser's treatise from 1779 and his arguments about the inviolability of the monarch and his property.

But the aim of protection changed rather quickly in Germany. The monarchical argument was no longer adequate in the phase of the *Vormärz* the period between 1815 and the revolutionary time of 1848. There has also been an early universalism of cultural heritage in Germany. Individually, both Friedrich Saalfeld in 1833 and Karl Salomo Zachariä in 1841 formulated the first universalism related to cultural heritage in international law doctrines of the 19th century. Saalfeld stated that works of art are the common property of all peoples (*Gemeingut aller Völker*) and limits the war booty on those things in this context.[34] Zachariä enhances that concept (without mentioning Saalfeld) by entrusting the state with these cultural treasures and collections.[35]

The first British efforts to justify the norm that prohibits seizure of cultural property in war were made in a completely different way. In the first half of the 19th century, the international law doctrine in Great Britain hardly dealt systematically with topics like the laws of war as the German jurists did.[36] An exciting opinion on the question of the lawfulness of the transfer of cultural patrimony in times of war can be found in the treatises of James Lorimer[37] and Henry Sumner Maine.[38] Both legal scholars put civilization in the center of their reflections. This had the consequence that Lorimer[39] and Maine[40] assumed that Napoleon had served the ends of civilization more with his practice of cultural transfers than he had damaged it. Thus, they saw the behavior of Napoleon and France as lawful because the benefits for civilization were higher when all these cultural assets are united at one place and not spread around Italy and Europe. Nevertheless, both consider the restitutions legitimate as the allies made it a condition for peace with France.

These three examples reveal the problems associated with the notion of progress in international law. If we compare the opinions of Klüber and Martens to

30 Klüber, 1819, § 253, p. 397.
31 Martens, 1821, § 280, p. 478.
32 For the international law doctrine of Johann Jakob Moser, see Wendehorst, 2015, pp. 303–324.
33 Moser, 1779, § 14, p. 159.
34 Saalfeld, 1833, § 96, p. 223.
35 Zachariä, 1841, p. 114.
36 Sylvest, 2004, p. 12.
37 Koskenniemi, 2016, pp. 415–429.
38 Mantena, 2010.
39 Lorimer, 1884, p. 79.
40 Maine, 1890, p. 195.

Saalfeld and Zachariä, we can easily state that the reasons for the protection by the latter (see earlier) seem to fit better to the current understanding. However, if we compare their positions with the attitudes of the two British jurists of the end of the 19th century, the assumptions of progress begin to wane as the earlier writers held views that seem to fit better to our present perspective.

Consequently, the term of progress must be considered carefully and aside from the master narratives mainly repeated by canonic authors of international legal doctrine. New narratives that consider developments nationally bring to light new actors and opinions. That helps to understand better the singularity of processes as well as overall tendencies in the legal discourse.

3.4.3 "The sound of silence": blind Eurocentrism

However, doctrinal questions did not cover all types of cultural property issues. A quite unconsidered part of cultural property law was the appropriation of cultural heritage in times of peace in the 19th century and throughout the interwar period. This issue arose especially in the context of archeological excavations. A survey of treatises showed that only Franz von Liszt[41] and Emanuel Ullmann[42] treated the so-called international cultural agreements mentioning excavation license treaties in their textbooks before the First World War. Both before and after the Great War, there existed several contracts for excavations and cultural exchange. In the aftermath of the Great War, the peace treaty of Sèvres included rules for the accessibility to the ruins and excavation grounds for the archeologists. The mandate treaties for Iraq and Syria-Libanon and the League of Nations contained such provisions. In both countries, Europeans ran the antiquities service. There were also bilateral excavation license treaties between various countries. In the 19th century, Greece concluded such contracts with Germany and France, Persia and Afghanistan even granted France in a treaty an exclusive right to carry out excavations and to keep a main part of their proceeds.

I want to give a short example of the legal framework in Syria-Lebanon to highlight some interesting aspects in times of colonial practices.[43] First, the mandate treaty 1922 under the aegis of the League of Nations expected a law of antiquities and outlined its content.[44] Particularly, the regulations regarding the authorization to excavate and the proceeds of excavations echoed European interests. In the ensuing *Règlement sur les antiquités en Syrie et au Liban* of 1926 and 1933, the archeologists were granted extensive possibilities to carry out excavations and expropriate locals for access to archeological sites.

Tadmur, better known under the name Palmyra, is a case in point. In the beginning of 2017, the Islamic State forces ("ISIL") carried out renewed brutal

41 Liszt, 1898, p. 189.

42 Ullmann, 1908, § 138, p. 412.

43 An interesting and critical account whether the mandate system was an instrument of colonization or decolonization in Schayegh, 2015, pp. 412–419.

44 "French Mandate for Syria and the Lebanon", 1923, pp. 177–182.

destructions of the ancient monuments at this archeological site, before the government of Syria, with Russian assistance, managed to retake Palmyra for the second time. Before the excavations started in Palmyra in the 1930s, the local people lived within the walls of the temples. They were relocated off the site by French archeologists in order to make the site more easily accessible for archeological work and to clear the impression of the antique monument from its "oriental" marks.[45] Half of the proceeds of the excavations came to Europe, and the other half in the newly founded and European-led domestic museums. However, a legal treatment of these issues hardly existed, as the administration lies in the hands of archeologists and not in those of (international) lawyers.

I suggest to see these practices as the surface of a colonial project.[46] The law enabled the archeologists to pursue the aims of attaining artefacts and findings. The scientific knowledge further helped to construct a national identity for the new states and at the same time become masters of that past. A famous example for that nation-building efforts is the archeological museum in Bagdad founded by Gertrude Bell, who was also a main figure in drafting the legal antiquity act for conducting excavations in Iraq. From a postcolonial perspective, these histories may suggest new interpretations of cultural heritage devastations like those carried out by "ISIL." So, these destructions could also be read as being directed against the colonial nation-building process and the mastering of the countries' past by western countries.

3.5 Conclusion – administering culture: new perspectives for a history of cultural heritage in international law

I want to conclude by stressing two points. First, in the international law doctrine of the 19th century and the interwar period, there was hardly any treatment of issues like archeological excavation license treaties or the administration of antiquities under the mandate system. This void is being repeated in the contemporary legal historical treatment of cultural heritage with very few exceptions.[47]

My argument is that the focus in international law doctrine regarding these objects has always been on their protection in the sense of physical integrity and the prohibition of illicit wartime transfer. I suppose that the reason for the blind spot in these matters lies on one side in the linguistic framing as "protection." On the other side, it lies in the missing respect that scholars of cultural heritage or cultural property protection pay to the importance that the concept of "civilization" played in international law in the 19th and 20th centuries.[48] The integration of these concepts in international law doctrine would shed light on the often obscured parts of history. It would illuminate how the so-called "standard of civilization" determined legal norms on the domestic and the international

45 Stucky, 2008, pp. 505–511.
46 See, e.g., Nafziger and Nicgorski (Eds.), 2009; Greenfield, 2007.
47 A good example is Vrdoljak, 2006.
48 Obregón, 2012, pp. 917–939; Pauka, 2012; Gong, 1984.

levels in this field for several purposes, such as to prove the compliance with the standard or to justify appropriations of cultural objects.[49]

In my opinion, the task for a history of international law that deals with the legal protection of cultural heritage is to embrace also topics, like the mandate administration of cultural heritage under the League of Nations. Although the law and its enforcement were hardly managed by lawyers in that field and there has scarcely been any doctrinal reflection about it, the administration of cultural heritage was legally regulated.

To foster such an extensive and global approach, I suggest to replace the terms "protection of cultural heritage" with "administering of culture." This broadens also the scope of histories of international law in that field and includes the important matter of civilization in the considerations of new narratives.

Second, the methodology of such a project has to reconsider international law doctrine critically and work interdisciplinary together with global history, cultural studies, and archeological studies. All those disciplines form the context for an analysis of legal rules on cultural heritage. To put these two sides in dialog should prevent the reproduction of inadequate canonizations like those I demonstrated in the history of cultural heritage protection.

By such canonizations in this field of international law, the problematic narrative of progress is being perpetuated in the general history of international law. The history I am trying to narrate is instead one that strives for approaching the ambivalence of "progress" in the legal protection and preservation of cultural heritage and even in the terminology of that field. These histories reveal the various interpretations of cultural conflicts which are on the rise nowadays. Thus, the problematic relation of valuing and protecting cultural heritage is eventually reflected in the increasing destruction of such items in armed conflicts today.

References

Matthijs de Blois, "French Mandate for Syria and the Lebanon", *American Journal of International Law*, vol. 17, no. 3, 1923, pp. 177–182.

Johann Caspar Bluntschli, *Das moderne Kriegsrecht der civilsirten Staten als Rechtsbuch dargestellt*, C.H. Beck, Nördlingen, 1866.

Johann Caspar Bluntschli, *Das moderne Völkerrecht der civilisirten Staten als Rechtsbuch dargestellt*, C.H. Beck, Nördlingen, 1868.

Guido Carducci, "L'obligation de restitution des biens culturels et des objets d'art en cas de conflit armé: Droit coutumier et droit conventionnel avant et après la convention de la Haye de 1954", *RGDIP*, vol. 104, 2000, pp. 289–392.

Dipesh Chakrabarty, *Provincializing Europe: Postcolonial Thought and Historical Difference*, Princeton University Press, Princeton, NJ, 2000.

49 My Ph.D. thesis (Spitra, 2018) deals with the implications of the "standard of civilization" for the development of international legal rules regarding cultural heritage.

Matthew Craven, "Introduction: International Law and Its Histories", in Matthew Craven, Malgosia Fitzmaurice and Maria Vogiatzi (Eds.), *Time, History and International Law*, Martinus Nijhoff Publishers, Leiden and Boston, MA, 2007, pp. 27–42.

Emer de Vattel, *Le droit des gens ou principes de la loi naturelle appliqués à la conduite & aux affaires des Nation & des Souverains*, vol. 2, Liberos Tutior, London, 1758.

Frederik Dhont, "Recent Research in the History of International Law", *Tijdschrift voor Rechtsgeschiedenis/Revue d'histoire du droit/The Legal History Review*, vol. 84, 2016, pp. 313–334.

Thomas Duve, "European Legal History – Concepts, Methods, Challenges", in Thomas Duve (Ed.), *Entanglements in Legal History: Conceptual Approaches*, Max Planck Institute for European Legal History Open Access Publication, Frankfurt am Main, 2014.

Thomas Duve, "Von der Europäischen Rechtsgeschichte zu einer Rechtsgeschichte Europas in globalhistorischer Perspektive", *Rechtsgeschichte*, vol. 20, 2012, pp. 18–71.

Robin Feldman, "Remarks in Honor of the Legal and Public Policy Legacies of John Henry Merryman: Cultural Property and Human Cells", *International Journal of Cultural Property*, vol. 21, no. 3, 2014, pp. 243–250.

Barbara Genius-Devime, *Bedeutung und Grenzen des Erbes der Menschheit im völkerrechtlichen Kulturgüterschutz*, Nomos, Baden-Baden, 1996.

Gerrit W. Gong, *The Standard of "Civilization" in International Society*, Oxford University Press, Oxford, 1984.

Jeanette Greenfield, *The Return of Cultural Treasures*, Cambridge University Press, Cambridge, 2007.

Christopher Greenwood, "Historical Development and Legal Basis", in Dieter Fleck (Ed.), *The Handbook of International Humanitarian Law*, Oxford University Press, Oxford, 2013, pp. 1–44.

Henry W. Halleck, *Elements of International Law and Laws of War*, J.B. Lippincott & Co., Philadelphia, PA 1866.

Henry W. Halleck, *International Law: Or, Rules Regulating the Intercourse of States in Peace and War*, D. Van Nostrand, New York, 1861.

Barbara T. Hoffman (Ed.), *Art and Cultural Heritage. Law, Policy and Practice*, Cambridge University Press, Cambridge and New York, 2006.

Johann Ludwig Klüber, *Droit des Gens Moderne de l'Europe*, vol. 2, J.G. Cotta, Stuttgart, 1819.

Martti Koskenniemi, "Histories of International Law: Dealing with Eurocentrism", *Rechtsgeschichte*, vol. 19, 2011, pp. 152–177.

Martti Koskenniemi, "On the Idea and Practice for Universal History with a Cosmopolitan Purpose", in Bindu Puri and Heiko Sievers (Eds.), *Terror, Peace, and Universalism. Essays on the Philosophy of Immanuel Kant*, Oxford University Press, Oxford, 2007, pp. 122–148.

Martti Koskenniemi, "Race, Hierarchy and International Law: Lorimer's Legal Science", *European Journal of International Law*, vol. 27, no. 2, 2016, pp. 415–429.

Martti Koskenniemi, "Why History of International Law Today?", *Rechtsgeschichte*, vol. 4, 2004, pp. 61–66.

Franz Liszt, *Das Völkerrecht systematisch dargestellt*, O. Haering, Berlin, 1898.

James Lorimer, *The Institutes of the Law of Nations. A Treatise of the Jural Relations of Separate Political Communities*, vol. 2, William Blackwood & Sons, Edinburgh and London, 1884.

Peter Macalister-Smith and Joachim Schwietzke, "Bibliography of the Textbooks and Comprehensive Treatises on Positive International Law of the 19th Century", *Journal of the History of International Law*, vol. 3, 2001, pp. 75–142.

Henry S. Maine, *International Law*, John Murray, London, 1890.

Karuna Mantena, *Alibis of Empire: Henry Maine and the Ends of Liberal Imperialism*, Princeton University Press, Princeton, NJ, 2010.

Georg Friedrich Martens, *Précis du droit des gens moderne de l'Europe fondé sur les traités et l'usage*, Dieterich, Göttingen, 1821.

John H. Merryman, "Cultural Property Internationalism", *International Journal of Cultural Property*, vol. 12, 2005, pp. 11–39.

John H. Merryman, "Two Ways of Thinking about Cultural Property", *American Journal of International Law*, vol. 80, no. 4, 1986, pp. 831–853.

Johann Jakob Moser, *Versuch des neuesten Europäischen Völker-Rechts in Friedens – und Kriegs-Zeiten vornehmlich aus den Staatshandlungen derer Europäischen Mächten, auch deren Begebenheiten, so sich seit dem Tode Kaisers Carls VI. im Jahr 1740. zugetragen haben*, vol. 9, no.1, Barrentrapp Sohn und Wenner, Frankfurt am Main, 1779.

James. A. Nafziger and Ann M. Nicgorski (Eds.), *Cultural Heritage Issues: The Legacy of Conquest, Colonization, and Commerce*, Marinus Nijhoff Publishers, Leiden, 2009.

Liliana Obregón, "The Civilized and the Uncivilized", in Bardo Fassbender and Anne Peters (Eds.), *The Oxford Handbook of the History of International Law*, Oxford University Press, Oxford, 2012, pp. 917–939.

Kerstin Odendahl, *Kulturgüterschutz. Entwicklung, Struktur und Dogmatik eines ebenenübergreifenden Normensystems*, Mohr Siebeck, Tübingen, 2005.

Marc Pauka, *Kultur, Fortschritt und Reziprozität. Die Begriffsgeschichte des zivilisierten Staates im Völkerrecht*, Nomos, Baden-Baden, 2012.

Roger O'Keefe, *The Protection of Cultural Property in Armed Conflict*, Cambridge University Press, Cambridge, 2006.

Friedrich Saalfeld, *Handbuch des positiven Völkerrechts*, E.F. Osiander, Tübingen, 1833.

Wayne Sandholtz, *Prohibiting Plunder: How Norms Change*, Oxford University Press, Oxford and New York, 2007.

Cyrus Schayegh, "The Mandates and/as Decolonization", in Cyrus Schayegh and Andrew Arsan (Eds.), *The Routledge Handbook of the History of the Middle East Mandates*, Routledge, London and New York, 2015, pp. 412–419.

Daniel Shapiro, "A Universalist: Fathering Fields", *International Journal of Cultural Property*, vol. 21, no. 3, 2014, pp. 237–242.

Thomas Skouteris, "Engaging History in International Law", in José María Beneyto, David Kennedy, Justo Corti Varela and John Haskell (Eds.), *New Approaches to International Law. The European and American Experiences*, T.M.C. Asser Press, The Hague, 2012, pp. 99–121.

Sebastian M. Spitra, *Die Verwaltung von Kultur im Völkerrecht. Eine postkoloniale Geschichte*, Nomos, Baden-Baden, forthcoming 2018.

Rolf Stucky, "Henry Seyrig – Engagierte Archäologe und Verwalter des Antikendienstes während der Mandatszeit", in Charlotte Trümpler (Ed.), *Das große Spiel. Archäologie und Politik zur Zeit des Kolonialismus (1860–1940)*, Dumon, Köln, 2008, pp. 505–511.

Caspar Sylvest, "International Law in Nineteenth-Century Britain", *British Yearbook of International Law*, vol. 75, 2004, pp. 9–70.

Jiří Toman, "The Control System under the 1954 Hague Convention and Its 1999 Second Protocol", in Paul Meerts (Ed.), *Culture and International Law*, TMC Asser Press, The Hague, 2008.

Jiří Toman, *The Protection of Cultural Property in the Event of Armed Conflict*, UNESCO Publishing, Dartmouth, 1996.

Emanuel Ullmann, *Völkerrecht*, J.C.B. Mohr (Paul Siebeck), Tübingen, 1908.

Roberto Unger, *The Critical Legal Studies Movement. Another Time, a Greater Task*, Verso, London and New York, 2015.

Sabine von Schorlemer, *Kulturgutzerstörung. Die Auslöschung von Kulturerbe in Krisenländern als Herausforderung für die Vereinten Nationen*, Nomos, Baden-Baden, 2016.

Ana Filipa Vrdoljak, *International Law, Museums and the Return of Cultural Objects*, Cambridge University Press, Cambridge, 2006.

Stephan Wendehorst, "Johann Jacob Moser: Der Reichspublizist als Völkerrechtler", in Stephan Wendehorst (Ed.), *Die Anatomie frühneuzeitlicher Imperien. Herrschaftsmanagement jenseits von Staat und Nation: Institutionen, Personal und Techniken*, De Gruyter, Berlin, München and Boston, MA 2015, pp. 303–324.

Rüdiger Wolfrum, "Cultural Property, Protection in Armed Conflict", in Rüdiger Wolfrum (Ed.), Max Planck Encyclopedia of Public International Law, 2012.

Karl Salomo Zachariä, *Vierzig Bücher vom Staate*, vol. 5, C.F. Winter, Heidelberg, 1841.

4 From spies to international criminals

The influence of the Austro-Hungarian counter-espionage service on the International Criminal Police Commission

Mark Lewis

4.1 Introduction

European attempts to internationalize police cooperation emerged in the conjuncture of new power relations, technologies, and economic forces. Historians have traced the history of the International Criminal Police Commission (ICPC) and Interpol, its successor organization, to an anti-anarchist conference of police officials in Rome in 1898, which spread the notion that political criminals should be subject to extradition (not asylum) and encouraged the use of the *portrait parlé* system to record and transmit suspects' physical characteristics. In 1904, ten countries signed a secret agreement in St. Petersburg to create police bureaus to keep files on anarchists, share that information with each other, and standardize rules for expelling them.[1] In the standard accounts of the history of international police cooperation, the First World War is considered a dormant period when cooperation was impossible because police forces, which had gained some bureaucratic independence from their interior ministries, were supposedly subjected to stricter political control, and governments that had signed the St. Petersburg Protocols were now enemies (Germany and Austria-Hungary on one side, Russia on the other).[2] Furthermore, it might appear that police turned away from international cooperation during the war because they prioritized domestic matters, such as locating saboteurs and spies, and had to maintain censorship of the post and press. Supposedly, the police's interest in recapturing the earlier spirit of cooperation was only resuscitated in 1923, when 131 police officials met in Vienna to form the ICPC. Superficially, this body was supposed to coordinate the fight against international, "non-political" criminals, including counterfeiters, fencers of stolen goods, drug traffickers, and confidence men who slipped over borders.[3] Yet, recent scholarship has shown that high-level policemen who were the official

1 Bach Jensen, 1981, pp. 323–347.
2 Jäger, 2006, p. 16; Deflem, 2002a, pp. 110, 119–121.
3 Schulz, 1926.

delegates to the ICPC used their contacts to deal with political matters and practice racial profiling. For example, Austrian and Yugoslav police officials developed a rocky relationship concerning the repression of Croatian terrorists between 1929 and 1934;[4] Swedish and Nazi German police officials, who had met through their ICPC contacts, worked together to exchange information about political refugees in 1937–1939 and destroy an anti-Nazi group of saboteurs (the Wollweber League) between 1938 and 1940; and the ICPC itself set up an international information bureau in 1936 to collect photos, fingerprints, and criminal records of "Gypsies."[5]

As a contribution to the history of international law, this chapter argues that new forms of legal thinking were not the sole generator of changes in international organization and actual state practice in the 19th and 20th centuries. International law was not only the domain of law scholars, foreign office officials, and humanitarian organizations. It was also territory traversed by police officials who first built new imperial networks of communication and repression in their countries, especially during the First World War, then wanted to apply these structures to international police cooperation after the First World War. Furthermore, they wanted to gain international legitimacy for methods they were already using by enshrining them in international legal conventions.

This chapter will show how political policing in Austria-Hungary during the First World War actually worked, and that the bureaucratic model for controlling sabotage and espionage in the Habsburg Empire was taken over by the ICPC for international crime after the war. The war was not a caesura but an important phase of police development, which has not been sufficiently covered in two of the main studies dealing with the evolution of international police organization.[6] Second, this chapter questions sociologist Mathieu Deflem's position that police forces became pure "Weberian" rational-purposive bureaucracies, only interested in fighting crime and wanted to liberate themselves from political bureaucracies.[7] In fact, they were deeply enmeshed in ideological and political matters, which is one of the reasons why they developed into independent executors of power in the 20th century.

4.2 A new security system: the *Defensive Kundschaftsdienst*

In May 1914, before the outbreak of the "Great War," the Austro-Hungarian military intelligence bureau, the Vienna Police Directorate, and the Hungarian border police formed a new type of domestic counter-intelligence system to track alleged spies and suspicious persons. Authorities wanted to create this system to counter Russian espionage in the dual monarchy, which had grown rapidly since

4 Lewis, 2014a, pp. 186–212.
5 Selling, 2017, pp. 329–353.
6 Jäger, 2006; Deflem, 2002.
7 Deflem, 2002, pp. 12–26, 147–152.

1906. Since 1910, provincial governments in Austria had instructed police to increase surveillance of bridges and military installations and report suspicious activity to the military, but they had no imperial-wide system to track convicted and potential spies. Officials believed that it was too easy for a convicted spy, who had been expelled from one province of the empire, to move to another.[8] The new system, called the *Defensive Kundschaftsdienst*, was supposed to permit quick responses to find and arrest wanted persons, and enable rapid communication between State Police officials, in charge of internal state security, and military intelligence, which spied on external countries.[9]

Austria-Hungary, a dual monarchy of more than 60 million persons, was governed by four administrations: Austria, Hungary, Bosnia,[10] and the Kingdom of Croatia, Slavonia, and Dalmatia. In the new domestic surveillance system, a Central Office (*Zentralstelle*) was established in each capital or provincial capital: Vienna, Budapest, Sarajevo, and Zagreb. Each one collected files on all known and suspected spies, then indexed the files; thus, this was not an imperial system with one center, but a linked network with four centers. They sent out regular bulletins of wanted persons and answered inquiries about suspects from lower-level police departments.[11] Each Central Office was the main point of contact with a military intelligence bureau (*Evidenzbüro*), the military's espionage branch, which sent them information about civilians prosecuted in military courts for espionage. Beneath the four Central Offices were Main Offices (*Hauptstellen*) which directed investigations and sent reports and descriptions of suspects to the Central Offices.[12] They were supposed to have investigative independence from the Central Offices though sometimes the latter issued urgent warnings about certain persons or told the Main Offices to pursue certain cases. Usually, the Main Offices were stationed in existing Police Directorates (higher police authorities in major cities) or in border police stations (the system in Hungary).

According to Austria's Interior Minister, the system would create a "reservoir of data"[13] which all offices could share. The Main Offices supervised the civilian population and watched foreigners on the dual monarchy's borders

8 Hrvatski Državni Arhiv (Croatian National Archive, Zagreb), Fond 79 [HR-HDA-79], Odjel za Unutarnje Poslove- Središnja defenzivna dojavna služba [UOZV-SDDS], Kut. 5687 (1), 9/1914, K.u.K. Chef des Generalstabes. K.Nr. 4444 von 1914, Protokoll über die Konferenz: "Schaffung der Zentral- und Hauptstellen für den defensiven Kundschaftsdienst" im Mai 1914, pp. 2–3. Hereafter, Protokoll 1914. On pre-war cooperation between the Maxilimian Ronge, the main Evidenzbüro official who created the new system, and the Vienna Police Directorate, see Moritz, Leidinger and Jagschitz, 2007, pp. 100–110.

9 The following two paragraphs are adapted from Lewis, 2018.

10 The Bureau of Bosnian Affairs was under the Joint Finance Ministry, and all major decisions required the approval of both the Austrian and Hungarian parliaments. See Okey, 2007, p. 30.

11 HR-HDA-79/UOZV-SDDS, Kut. 5687 (1), 9/1914, K.k. Minister des Innern to all Landeschefs, Schaffung einer Zentralstelle für den defensiven Kundschaftsdienst, 5319/M.I., 25 May 1914. On the Zagreb Central Office, see Stanišić, 1993, pp. 181–206.

12 Protokoll 1914, Beilage 2, Übersicht über die Z.St. und H.St., sowie über die betreffenden Haupt K.Stellen. The latter (Kundschaft-Stellen) were military intelligence bureaus.

13 Protokoll 1914, p. 13.

who might be spying.[14] Both functions were long established in Austria, part of the Higher State Police system under Anton Graf von Pergen and later Police Minister Count Joseph Sedlnitzky.[15] In 1914, the system did not require special approval from the Austrian and Hungarian parliaments and was formed with the approval of the different interior ministries; furthermore, it was strictly an internal sovereign matter, not subject to international law. Once the war began, the Emperor suspended civil liberties in the Austrian half of the empire by declaring a state of emergency under an 1869 law, broadening police powers to search houses, detain suspects, and open letters without a judge's permission.[16] The surveillance system was integrated with mail censors and police forces, which used their own detectives and officers to investigate cases. Investigations started from a censor's warning, information from a police informant, a notification from military intelligence, or a tip from a member of the public, who reported a "suspicious" neighbor. During the war, the authorities made various changes to the system because communication between parts of the empire was not always smooth, the military's aggressive prosecutions clogged the court systems, and there were shortages in personnel since policemen were drafted.[17]

Nevertheless, from the police's point of view, the system prevented major instances of espionage and sabotage inside the empire from 1914 to 1917. In fact, the authorities were so confident in March 1917 that Austria-Hungary would win the war that they discussed how to convert the system for counter-espionage during peacetime.[18] In May 1918, after the Treaty of Brest-Litovsk, the chiefs discussed expanding the system to deal with the occupation of Ukraine, the Romanian border, and the increased surveillance of weapons factories in Vienna.[19] Their belief in the efficacy of the system was not really shaken by the massive factory strikes in Vienna in January 1918, either. The Viennese State Police regularly reported on these strikes and the resumption of work, advising

14 Protokoll 1914, p. 23.

15 Emerson, 1968, pp. 31–56.

16 Koller (Ed.), 1914, pp. 1–6, Art. 4–5; Rauchensteiner, 1993, pp. 107–109.

17 Österreichisches Staatsarchiv, Allgemeines Verwaltungsarchiv, Ministerium des Innern (OeStA, AVA, MdI), K. 1931, 20, Protokoll N. ad 5338 ex 1915, PolDion in Wien to the Präsidium des k.k. Ministeriums des Innern, Pr.Z.968. Z.St./2, 22 March 1915; HR-HDA-79, UOZV-SDDS, Kut. 5717 (31), 596/1917, K.u.k. Armeeoberkommando. Nachrichtenabteilung. Evb. Nr. 5125/I, Protokoll zu der am 21. und 22. Mai l.J. stattgefundenen Besprechung mit den Leitern der vier Zentralstellen für den Spionageabwehrdienst im k.u.k. Kriegsministerium (Evb. d. Gstbs.), 22 May 1918. Hereafter Protokoll May 1918.

18 HR-HDA-79, UOZV-SDDS, Kut. 5717 (31), 596/1917, Nachrichtenabteilung des k. und k. Armeeoberkommandos, Protokoll zu der am 20. und 21. März 1917 stattgefundenen Besprechung mit den Leitern der vier Zentralstellen für den defensiven Nachrichtendienst im Evidenzbureau des k.u.k. Generalstabes, Evb.Nr. 2308 res.

19 Protokoll May 1918.

the government that it should negotiate with moderate Social Democratic leaders and arrest radicals who wanted to continue striking.[20]

The greatest challenge the system faced was dealing with Czech, South Slavic, and Polish nationalist politicians and activists who were seeking independence and went into exile abroad. There they raised money for legions to fight Austria-Hungary and established diplomatic contacts with the Entente, seeking their support to establish independent states. The problem of breakaway nationalities reached a crisis point during 1918, at the same time Vienna city police had to deal with streams of returning soldiers (with weapons) and a public that was hungry, disillusioned, and suffering social breakdown.[21] When the empire collapsed in the fall of 1918, the Austro-Hungarian military was immediately dissolved—and the new Vienna police chief, Johannes Schober, boasted that his policemen were the only state instrument to keep the peace and save the state from Bolshevism.[22]

This sketch describes the structure of the system in the abstract. Two cases demonstrate how police, censors, military intelligence, and government officials communicated and built an investigation. The cases also show that police surveillance and detention were directed against subject nationalities, especially those linked to areas where Austria-Hungary was involved in intensive combat against Serbia and Russia. The first case concerns a 65-year-old Serbian businessman from Hungary, exemplifying how the "suspect's" privately expressed sentiments were amplified into grounds for his internment. The second deals with a 40-year-old Polish parliamentary representative from Galicia, arrested because of his nationalist politics.

4.3 Arbitrary internment based on private sentiments: the case of Johann Notaroš[23]

Notaroš, born in 1849, was a Serbian businessman with Hungarian citizenship.[24] In August 1914, he came to Vienna with his wife, Danica Nikolić, and rented an apartment. On 25 August 1914, about a month after Austria-Hungary declared war on Serbia,[25] he received a one-line telegram from Vojvodina, an area of mixed nationalities that was part of Hungary. The telegram read, "Due to well-known circumstances advise you to remain there / would like to come there." A censor pulled the telegram, determining that the sender was a Serbian

20 OeStA, AVA, MdI, Präsidale, K. 2074, Protokoll Nr. 2414 ex 1918/M.I., Pr.Z.52356/23 K., 21 Jänner 1918. Arbeitseinstellungen in Wien.

21 Healy, 2004, pp. 300, 306.

22 Landespolizeidirektion Wien, Archiv (Vienna Police Directorate, Archive [LPDW]), Interpol/1925, Johannes Schober, Speech to the International Police Conference in New York, attached to Schober to Enright, 9 August 1925.

23 All documents about this case come from LPDW, 1914, Scha. V/7, 433/914/K.

24 He was a director of a warrant bank (*Versatzbank*) in Belgrade.

25 28 July 1914. See Rauchensteiner, 1993, p. 95.

woman, and the addressee was her brother-in-law, Johann Notarosch (Notaroš). The censor said Notaroš had lived for many years in Belgrade, was known to be a "Great Serb" (meaning he supported the expansion of the Serbian Kingdom with territory taken from Austria-Hungary), and was "probably politically unreliable." The censor twisted the meaning of the single line, claiming that Notaroš's sister-in-law was warning him that if he came back to Vojvodina, he would be arrested. This information was sent to the Vienna Police Directorate, where he was investigated by Dr. Otto Steinhäusl, who became Vienna's Police President 24 years later under the Nazis.[26] The police found Notaroš in Vienna, questioned him and his wife, and searched their apartment. When checking Notaroš's residency registration, police found out he had not told the truth on the form; he was a widower and not actually married to Danica. For this offense, he was fined and given 12 hours in jail.

Several months passed. Austria-Hungary had invaded Serbia and marched into Belgrade, but then was kicked out in a stunning reversal in December 1914. This defeat may have made the censors more zealous. They intercepted a postcard that Notaroš sent to a business partner in Geneva. Mainly, it was a business letter, but the censor objected to two statements. Notaroš wrote that while he was sad to have to celebrate his family's saint's day in Vienna, he still had cause "to be happy and sing"; second, he stated that he had read in the newspaper that "the Germans have used violent measures to take everything they need from everyone." These remarks triggered a State Police investigation because police thought he sympathized with Serbia. Local police interrogated him and searched his residence, confiscating letters and cards written in Serbian, which a police translator interpreted. Two letters, neither actually written by Notaroš, got him in trouble. One was written by his female companion, but the censors had not allowed it to reach the recipient. It contained a line stating, "Yesterday Anka wrote us that they are well and that a new medical inspection [for military service] will happen in February. This is just what we need." The other letter was written to Notaroš by his grandson, a first-year volunteer in the Austro-Hungarian army. The young soldier, a Serb stationed in Cracow, complained that he did not know anyone in his unit, did not speak Polish, and had to work on Sundays.

The data from the censors, the local police investigations, and the police translator were sent to the State Police, which decided in January 1915 that Notaroš was a "Great Serb" who was "politically questionable"—a polysemous phrase which meant there was something about the subject's attitude (*Gesinnung*) requiring the person's removal from normal society. This could mean different things, depending on the situation: He/she was too devoted to nationalist ideas and committees, exhibited pronounced anti-Habsburg

26 Some police officials in the First World War era were not simply supporters of non-nationalist bureaucratic absolutism but developed anti-Slavic and German nationalist views. Steinhäusl, for example, became the head of the Vienna criminal police, was involved in the Nazis' 1934 putsch plans in Austria, and was removed from the force in 1934. He returned in 1938 to become the Police President under the Nazis. Weisz, 1991, p. 40; Rothländer, 2012, p. 444.

views, participated in radical socialist or communist organizations, or was in some way "untrustworthy." In Notaroš' case, the Austrian governor's office (*Statthalterei*) said he was "politically questionable" because he had allegedly not told the truth when he registered Danica as his wife. His comments to his associate in Geneva that he had reason to celebrate during his saint's day supposedly referred "openly to the Austrian misfortune in Serbia." His companion Danica had commented negatively about a new draft, and Notaroš' grandson complained about army life. The authorities had no evidence that he committed a crime; they evaluated his political attitude, his *Gesinnung*.[27] On the police's order, Notaroš was interned in a "confinement station" in Salzerbad, south of Vienna in January, transferred to an internment camp at Raabs, Lower Austria in May 1915, and then interned in Hungary (Kismarton, Sopron County). He was still there in May 1916 when he petitioned the Vienna Police Directorate about whether he could travel to Vienna when his internment was over to visit his wife/companion, who had an eye disease. His ultimate fate is unknown.[28]

The case shows how the chain of information passed from the censor to the police and ultimately the State Police, and how the internment of a Hungarian subject, who was Serbian, was considered a legitimate form of "defensive policing" to remove any alleged Serbian threat from the Austrian capital. The filing system ensured that when he appeared again in 1916 (with his petition to the Vienna police), the police knew his prior history. The Austrian police excelled in this type of record-keeping, and the Hungarian and Croatian Central Offices had sent representatives to Vienna in 1914 to learn it.[29] Centralized filing systems were not new for the war. Vienna already had a central registry of alleged anarchists, as well as prostitutes allowed to work in regulated bordellos.[30] It also maintained a *Zentralpolizeiblatt* (a blotter of everyone arrested); a list of search notices (*Fahndungsblatt*) that was sent to all Austrian and German authorities; and an *Evidenzblatt*, a registry of all people sentenced by Vienna courts, Viennese residents sentenced by foreign courts, and all people expelled from Austria. It exchanged this registry with Budapest and Pressburg (Bratislava). But before the war, it did not share the *Zentralpolizeiblatt* and *Fahndungsblatt* with Zagreb or Sarajevo, so the wartime system was expanded to cover more cities. [31] In addition, all the Central Offices were now in contact with military intelligence, adding that dimension to the network.

27 Healy, 2004, pp. 191–193.

28 We do not know the police's answer because only the first page of the reply survives in the file, and it just states his request.

29 Protokoll 1914, pp. 13–15.

30 Wingfield, 2017, pp. 20–21, 51–52.

31 Protokoll 1914, pp. 15–16. Austria established a Central Bureau for the Supervision of Anarchists on 29 April 1899, which is mentioned in connection to the wartime Zentralstelle in OeStA, AVA, MdI Präsidium, K. 1931, Protokoll N. ad 5338 ex 1915, Pr.Z.968. Z.St./2, 22 March 1915.

4.4 Police and military cooperation: the case of Jan Zamorski[32]

The police took the leading investigative role in Notaroš' case, while military intelligence directed investigations aimed at breaking a faction of the National Democratic Party, a Polish nationalist party. The main thrust of the investigation was directed at politicians and intellectuals from the Eastern Galician city of Lemberg (Lwów, L'viv). Jan Zamorski, however, was from Cracow. Born in 1874, he was a secondary school professor who became a Polish deputy in the Austrian parliament. His case demonstrates how the military intervened in the legal and police system in Galicia to suppress the Polish independence movement; then, the Austrian state police got involved, providing intelligence to civilian leaders who wanted to suppress Polish nationalists in Eastern Galicia in 1917–1918. Information was freely shared between military intelligence and the state security police, demonstrating that the police, as part of the civilian bureaucracy, worked closely with the military, as typically occurs during a war.

In August 1914, different Polish political parties in Galicia formed the Polish Supreme National Committee to organize Polish troops in Galicia, ostensibly to fight for the Habsburgs. The Army High Command (*Armeeoberkommando, AOK*) agreed to this arrangement, forming a Western and Eastern Legion.[33] However, Polish soldiers in the Eastern Legion thought the rations and weapons the AOK gave them were substandard, so they refused to swear an oath of allegiance to the Habsburg Emperor. They were encouraged to do this by Galician politicians and intellectuals who formed a splinter group in the National Democratic Party (one of the Polish parties that controlled the Supreme National Committee). The splinter group was more pro-Russian than pro-Habsburg: it wanted to build bridges to Roman Dmowski's National Democratic Party in Russian-controlled Congress Poland, with the eventual goal of unifying partitioned Poland. Therefore, after the soldiers refused to take the oath, the Habsburg military intelligence bureau (*Evidenzbüro*) accused this faction of treason and decided to prosecute their leaders.[34]

In November 1914, the AOK's Intelligence Department (*Nachrichtenabteilung*) told the Cracow Police Directorate to arrest two directors of the East Galician Legion, as well as Zamorski. He was accused of helping dissolve the Legion by propagating the idea that the men should refuse to take the oath of allegiance. When the police searched his house, they found 500 copies of a report that the Military Committee of the Supreme National Committee had prepared about the legion's problems. Although he had not written the report, military prosecutors claimed he disseminated it to cause the legion's demise. And though

32 All documents about this case come from OeStA, AVA, MdI, Präsidale, K. 2076, Präs. No. 8567 ex 1918/M.I. and Präs. No. 8905 ex 1918/M.I.

33 Wandycz, 1974, pp. 332–337.

34 For the empire's use of treason trials during the war to stifle dissent, see Cornwall, 2015, pp. 113–134.

he was not a member of the National Democratic Party, prosecutors alleged that he was an “intellectual instrument” of the party’s Eastern Galician faction, centered around Dr. Alexander Graf Skarbek, chief of the military department of the Eastern Legion. Prosecutors alleged that this group had committed treason by working out an agreement with Dmowski in Russian Poland. They stated that they were not directing their case against Zamorski alone, but against “the idea of political unification of all Poles under a unified state government,” an idea propagated by Zamorski and “his party colleagues.” Zamorski was investigated between February and March 1915, a period when seven-eighths of Galicia had been conquered by Russia, which was also occupying Lemberg and working with certain Galician National Democratic politicians; the Austrian government viewed them as collaborators. Thus, the stage was set for the Austrians to attempt to eliminate the anti-Habsburg wing of Polish national movement. Zamorski was sentenced to nine months for his association with the Galician National Democrats while Skarbek escaped prosecution because he had fled to Switzerland. However, military prosecutors were not able to find substantial evidence proving Zamorski committed treason, so he was released in August 1915 and placed under observation by the gendarmerie in Upper Austria.

In November 1915, Zamorski, then 41 years old, was drafted for military service. The AOK’s Intelligence Department ordered that he had to join a unit on the Italian front, where conditions were extremely harsh. He was required to join a German-speaking unit, probably to punish him for his Polish nationalism. He applied for a reserve officers’ school but was rejected, so he became an infantryman in a battalion of soldiers half his age. In November 1916, he was captured and interrogated by an Italian intelligence officer, who sympathetically viewed Zamorski as an exhausted man who had suffered incredible privations because of his support for Polish independence. (Amazingly, we know about Zamorski’s fate and this encounter because the Austrian army found the Italian intelligence report when it captured a castle where the Italian Third Army Command had been located.) The Italian army released Zamorski, who went to live in Viterbo, Italy in spring 1917. Then, with the help of Italian friends, he went to Paris, where he became active in the Polish National Democratic Party. The Austrian government knew about this because in 1917, censors had picked out Zamorski’s name from various pieces of mail coming into the empire.

In 1918, the Interior Ministry wanted the Galician governor to find out whether Zamorski was still collecting a salary as a professor. This was connected to a new initiative to counter the Galician National Democrats in 1918 and cultivate the support of moderate Polish parties to pass the military budget. Minister President Ignaz von Seidler had received reports that the Interior Ministry was not acting ruthlessly enough against this “all Polish” party, so he issued an order in March that the Interior Minister should repress nationalist publications in Galicia, expand military trials to cover the widest circles of Polish nationalists, and “unmask” the professoriate at Lemberg University for its unreliability. The State Police in Vienna provided several key reports—summaries of military intelligence investigations of Zamorski and Grabek, as well as background reports on the National Democrats—that the Minister President and Interior Ministry used to form their proposals. Thus, the police helped legitimize the repressive campaign though it was started by the military. There were limits, however, about what the authorities could do about the Polish nationalists. Several figures that the Minister President wanted to prosecute (Zamorski, Skarbek, and others) were all abroad. Extradition requests, obviously, would not be honored by enemy countries.

4.5 The post-war influence of the counter-espionage system on the ICPC

Austria-Hungary collapsed as a result of the war, and the central files of the *Defensive Kundschaftsdienst* were taken over by each successor state. In the new Austrian Republic, Vienna's files remained with the Austrian State Police, which then built a post-war intelligence service with a similar filing system.[35] Vienna lost its status as an imperial capital and experienced continuing hunger and housing shortages into the 1920s, as well as social conflicts between workers, independent proprietors, and the middle class.[36] Vienna became a center of revolutionary movements on the extreme left and right, as well as a center of operations for various European nationalities that had not received their own states at the Paris Peace Conference. The Viennese police initially sought a modus vivendi with the Social Democratic government, then veered in an authoritarian direction, aligning with the Austro-fascist *Heimwehr*. Internationally, it sought a means to recover its status as an institution skilled at scientific policing and tracking suspects.

Between 1922 and 1926, the Viennese police played a decisive role in forming a new international police organization to track and find "international criminals," defined as thieves, swindlers, and counterfeiters who committed crimes outside their home countries.[37] Johannes Schober, Vienna's Police President (chief of police), hosted a conference in Vienna in 1923 to discuss international policing; 131 police officials from Europe, Egypt, Japan, China, and the U.S. attended.[38] During the war, he had been head of the political department of the Vienna Police Directorate and had devised the *Defensive Kundschaftsdienst* with Major Maximilian Ronge, chief of the military's intelligence service.[39] At the 1923 conference, police officials decided to form a new organization, the ICPC, to improve police collaboration to fight "common crime," not political crime. At their first meeting in 1924, Dresden's Police President Robert Heindl proposed a system in which different police agencies, each acting autonomously in its own country, would send information about known international criminals to a central office in Vienna,

35 Jagschitz, 1978, pp. 49–95.
36 Botz, 2008, pp. 15–23, 177–178, 373–374, 393–395, 577–584.
37 Schulz, 1926.
38 Deflem, 2002, p. 126.
39 On Ronge, see Moritz, Leidinger, and Jagschitz, 2007, pp. 100–110.

which would compile the data into a card-index system. Bruno Schulz, a Director with the Vienna Police Directorate, proposed that Vienna also create a searching service for wanted persons (*Internationale Fahndungsevidenz*) and a publication containing wanted notices (*Polizeiblatt*). An ICPC administrative committee determined that police departments would use standardized forms and confirmed that Vienna's Police Directorate would house the central filing system, answer inquiries from other police forces, and publish wanted notices in a publication called *International Public Security* (*Internationale Öffentliche Sicherheit*), which began in January 1925. These plans were finalized in 1926.[40]

Many components came directly from the *Defensive Kundschaftsdienst* during the war: the central filing system, the international police blotter, and the notion that main offices should autonomously direct investigations. During the war, the Main Offices (based in Police Directorates, for example) carried out the investigations and reported the results to a Central Office (Vienna, Budapest, Zagreb, or Sarajevo). This was similar to the ICPC system, in which a city police force (Paris, Brussels, Berlin, or Dresden, for example) conducted its own investigation and sent case file information to Vienna, which compiled the information. Vienna would then notify other police agencies, which could track or arrest the person. Although the Vienna Police Directorate had operated many types of central registries in the past—and many European police bureaus published their own police blotters of wanted notices—Vienna gained the position as the central ICPC office. This was not simply because it had a high degree of technical competence,[41] but because it was able to deal with multiple languages,[42] and, as a former imperial capital, had experience with the police in many provinces that later became parts of successor states.

One major difference between the *Defensive Kundschaftsdienst* and the ICPC was that the former intended to concentrate on spies while the latter targeted "international criminals." The European police's focus on counterfeiters, drug smugglers, and confidence men was not a new phenomenon; police in the 1880s–1890s believed a new type of skillful international criminal was outsmarting the police using modern communications and transportation.[43] For the police, this criminal was a distinctly modern type, a technologically savvy shape-shifter. The police connected this modern mobile criminal, who easily crossed borders, with the massive changes wrought by the war—flows of refugees, new political borders, and the disintegration of old structures of authority, ranging from empires to the patriarchal family. Not only was crime supposedly on the rise but so was international crime. Hence, a new type of international organization was necessary to counter it.

40 Schulz, 1926, pp. 2–5.

41 Deflem, 2002, p. 137, only emphasizes Vienna's technical capabilities and history of trying to establish international police cooperation but does not mention the *Defensive Kundschaftsdienst* or the Vienna police's imperial legacy.

42 Schulz, 1926, p. 7.

43 Jäger, 2006, pp. 115–126; Knepper, 2010, pp. 12–42.

There were, however, connections between the authorities' concepts of the spy and international criminal: the use of deceptive masks. In 1925, Oskar Dressler, a Viennese police official involved with the ICPC, stated that the essence of the international criminal was that he operated by deception and fraud, always telling a new story wherever he turned up.[44] This is quite similar to the idea of the spy, who masks his/her identity with fictions and impersonations. The historical development of the "confidence man" is an under-investigated figure. The police imagination and the minds of writers associated this figure with 19th-century economic booms and also with wartime profiteering. Both the spy and confidence man had to be "unmasked" to protect the public. The spy who threatened one state (or empire) was an enemy agent while the international criminal was the "enemy of public order," meaning all states had an interest in stopping this figure. Both the spy and international criminal were shape-shifters, and both, the police believed, could be exposed through a more efficient police system that relied on "reservoirs of data" and rapid communication among police agencies.

The creation of the ICPC occurred outside the framework of international law though prior international legal agreements contributed to it. For example, the International Anti-Anarchist Conference in Rome in 1898 agreed that each participating state would create a central agency to surveil anarchists and directly exchange information with agencies in other states, and Austria-Hungary acceded to this agreement. Yet, Britain never signed the final protocol and France was opposed to creating an international police bureaucracy.[45] The 1904 International Agreement for the Suppression of the "White Slave Traffic" instructed contracting governments to establish authorities to centralize information "concerning the procuration of women or girls with a view to their debauchery in a foreign country" and have these authorities (such as special bureaus within the police) communicate directly with each other, without having to go through consulates.[46] Austria-Hungary did this as well.

Yet, there are two important points to keep in mind. Before 1913, the Viennese Police Directorate communicated information about criminal investigations directly with police in several states (the German Empire and the Netherlands) and cities (including Belgrade, Bucharest, London, Stockholm, and Venice). The police believed that direct communication led to quicker arrests because they did not have to go through diplomatic channels. Yet, direct communication with the Paris police was limited to dealing with anarchism and "white slave trafficking" since these were specified under international agreements. Direct communication about other types of crimes, such as theft, counterfeiting, and murder, was not allowed because of legal restrictions. The French government said that all

44 LPDW, Interpol/1925, Oskar Dressler, Material für die Skizze eines Vertrages, 16 April 1925, Pr.Z.II-286/1/2/a.

45 Jensen, 1981, pp. 334–335.

46 Suppression of White Slave Traffic, 18 May 1904, Art. 1, available at: www.loc.gov/law/help/us-treaties/bevans/m-ust000001-0424.pdf (accessed 16 September 2017). See also Limoncelli, 2010, pp. 9–11, 19–41.

Austrian requests had to be made by a judge (acting as a *commission rogatoire*) and transmitted by Austria's Justice Ministry to the French government. The Vienna police and Austrian government thought this would lead to unnecessary delays and wanted to negotiate an international agreement with France, but this did not materialize before the First World War.[47] Second, even after the ICPC became operational in the mid-1920s, it could only coordinate the storage and sharing of information about wanted criminals and suspects on the run. It had no power to order arrests or to require extraditions, which were governed by bilateral extradition treaties.

In the 1920s, the Vienna police tried to position itself as the international center for different national police bureaus to communicate with each other, as well as serve as a central database of criminals, their techniques, and authoritative information police could use for investigations. This ran in advance of international law. For example, Dutch police proposed in 1923 that all states create bureaus to monitor the counterfeiting of currency and other financial instruments, as well as send examples of their currency to a central office, a position that Vienna wanted. The Dutch concern was driven by the fact that out-of-control inflation after the First World War made counterfeiting the stable Dutch currency attractive while Vienna was concerned that controls against counterfeiting were weak in the successor states, which were still using the old imperial currency (only adding their own stamps). More broadly, governments feared that counterfeiting posed a threat to their debt-ridden economies, and that weakened economies would cause the Paris Peace Treaties to unravel.[48] Following the first ICPC conference in 1923, European police formed 27 bureaus to centralize information on counterfeiting and discussed making Vienna the *provisional* center for the exchange of information.[49] In 1926, the ICPC (or really the Vienna Police) was able to position itself favorably when negotiations were underway in the League of Nations to create the Convention for the Suppression of Counterfeiting Currency.[50] Completed in 1929, it provisionally allowed the ICPC to serve as an international clearinghouse of information about counterfeiters and counterfeiting techniques.

After Croatian separatists (the Ustaša) organized the assassination of King Aleksandar of Yugoslavia and French Foreign Minister Louis Barthou in Marseille in 1934, the ICPC, led by Vienna, tried to leverage its position as the central anti-counterfeiting office to take over a similar role to coordinate the sharing of information about international terrorists. In January 1935, it lobbied the League of Nations to send a representative to the legal committee that

47 OeStA, AVA, MdI, Allgem., K. 2088, Protokoll Nr. 206050 ex 1913.

48 Petruccelli, 2016, pp. 511–514.

49 Schulz, 1926, pp. 9–11; League of Nations, *Proceedings of the International Conference for the Adoption of a Convention for the Suppression of Counterfeiting Currency*, Geneva, 1930. C.328.M.114.1929.II, Netherlands Legation to Secretary-General, 21 June 1926.

50 League of Nations, *Proceedings*, C.328.M.114.1929.II, Austrian Federal Government to Secretary-General, 20 August 1926.

drafted what became the 1937 Convention for the Repression and Punishment of International Terrorism.[51] In 1935, it also presented a draft convention, borrowing the definition of terrorism used in an earlier French proposal ("attacks on the life and freedom" of state officials, civil servants, and "private persons due to their political views.")[52] While the Austrian police had aimed to suppress espionage and sabotage across the empire during the First World War, it now thought in international terms, wanting to suppress the production of counterfeit passports and ensure that terrorists could not obtain political asylum. The President of the ICPC, Michael Skubl (who was Vienna's Police President under an Austro-fascist government), was really playing a double game. On one hand, he wanted the ICPC (and specifically Vienna) to become the central information clearinghouse for terrorist investigations, but on the other, he protected a key member of the Croatian Ustaša—Ivan Perčević, a former Austro-Hungarian military intelligence officer who resided in Vienna and was involved in the Marseille assassinations.[53] In his capacity as ICPC President, Skubl contacted ICPC Vice President Kurt Daluege (who was head of the police department in Nazi Germany's Interior Ministry) and informed him about his request to send a technical expert to work on the League's anti-terrorism committee.[54] Daluege replied that since Germany had withdrawn from the League, he hoped the ICPC's cooperation would protect the interests of states not in the League (i.e. Germany). He requested that Skubl consult with him about the choice of an ICPC representative, "taking into account German wishes."[55] This did not happen, however, because French and British representatives objected to giving the ICPC a seat at the table. The final anti-terrorism convention did not give Vienna the powerful position of serving as a central clearinghouse of information about terrorist suspects.[56] Following Germany's takeover of Austria in 1938, Skubl was removed from his position and arrested. The Nazi police engineered a way to put the leadership of the ICPC under Reinhard Heydrich (head of the Nazi *Sicherheitsdienst*) and move the central office from Vienna to Berlin in 1940.[57]

4.6 Conclusion

This chapter's argument—that the creation of a new type of counter-espionage network inside Austria-Hungary influenced the bureaucratic structure of the ICPC—demonstrates that some aspects of international police cooperation

51 Bundesarchiv (Berlin-Lichterfelde), R 901/78049, P.K. 10/35, Skubl to Secretary-General, 3 January 1935 (copy of a German translation sent to Daluege).

52 Ibid., deutsche Übersetzung, Vorentwurf eines Übereinkommens, Art. 3; Motiven-Bericht, pp. 2–3.

53 Lewis, 2014a, pp. 203–205, 210.

54 Bundesarchiv, R 901/78049, I.K.P.K. 10/2/35, Skubl to Daluege, 13 January 1935 (copy).

55 Ibid., I.K.P.K. II A 1 p/13.1, Daluege to Skubl, 6 February 1935 (copy).

56 Lewis, 2014b, pp. 140–143.

57 Mathieu Deflem, 2002b, pp. 21–44.

developed outside of international diplomatic and legal agreements. The First World War was not a hiatus from the search for new means of police control; instead, the Austro-Hungarian example shows how different police agencies (police directorates, border police, local police) and the military formed a new type of system with four central offices (not just one). This system was supposed to function in multiple administrative areas and regions with different languages. This model influenced international police organization in the interwar period. Therefore, when writing the history of international law, scholars should note that the police in the 19th and 20th centuries saw extradition law as a hindrance to their work and developed international cooperation to circumvent it legally, first informally, then formally. They developed new categories, such as "politically suspicious persons" and "international criminals" before laws were erected to set other parameters for these concepts. They developed information technologies in advance of law, later seeking confirmation and recognition in international legal agreements.

References

Richard Bach Jensen, "The International Anti-Anarchist Conference of 1898 and the Origins of Interpol", *Journal of Contemporary History*, vol. 16, no. 2, 1981, pp. 323–347.

Gerhard Botz, *Nationalsozialismus in Wien. Machtübernahme, Herrschaftssicherung, Radikalisierung, 1938/39*, Mandelbaum Verlag, Vienna, 2008.

Mark Cornwall, "Traitors and the Meaning of Treason in Austria-Hungary's Great War", *Transactions of the Royal Historical Society*, vol. 25, 2015, pp. 113–134.

Mathieu Deflem, *Policing World Society: Historical Foundations of International Police Cooperation*, Oxford University Press, New York, 2002a.

Mathieu Deflem, "The Logic of Nazification: The Case of the International Criminal Police Commission ("Interpol")", *International Journal of Comparative Sociology*, vol. 43, no. 1, 2002b, pp. 21–44.

Judith Devlin, Maria Falina, and John Paul Newman (Eds.), *The Other Great War: World War I in Central and Eastern Europe- Experience and Memory*, I.B. Tauris, London, forthcoming 2018.

Donald E. Emerson, *Metternich and the Political Police. Security and Subversion in the Habsburg Monarchy (1815–1830)*, Martinus Nijhoff, The Hague, 1968.

Maureen Healy, *Vienna and the Fall of the Habsburg Empire: Total War and Everyday Life in World War I*, Cambridge University Press, New York, 2004.

Gerhard Jagschitz, "Die politische Zentralevidenzstelle der Bundespolizeidirektion Wien. Ein Beitrag zur Rolle der politischen Polizei in der ersten Republik", *Jahrbuch für Zeitgeschichte*, 1978, pp. 49–95.

Jens Jäger, *Verfolgung durch Verwaltung. Internationales Verbrechen und internationale Polizeikooperation 1880–1933*, UVK Verlagsgesellschaft, Konstanz, 2006.

Alexander Koller (Ed.), *Ausnahme-Gesetze und Verordnungen für den Kriegsfall*, Manzsche k.u.k. Hof-Verlags- und Universitätshandlung, Vienna, 1914.

Paul Knepper, *The Invention of International Crime: A Global Issue in the Making, 1881–1914*, Palgrave Macmillan, New York, 2010.

Mark Lewis, "The Failure of the Austrian and Yugoslav Police to Repress the Croatian Ustaša in Austria, 1929–1934," *Austrian History Yearbook*, vol. 45, 2014a, pp. 186–212.

Mark Lewis, *The Birth of the New Justice: The Internationalization of Crime and Punishment, 1919–1950*, Oxford University Press, Oxford, 2014b.

Mark Lewis, "The Failed Quest for Total Surveillance: The Internal Security Service in Austria-Hungary during World War I", in Judith Devlin, Maria Falina, and John Paul Newman (Eds.), *The Other Great War: World War I in Central and Eastern Europe-Experience and Memory*, I.B. Tauris, London, forthcoming 2018.

Stephanie A. Limoncelli, *The Politics of Trafficking: The First International Movement to Combat the Sexual Exploitation of Women*, Stanford University Press, Stanford, CA 2010.

Verena Moritz, Hannes Leidinger, and Gerhard Jagschitz, *Im Zentrum der Macht: die vielen Gesichter des Geheimdienstchefs Maximilian Ronge*, Residenz Verlag, St. Pölten, 2007.

Robin Okey, *Taming Balkan Nationalism: The Habsburg 'Civilizing Mission' in Bosnia, 1878–1914*, Oxford University Press, New York, 2007.

David Petruccelli, "Banknotes from the Underground: Counterfeiting and the International Order in Interwar Europe", *Journal of Contemporary History*, vol. 51, no. 3, 2016, pp. 507–530.

Manfried Rauchensteiner, *Der Tod des Doppeladlers. Österreich-Ungarn und der Erste Weltkrieg*, Verlag Styria, Graz, 1993.

Christiane Rothländer, *Die Anfänge der Wiener SS*, Böhlau, Vienna, 2012.

Bruno Schulz, "Bericht über die Tätigkeit der 'Internationalen Kriminalpolizeilichen Kommission' (umfassen die Zeit vom September 1923 bis September 1926)", in *Internationaler Polizeikongress, Berlin 1926. Sammlung der Referate und Beschlüsse*, 1926.

Jan Selling, "The Obscured Story of the International Criminal Police Commission, Harry Söderman, and the Forgotten Context of Antiziganism", *Scandinavian Journal of History*, vol. 42, no. 3, 2017, pp. 329–353.

Biserka Stanišić, "Odsjek IV-B Res. za pogranična redarstevna satništva odjela za Unutarnje poslove Kraljevske hrvatsko-slavonsko-dalmatinske zemaljske vlade u Zagrebu", *Arhivski Vjesnik*, vol. 36, 1993, pp. 181–206.

Piotr S. Wandycz, *The Lands of Partitioned Poland, 1795–1918*, University of Washington Press, Seattle, 1974.

Franz Weisz, "Die Geheime Staatspolizei, Staatspolizeileitstelle Wien 1938–1945, Organisation, Arbeitsweise und personale Belange", Ph.D. thesis, University of Vienna, 1991.

Nancy M. Wingfield, *The World of Prostitution in Late Imperial Austria*, Oxford University Press, Oxford, 2017.

5 Authority, legitimacy and military violence

De facto combatant privilege of non-state armed groups through amnesty[1]

Pål Wrange

5.1 Introduction

The US Department of Defence's Law of War Manual of 2015 states that "[o]ne longstanding criterion for a just war is that war must be ordered by a competent authority for a public purpose. This jus ad bellum principle (sometimes called right authority) acknowledges that the resort to military force is a prerogative of the State. [This] is reflected in the requirement that armed groups must belong to a State to receive the privileges of combatant status."[2] "[M]embers of a non-State group may be subject to prosecution under a State's domestic law for their participation in hostilities against it."[3] The manual further says that "[a] State may exercise both sovereign and belligerent rights over non-State armed groups."[4]

Three pages later, the manual notes that "[a]lthough amnesty is normally left to the discretion of the State, [Article 6(5) of the Second Additional Protocol to the 1949 Geneva Conventions] provides that, at the end of hostilities, the authorities in power shall endeavour to grant the broadest possible amnesty to persons who have participated in the armed conflict, or those deprived of their liberty for reasons related to the armed conflict, whether they are interned or detained."[5] The history of Article 6(5) shows, in a grain of sand, the relation between sovereign and belligerent rights as manifestations of conceptions of right authority, as suggested by my selection of quotations from the US Law of War Manual.

This chapter is part of a project on the use of force and non-state actors, in which I ask whether the current state-centric view of authority and force is

1 Thanks to participants in various presentations of different iterations of this paper, including the conference in Uppsala in 2016, a presentation at Melbourne Law School on 16 November 2017 and my presentation at the International Studies Association Convention in San Francisco, 7 April 2018. Special thanks to Jens Bartelson, Anne Orford, Bruce "Ossie" Oswald. It is unnecessary to say that none of them bears responsibility for remaining weaknesses of the text.

2 Law of War Manual, 2015, p. 40.

3 Law of War Manual, 2015, p. 81.

4 Law of War Manual, 2015, p. 1025.

5 Law of War Manual, 2015, p. 1028.

changing in international law. Through the lens of the just war concept of right authority, I ask how international law deals with the authority to use military means, as well as with political and other forms of authority in general. My interest in these questions is twofold: I want to understand the current regulation of the use of force in a contemporary legal environment of human rights, international criminal law, transitional justice and counter-terrorism law. But I am also interested in the construction of authority as such. This brief text will limit itself to trace the development of one particular provision – article 6(5) of the Second Additional Protocol to the 1949 Geneva Conventions (AP II) – and its implications for right authority. Before I proceed to this presentation, I will first explain how these ideas connect.

As implied by the quote from the US Law of War Manual, it may be useful to describe the problem as sovereign rights versus belligerent rights.[6] Under international law, a sovereign government (the sovereign) has both rights and obligations towards her subjects (or citizens), the subjects being members of the same political body as the sovereign. A sovereign can, of course, also be a belligerent, but the relation between belligerents is different: It is one of enmity *and* equality, regulated by the law of war (or international humanitarian law [IHL] or *jus in bello*). The subjects of a sovereign who use arms against that sovereign can be punished for rebellion, but soldiers of a belligerent cannot. Some political and legal theorists think that the two relations – sovereignty and belligerency – exclude one another (an enemy cannot also be a subject) while others believe that the sovereign rights and belligerent rights can apply at the same time in a civil war.

This dichotomy is related to the concept of right authority. Just war doctrine, from the 13th to 16th centuries, generally held that there were three requirements for a war to be just: just cause, right intention and, thirdly, the war had to be pursued by the right or proper authority. This third requirement had profound political implications in the fragmented politics of medieval Europe. As just war doctrine morphed into international law in the 16th and 17th centuries, right authority came to be vested in "the prince," and later "the state."

Ever since then, international law has – as a main rule – assumed that only states have the authority to use military force, that is, belligerent rights. In rebellions and civil wars, the use of violence by members of governmental armed forces will be legal while rebels are criminally liable for various violations of domestic law, even if they have complied with the laws of war. However, as will be explained, in present international law, this requirement of right authority is undermined by certain tendencies in the *jus in bello.* To the extent that non-state armed groups (NSAGs) can start a war without negative legal consequences and thus acquire belligerent rights, they actually have a de facto authority, or at least they are undermining the state's exclusive authority. But first a few more words of background.

6 Neff, 2005, p. 257. Cf also Chinkin and Kaldor, 2017, p. 85.

International humanitarian law not only limits but also empowers actors to use force; legitimate combatants are permitted to use violence under certain conditions and they are provided "combatant immunity" (or "privilege"), "which is, in effect, a limited license to take life and cause destruction."[7] By proscribing illegitimate warfare, IHL determines what is legitimate warfare and thereby allows belligerents to do things that in peacetime would constitute violations of human rights (like the killing of sleeping enemy fighters).[8] If IHL would allow others than states to do that, it would widen the scope of permissible force, beyond the traditional monopoly of states (and inter-state organizations).

Although only states (and perhaps the UN) have an explicit right to use force under some circumstances, the authority provided by the *jus in bello* is more important in legal practice.[9]

The arguably most important legal consequence of a decision to go to war is the creation of a state of armed conflict ("war"). The application of international humanitarian law is triggered when a conflict reaches the threshold of armed conflict, regardless of the express will of the parties. Hence, the state of war may be triggered not only by the acts of governments but also by the acts of non-state actors.

A state of war entails some important legal consequences. One is that the parties to the conflict may use violence that would otherwise be prohibited, for instance as violations of the human right to life. This is most relevant to governments, who are bound by human rights obligations in peace. However, there are important useful consequences also for a NSAG. If the armed struggle is conducted properly, the group will be able to employ violence without being classified as a terrorist group, and thereby avoid being subjected to various types of counter-terrorism measures.

An even more important consequence would be if individuals involved as combatants would be relieved of the risk of prosecution for their acts in the war. In an international war between states, soldiers have no criminal responsibility for taking part in the war; as mentioned, they have combatant immunity, that is, "a limited license to take life and cause destruction."[10] By contrast, in a non-international armed conflict, or civil war, the baseline position is that the members of the non-state armed forces are guilty of rebellion, and they may thus be prosecuted by the territorial state under its domestic law (as an exercise of its sovereign right).[11] Nevertheless, there are plenty of historical examples where rebels have been given that "privilege," and the amnesty provision that

7 Fleck para 1202, p. 612. See also Kennedy, 2009, pp. 167 and passim.

8 Of course, when states negotiate IHL conventions, they may very well hold that the background norms, the baseline, are set of customary rules that give states considerable leeway, but that argument may not necessarily withstand scrutiny, given the fact that the human rights conventions in general are more recent, they are lex posterior.

9 Cf Watkin, 2005, p. 27.

10 Fleck, 2013, p. 590.

11 This is the classical dichotomy. See Schmitt, 1991, p. 33, who said that a technical definition is that war is armed struggle between organized political entities while civil war is armed struggle within a politically organized entity.

I will discuss below, may – retroactively – provide such immunity. In effect, this has meant that states have given belligerent rights to NSAGs and renounced a part of their own sovereign rights. Before the Second World War, governments sometimes recognized rebels as belligerents, thus putting such combatants on equal legal terms. During the negotiations in Geneva leading to the 1949 Geneva conventions and the 1977 additional protocols, negotiators were faced with different options – including complete legal equality – but in 1977, they finally chose to uphold the state prerogative to use military violence but recommend discretionary amnesties for NSAG combatants.

The question that will be pursued in my brief historical review concerns the relation of the non-state party to the sovereign – is it one of subordination or equality? In particular, I will focus on the question if fighters in an NSAG are permitted to fight, that is, if they have combatant immunity, which is an issue that "goes to the heart of the IHL system."[12]

Another – secondary – question is who regulates. The choice is typically between the sovereign and the international community (international law). Relatedly, there is an issue who triggers the application of the law – is it triggered by a decision by someone (typically the sovereign) or by a legal fact (like "protracted armed violence"), which means that anyone who can create that fact can trigger such application.

While the position of the NSAG fighter can easily be discussed in terms of right authority or the sovereign/belligerent right dichotomy, as I will do, much of the legal and political discussion on this issue has invoked other reasons. One humanitarian argument has been that if the parties are equal – meaning that captured rebels will not be executed or otherwise maltreated – then there will not be a "spiral of revenge" between the parties. Furthermore, if NSAG fighters have the combatant privilege for mere fighting, then they will have an incentive to respect the laws of war (or IHL) to avoid punishment, and that will spare civilians. Another important argument is that combatant immunity will facilitate reconciliation at the end of a conflict.[13] In fact, these basically humanitarian considerations – which I sympathize with – have overshadowed the more basic considerations about who has the authority to engage in war.

5.2 Historical review

5.2.1 Recognition of belligerency

Emer de Vattel, one of the most important figures in the history of international law, was a transitional writer between the natural law tradition and the later positivist tradition. His "*Le droit des gens*" (1758) was hugely influential for more than a century, not least in the United States. For Vattel, there was no right to

12 Crawford, 2010, p. 69.

13 A much less often used argument, and one that is related to the question of right authority, is suggested by Lauterpacht in Oppenheim, 1952, p. 211.

make war against the government, but like for instance Hobbes and Locke, he provided exceptions. When rebellious subjects wholly rejected their ruler's right to govern them, there was a true civil war, that is, the same situation as in a war between two different nations, and this made the conflict equivalent to a war between states. Therefore, both parties had to respect the common laws of war.[14] Hence, in a true civil war, the relation is one of belligerency, not sovereignty.

In international practice, the question of the status of rebels was dealt with through the institution of recognition of belligerency. The recognition of belligerency was a rather frequent occurrence, not least in the various rebellions against the Ottoman and Spanish empires, and it was a living concept in international law at least until the adoption of the 1949 Geneva Conventions.[15] It fell into disrepute during the Spanish Civil War in 1936–39 and has since then only been invoked occasionally.[16]

After a recognition of belligerency, the rebel party was recognized as an equal to the state, and its combatants were given combatant immunity. Hence, at least for the purpose of the armed struggle, there was equality between the parties and "the relationship between the parent State and the rebels, and between them and outside States, is … the same as when there is a state of war between two independent States."[17]

The reasons for this institution were largely humanitarian. The US Supreme Court emphasized in 1877 that "[t]his concession is made in the interests of humanity, to prevent the cruelties which would inevitably follow mutual reprisals and retaliations."[18] However, there were also gains to be made by the government – it could, for instance, institute blockades and exercise visit and search rights for contraband against third states on the high seas.

There was, however, ambivalence in several respects. First, was belligerency an automatic consequence of fighting on a large scale (as Vattel seems to have held) or was a recognition necessary (in other words, was recognition declaratory or constitutive)?[19] Many scholars, including the prominent Swiss scholar J.C. Bluntschli, held the former position, but most state practice and doctrine seemed to suggest that recognition was a requirement although it could be implied, for instance by the institution of a blockade.[20]

Second, was the recognition of belligerency a duty upon objective conditions or was it a discretionary prerogative of states?[21] Lauterpacht held that it was a duty, but that was a minority opinion.[22]

14 Vattel, Book III, Ch XVII §294.
15 Neff, 2005, p. 262.
16 Boczek, 2004, p. 104; Wilson, 1988, p. 27.
17 McNair & Watts, 1966, p. 32.
18 US Supreme Court, Williams v. Bruffy (1877), 96 US 176, at 186. 35 Ibid., at 187.
19 See Neff, 2005, p. 251.
20 McNair & Watts, 1966, p. 33. Neff, 2005, p. 264.
21 Cullen, 2010, p. 21.
22 Oppenheim, 1952, p. 249.

At any rate, there was agreement that the state of belligerency could only apply to what looked like "true civil wars."[23] As the US Supreme Court pronounced in 1863, a civil war

> becomes such by its accidents – the number, power, and organization of the persons who originate it and carry it on. When the party in rebellion occupy and hold in a hostile manner a certain portion of territory; have declared their independence; have cast off their allegiance; have organized armies; have commenced hostilities against their former sovereign, the world acknowledges them as belligerents, and the contest as a war.[24]

To sum up, if belligerency had been an automatic consequence of certain facts (like fighting at a certain level), then there would have been equality between two belligerent parties who, in Vattel's terms, constitute two distinct nations. However, state practice indicates that it is still the sovereign's prerogative to give such status to the rebels.

5.2.2 The Geneva conventions of 1949

At the 1949 conference that adopted the four Geneva Conventions, the states parties had to decide whether IHL should apply also to non-international armed conflicts, whether such application should be *ipso facto* on certain facts or only after a recognition of belligerency and – crucially – whether fighters on the rebel side should have combatant immunity.[25]

The early drafts from the International Committee of the Red Cross (ICRC) (common article 2) stipulated that the conventions should apply to all situations of armed conflict, including non-international ones, "whatever the legal status of the Parties to the conflict and without prejudice thereto."[26]

This line was supported by some countries — most persistently Norway but also the USSR and Romania, Mexico, Denmark and Hungary.[27] However, at the conference, sovereignty was invoked by numerous delegations, including by leading western states like France and the UK. The potential for the impingement on state sovereignty was well recognized and led many states to oppose the inclusion of a provision relating to situations "not of an international character."[28] The United Kingdom's delegation objected strongly to draft Article 2, claiming that it would "strike at the root of national sovereignty and endanger national security." Holding that the application of the Conventions should be limited to situations of (international) "war," the UK was concerned that "the

23 Neff, 2005, p. 264.
24 Neff, 2005, p. 259, quoting Prize Cases, 67 US (2 Black) 635 (1863), at 666–667.
25 See, generally, Best, 1994, pp. 168 et seq. See also Draper, 1983.
26 Cullen, 2010, p. 28.
27 Cullen, 2010, p. 35
28 Cullen, 2010, p. 29.

application of the Conventions would appear to give the status of belligerents to insurgents, whose right to wage war could not be recognized."[29] The Greek delegate warned that the draft Article could "prevent rebels from being charged with crimes under common law committed before their arrest, and they would automatically be granted a pardon at the end of disturbances."[30]

After deliberations, a new formula was proposed, namely that the Conventions should be applicable to non-international armed conflicts "provided (a) that the de jure Government has recognized the status of belligerency of the adverse party... or (b) that the adverse party possesses an organized civil authority exercising de facto governmental functions over the population of a determinate portion of the national territory, an organized military force under the direction of the above civil authority, and the means of enforcing the Convention and the other laws and customs of war...."[31] This was a combination of the two opposing theories on the traditional institution of belligerency, and it effectively meant that the Conventions could be applicable to civil war ipso facto, even against the will of the sovereign, under (b).

That idea did not meet with approval and the actual solution went in a different direction, the so-called common Article 3 of the four conventions, which applies "[i]n the case of armed conflict not of an international character occurring in the territory of one of the High Contracting Parties" and provides for a short list of minimum obligations, such as a prohibition of "murder, mutilation, torture, cruel, humiliating and degrading treatment." Hence, the scope of application was broad, but the range of obligations was narrow, and it did not provide any combatant status for NSAG fighters.[32]

The important Paragraph 3 of Article 3 stated that "[t]he application of the preceding provisions shall not affect the legal status of the Parties to the conflict." The commentator Pictet noted that this clause was "essential. Without it Article 3 would probably never have been adopted. It meets the fear – always the same one – that the application of the Convention, even to a very limited extent, in cases of civil war might interfere with the *de jure* Government's suppression of the revolt by conferring belligerent status, and consequently increased authority and power, upon the adverse Party."[33] Even this minimal provision was controversial, though. Of the 47 delegates in attendance, 34 delegates voted in favour, 12 against and 1 abstained. The Burmese representative, speaking on behalf of the Asians, described Article 3 as "an encouragement and incentive to [...] insurgents."[34]

As to trigger, there were divided views regarding whether this "mini-convention" would apply without an express recognition or not, but it was clear

29 Cullen, 2010, pp. 31–32, ref to Final Record, vol. II-B, Summary Records, 1st Meeting, p. 10.
30 Cullen, 2010, p. 34, Final Record, vol. II-B, Summary Records, 1st Meeting, pp. 10–11.
31 Cullen, 2010, p. 38; Final Record, vol. II-B, Seventh Report, 16 July 1949, Annex B, p. 125.
32 Cf Cullen, 2010, p. 40.
33 Pictet, 1960, p. 38.
34 Cullen, 2010, p. 45, referring to Final Record, vol. II-B, Minutes, 28 July 1949, p. 330.

that many if not the overwhelming majority of states parties held that it applied only to armed conflicts of such magnitude that a recognition of belligerency would have been appropriate under the old doctrine. The US explained, "[T]he Convention should be applicable only where the parent government had extended recognition to the rebels or where those conditions obtained which would warrant in recognizing the belligerency of the rebels whether or not such recognition was accorded by the Power on which they depend in this latter eventuality."[35] The ICRC's commentary found that "the terms of this paragraph support the finding evidenced in the [preparatory works] of the Geneva Conventions, that the term 'armed conflict not of an international character' was generally understood to have the same meaning as that of 'civil war'."[36]

At any rate, it was clear that the application of Article 3 did not entail any recognition of belligerency, let alone equality between the parties. And it was abundantly clear that states wanted to retain their sovereign rights, for instance to prosecute.

5.2.3 The 1977 additional protocols

The negotiations to the two additional protocols of 1977 proved to be even more complicated. The process started in the UN in 1968 and was then taken over by the ICRC in 1971, culminating in the four-year long diplomatic conference that began in 1974.

It was generally agreed at the time that the phenomenon of guerilla warfare – as seen in Vietnam, the Middle East, etc. – needed to be addressed, but soon much of the energy came to focus on the position of a particular type of guerrilla – national liberation movements. After difficult discussions, it was eventually – but still controversially – agreed in 1974 that wars of national liberation should be treated as international armed conflicts (war between states) in Protocol I.[37] That, of course, meant that colonial conflicts were no longer covered by the concept of non-international armed conflict. The Indian delegate explained the significance of this:

> It must be remembered here that the newly independent developing countries which are endeavouring to consolidate their newly earned independence are jealous of their sovereignty and will guard it against any action which might constitute an interference in their internal affairs under whatever form or guise. … The adoption of the United Nations Charter after the Second World War gave an impetus to the intensification of wars of national liberation in the erstwhile colonial world. The imperial and colonial powers

35 Cullen, 2010, pp. 32, 23, referring to Final Record, vol. II-B, Summary Records, 2nd Meeting, p. 12.

36 Cullen, 2010, p. 54, citing an earlier edition of Pictet.

37 This has been a hotly debated issue in international law. See, for instance, Wilson, 1988, in particular pp. 135–136.

> had, however, a clever pretext that the colonies were overseas parts of their metropolitan empires and hence armed liberations struggles were [non-international] armed conflicts. Fortunately, Article 1 of Protocol I would now cover the wars of national liberation.[38]

In 1972, the ICRC had concluded that a clear majority of states would not be willing to adopt the same regulations for non-international as for international armed conflicts. Certain experts had found that "proposals based on the abolition of the distinction between internal and international conflicts [would] alter the entire structure of the Geneva Conventions and indeed of international law in general."[39] Consequently, the ICRC submitted two draft protocols,[40] of which the second one (AP II) was to cover non-international conflicts. ICRC explained that the legal status "of the parties was fundamentally unequal, since a part of the population would be fighting against the Government in power, acting in the exercise of its original public authority."[41] Even this proposal, however, met scepticism among many Third World delegations who feared that "the Protocol would undermine state sovereignty and provide a pretext for external interference in the internal affairs of states."[42] The delegate from Zaïre remarked that "dissident armed forces are primarily a group of rebels with no international legal personality. Their only legal status is that granted them under the domestic laws of their national State. To claim otherwise is to place a sovereign State on the same footing as a rebel movement, and that would imply de facto recognition of the movement."[43]

As for trigger, the Saudi Arabian delegation wanted to retain the prerogative of the state to activate the protocol and "wished to make it clear that any definition of the terms of the article was solely the concern of the State on whose territory the armed conflict was taking place. Decision by any other country would constitute interference in the domestic affairs of the State concerned and an infringement of that State's sovereignty."[44] Brazil had proposed the words "recognized as such by the High Contracting Party on whose territory the armed conflict is considered to exist…"[45] However, in distinction to 1949, western states did not argue for a requirement of recognition of belligerency, and this proposal was defeated.

In the end, the conference came to adopt a much scaled-down version of Protocol II. As in 1949, there was a trade-off between the threshold for the application of AP II and the scope of the regulations though this time the threshold was a bit higher while the scope was broader, albeit much reduced compared to the initial proposals.

38 Official Records, Vol. VII, p. 81.
39 1972 Report A, p. 64.
40 1972 Report B, pp. 61–62.
41 Official Records, Vol. VIII, p. 203.
42 Cullen, 2010, p. 96.
43 Official Records, Vol. VII, p. 104.
44 Official Records, Vol. VII, p. 70.
45 Official Records, Vol. VII, p. 75.

As was abundantly clear, the delegates were not ready to provide any form of legitimation or subjectivity to NSAGs.[46] Article 3(1) provides,

> Nothing in this Protocol shall be invoked for the purpose of affecting the sovereignty of a State or the responsibility of the government, by all legitimate means, to maintain or re-establish law and order in the State or to defend the national unity and territorial integrity of the State.

One of the most prominent commentators found that "[t]he concern ... was based, ... on uneasiness about the legal implications for the status of parties to the conflict, and, in particular, on states' concerns about restrictions on their ability to prosecute and punish individuals under domestic law for their belligerent acts which constituted crimes under that law."[47]

Given the attitude of a number of states mentioned earlier, it is not surprising that it would not be easy to provide any form of combatant privileges for NSAG fighters. The ICRC had suggested, in draft Article 28, that combatants who have at least... "distinguished themselves from the civilian population by some distinctive sign or by any other means and who had complied with the provisions of the present Protocol, shall not be punishable by death if they become the object of penal prosecutions only by reason of having taken part in hostilities or having been members of armed forces."[48] The proposal aimed, "in addition to ensuring respect for the human person as such, at preventing, in the interests of both Parties to the conflict, an endless spiral of retaliation. Indeed, to outlaw the rebels would by no means encourage them to respect the rights of the combatants captured by them."[49] The Netherlands introduced a slightly redacted version of this proposal which would have spared all combatants from *any* penalties for having taken part in the hostilities.[50] Sweden submitted a similar draft.[51] None of them was accepted. One expert noted that this related to matters "within the jurisdiction of the State."[52] The delegate of Pakistan objected to the possibility of a rebel avoiding punishment "when his fellow citizen in peacetime would be prosecuted for similar activities." In Pakistan "insurgents would be executed, and any attempt to impose international legislation [of this kind] would, in his opinion, constitute interference with the sovereign rights of States."[53]

However, and interestingly, "[a] number of experts were of the opinion that the articles should contain references to the provisions applicable to war crimes, by means of an additional paragraph in Article 28 stating that violations of the

46 However, Cassese suggested that rebels might have the right to reprisal. Cassese, 1981.

47 Fleck, 2008, para 1202, pp. 611–612.

48 1972 Report B, p. 84.

49 1972 Report B, p. 83.

50 1972 Report B, p. 86. See also 1972 Report, Vol. II 40, Conf Doc CE/COM II/39.

51 Official Records, vol. IV, p. 34.

52 1972 Report B, p. 84.

53 Official Records, vol. VIII, p. 360. Pakistan referred to a later version of this article, numbered 10.

law of armed conflict ... could always be subject to the penalties provided."[54] The ICRC expert noted that draft Article 28 "applied only to the sole fact of having taken part in the hostilities; it did not apply in the case of grave breaches of the laws of armed conflicts."[55] The Eastern bloc introduced a draft amendment reading "[n]othing in the present Protocol shall be invoked to prevent the prosecution and punishment of persons charged with crimes against humanity or who participate in the conflict as foreign mercenaries."[56] Like the rest of Article 28, this proposal was not adopted.

Eventually, a modest draft provision was submitted by the United States, providing that "at the conclusion of hostilities the Parties to the conflict should grant amnesty as widely as possible."[57] After some debate, this was eventually adopted as Article 6(5). It did not limit the governments' prerogatives in a technical sense, but it still put an onus on them to provide amnesties. As we will see, this has been a quite prevalent practice.

5.2.4 The practice from 1990s

In the post-Cold War era, almost the whole of international humanitarian law came to be regarded as applicable to all belligerent parties even in civil war, only triggered by facts (fighting of a certain type and magnitude).[58] Still, there was no explicit recognition of combatant privilege for NSAGs.

Article 6(5) of AP II, referred to above, provides that

> [a]t the end of hostilities, the authorities in power shall endeavor to grant the broadest possible amnesty to persons who have participated in the armed conflict, or those deprived of their liberty for reasons related to the armed conflict, whether they are interned or detained.

This provision, which invites the winning party to be magnanimous to create reconciliation between the parties, means that rebels should not face prosecution for treason, rebellion or some similar crime.

As pointed out by Crawford, amnesty is a voluntary policy and "[p]articipants in a non-international armed conflict cannot assume that they will be granted amnesty at the end of the armed conflict in the same way a combatant in an international armed conflict can rely on his combatant immunity."[59]

Nevertheless, both states acting unilaterally and peace agreements after internal conflicts often follow this recommendation and provide that members of the rebel party will not be prosecuted for taking part in the war. In state practice,

54 1972 Report B, p. 86.
55 1972 Report B, p. 83.
56 Official Records, vol. IV, p. 34. See also Official Records, vol. VIII, p. 365.
57 1972 Report B, p. 85. 1972 Report, Vol II 41, Conf Dec CE/COM II/49.
58 See, generally, Henckaerts, 2005, p. 189.
59 Crawford, 2010, p. 104.

there are a great many agreements and laws that provide amnesty for rebellion after a civil war. Crawford finds that "the increasing prevalence of amnesty agreements does demonstrate an emerging trend" towards what might be called "retroactive combatant immunity…."[60] A recent example is the peace agreement in Colombia.[61] This development has been promoted and supported by the UN and other international organizations.[62]

This trend has been supported by efforts to facilitate reconciliation as well as to induce NSAGs to comply with international humanitarian law. A considerable number of NSAGs have made commitments to respect IHL to the ICRC, and a non-governmental organization (NGO), Geneva Call, has drafted three "Deeds of Commitments."[63] Of course, incentives to comply with IHL will be significantly strengthened if NSAGs can enjoy combatant immunity if they respect IHL. In 1996, the ICRC found that article 6(5) had been designed to offer "the equivalent of what in international armed conflicts is known as 'combatant immunity'. … It does not aim at an amnesty for those having violated international humanitarian law."[64]

When the ICRC presented its monumental study on customary international humanitarian law in 2005, article 6(5) was paraphrased as customary rule 159, with the not insignificant change that the authorities *must* "endeavour to grant the broadest possible amnesty to persons who have participated in a non-international armed conflict."[65] This contention is backed up with a review of practice.[66]

Hence, the recommendation in Article 6(5) has been strengthened over time. But its scope has also been restricted. In the 1970s and 1980s, amnesties were viewed favourably[67] and where even "one of the standard domestic policy options" for restoring normality after political violence.[68] A number of domestic courts have referred to Article 6(5), generally to uphold amnesties even for serious crimes like war crimes.[69] In the 1990s, however, blanket amnesties came to be increasingly questioned in the fight against impunity.[70]

60 Crawford, 2010, pp. 104–105.

61 See the part of the Agreement entitled Special Jurisdiction for Peace I. Basic Principles of the Judicial Component of the Comprehensive System for Truth, Justice, Reparations and Non-Recurrence, para 37, in the Final Agreement to End the Armed Conflict and Build a Stable and Lasting Peace, 24 November 2016, p. 160, http://especiales.presidencia.gov.co/Documents/20170620-dejacion-armas/acuerdos/acuerdo-final-ingles.pdf accessed on 15 November 2017.

62 Crawford, 2010, p. 108.

63 Geneva Call. See also Bangerter, 2011 and Herr, 2010.

64 Letter of Dr Toni Pfanner, Head of the Legal Division, ICRC Headquarters, cited in Roht-Arriaza, 1996, p. 93. See also Naqvi, 2003, p. 583.

65 Henckaerts, 2005, p. 212. The call for amnesty makes an exception for "persons suspected of, accused of or sentenced for war crimes," as will be discussed below.

66 Henckaerts and Doswald-Beck, 2005, pp. 611–614.

67 Freeman, 2009, pp. 1 et seq.

68 Du Bois-Pedain, 2007, p. 302 See also Bell, 2008, pp. 240–241.

69 Freeman and Pensky, 2012, p. 44.

70 Bell, 2008, pp. 240–241; Du Bois-Pedain, 2007, pp. 302 et seq. For a good overview, see Laplante, 2009.

The ICRC gave an explanatory interpretation of Article 6(5), in which it found that this provision "does not aim at an amnesty for those having violated international humanitarian law."[71] The Inter-American Commission on Human Rights and the UN Human Rights Committee have concurred with this interpretation.[72] In 1999, the UN Secretary-General issued "Guidelines for United Nations Representatives on Certain Aspects of Negotiations for Conflict Resolution" which provided that the UN "cannot condone amnesties regarding war crimes, crimes against humanity and genocide."[73] As already indicated, this interpretation is in line with what many states and the ICRC thought in 1977.[74]

Freeman notes that "we have gone from a time when amnesties were treated above all as a political issue, fully within the exclusive and sovereign domain of states, to a time when they are treated above all as a legal issue that extends beyond the prerogative of any one state."[75] Not accepting the limitations on amnesties could engender opposition from the UN and endanger external economic and other forms of support for amnesty-related or other peace-building programmes.[76]

Hence, the effect of these two developments has been that there is now a potential, retroactive combatant immunity for lawful belligerent acts combined with individual responsibility for war crimes and other international crimes. The sovereign right to prosecute or not has been curtailed, from both ends.

5.3 Conclusion and afterthoughts

To the extent that non-state actors are de facto treated as legitimate combatants that means that they, for all practical purposes, have a status which can be described as *justus hostis* in classical international law, that is, as legitimate enemies in a war between equals with belligerent rights.

A state involved in a civil war has a strong incentive not to provide any authority or legitimacy to rebel groups. During the age of recognition of belligerency, recognition was often – but not always – brought about by third states, who

What came to be called the fight against impunity was codified in the preamble of the Rome Statute of the International Criminal Court: "Affirming that the most serious crimes of concern to the international community as a whole must not go unpunished and that their effective prosecution must be ensured by taking measures at the national level and by enhancing international cooperation, Determined to put an end to impunity for the perpetrators of these crimes…

71 Letter of Dr Toni Pfanner, Head of the Legal Division, ICRC Headquarters, cited in Roht-Arriaza, 1996, p. 93. See also Naqvi, 2003, p. 583.

72 Freeman, 2009, p. 36.

73 Freeman, 2009, p. 89, referring to Slye, 2000, pp. 173, 177. On Sierra Leone, the cause célèbre of this new policy, see Meisenberg, 2004, p. 837.

74 Pace Bell, 2008, pp. 245–246; Freeman, 2009, pp. 35–36.

75 Freeman, 2009, p. 91. For a good discussion related to one of the most debated applications, the conflict in Northern Uganda, see Ssenyonjo, 2005.

76 Freeman, 2009, p. 91.

invoked neutral rights. Today, there is pressure from the UN, NGOs and other representatives of "the international community" to provide immunity for acts of rebellion. Pressure and incentives come from contradicting tendencies, connected to different ways of talking about IHL: The underlying will to protect sovereignty, humanitarian ambitions to incentivize compliance with IHL and the peacemakers' will to promote reconciliation.[77]

The practice of amnesties is now so common that a NSAG fighter has a reasonable chance of avoiding the exercise of sovereign rights in the form of prosecution. This gives her belligerent rights though retroactively. And this, in turn, means that the monopoly of authority on the use of military means is undermined. And, as appeared above (although I did not emphasize that aspect), when de facto privilege has been awarded, international law (like international institutions) has been completely indifferent to the substantive legitimacy of the struggle – the only factor has been the capacity to create a state of war, that is, the capacity to kill, maim and destroy. This development has been spurred by humanitarian considerations and of ambitions to resolve conflicts, and it has had very real positive effects in many places.[78] But, it has also come at a cost: the undermining of the monopoly on the use of military violence.

References

Oliver Bangerter, "Reasons Why Armed Groups Choose to Respect International Humanitarian Law or Not", *International Review of the Red Cross*, vol. 93, 2011, pp. 353–384.

Christine Bell, *On the Law of Peace: Peace Agreements and the Lex Pacificatoria*, Oxford University Press, Oxford, 2008.

Geoffrey Best, *Law and War since 1945*, Clarendon Press, Oxford, 1994.

Boleslaw A. Boczek, *International Law: A Dictionary*, Scarecrow Books, Lanham, 2004.

Antonio Cassese, "The Status of Rebels under the 1977 Geneva Protocol on Non-International Armed Conflicts", *International and Comparative Law Quarterly*, vol. 30, 1981, pp. 416–439.

Christine Chinkin and Mary Kaldor, *International law and new wars*, Cambridge University Press, Cambridge, 2017.

Emily Crawford, *The Treatment of Combatants and Insurgents Under the Law of Armed Conflict*, Oxford University Press, Oxford, 2010.

Anthony Cullen, *The Concept of Non-International Armed Conflict in International Humanitarian Law*, Cambridge University Press, Cambridge, 2010.

Department of Defence, *Law of War Manual*, Washington, 2015 [Law of War Manual].

Antje Du Bois-Pedain, *Transitional Amnesty in South Africa*, Cambridge University Press, Cambridge, 2007.

77 In international law, these issues could be approached as modern IHL, as international criminal law, as international human rights law, as what Christine Bell calls lex pacificatoria, and as remnants of the old regime of recognized belligerency. Hence, it could be discussed in terms of the contemporary debate on the fragmentation of international law.

78 For a good discussion, see Bell, 2008, pp. 239–258.

Gerald Irving A. Dare Draper, "Humanitarian Law and Internal Armed Conflicts", *Georgia Journal of International & Comparative Law*, vol. 13, 1983, pp. 253–278.

Dieter Fleck, "Non-International Armed Conflict", in Dieter Fleck (Ed.), *The Handbook of International Humanitarian Law* (2nd ed.), Oxford University Press, 2008, pp. 580–611.

Mark Freeman, *In Necessary Evils: Amnesties and the Search for Justice*, Cambridge University Press, Cambridge, 2009.

Mark Freeman and Max Pensky, "The Amnesty Controversy in International Law", in Francesca Lessa and Leigh A. Payne (Eds.), *Amnesty in the Age of Human Rights Accountability: Comparative and International Perspectives*, Cambridge University Press, Cambridge, 2012, pp. 42–66.

Geneva Call, *Deed of Commitment*, available at: www.genevacall.org/how-we-work/deed-of-commitment/ (accessed 23 April 2018).

Jean-Marie Henckaerts, "Study on Customary International Humanitarian Law: A Contribution to the Understanding and Respect for the Rule of Law in Armed Conflict", *ICRC Review*, vol. 87, 2005, pp. 175–212.

Jean-Marie Henckaerts and Louise Doswald-Beck, *Customary International Humanitarian Law - Vol I: Rules*, Cambridge University Press, Cambridge, 2005.

Stefanie Herr, "Binding Non-State Armed Groups to International Humanitarian Law Lessons from Sudan", PRIF Report No 95, Peace Research Institute, Frankfurt Frankfurt am Main, 2010.

David Kennedy, *Of War and Law*, Princeton University Press, Princeton, NJ, 2009.

Lisa J. Laplante, "Outlawing amnesty: the return of criminal justice in transitional justice schemes", *Virginia Journal of International Law*, vol. 49, 2009, pp. 915–984.

Lord McNair and Arthur D. Watts, *The Legal Effects of War* (4th ed.), Cambridge University Press, Cambridge, 1966.

Simon. M. Meisenberg, "Legality of Amnesties in International Humanitarian Law. The Lomé Amnesty Decision of the Special Court for Sierra Leone", *International Review of the Red Cross*, vol. 86, 2004, pp. 837–851.

Yasmin Naqvi, "Amnesty for War Crimes: Defining the Limits of International Recognition", *International Review of the Red Cross*, vol. 85, 2003, p. 583–625.

Stephen C. Neff, *War and the Law of Nations: A General History*, Cambridge University Press, Cambridge, 2005.

Lassa Oppenheim, *International Law*, Vol II, Hersh Lauterpacht (Ed.), (7th ed.), Longmans, Green, London, 1952.

Jean S. Pictet and Jean De Preux, *Geneva Convention Relative to the Treatment of Prisoners of War*, International Committee of the Red Cross, Geneva, 1960.

Naomi Roht-Arriaza, "Combating Impunity: Some Thoughts on the Way Forward", *Law & Contemporary Problems*, vol. 59, 1996, pp. 93–102.

Carl Schmitt, *Der Begriff des Politischen. Text von 1932 mit einem Vorwort und drei Corollarien* (3rd ed., 1963), Duncker & Humblot, Berlin, 1991.

Ronald C. Slye, "Amnesty, Truth, and Reconciliation: Reflections on the South African Amnesty Process", in Robert I. Rotberg and Dennis Thompson (Eds.), *Truth v. Justice: The Morality of Truth Commissions*, Princeton University Press, Princeton NJ, 2000, pp. 170–188.

Manisuli Ssenyonjo, "Accountability of Non-State Actors in Uganda for War Crimes and Human Rights Violations: Between Amnesty and the International Criminal Court", *Journal of Conflict and Security Law*, vol. 10, 2005, pp. 405–434.

Emer de Vattel, *The Law of Nations; or, Principles of the Law of Nature: Applied to the Conduct and Affairs of Nations and Sovereigns* (transl. from the French by unknown), J. Newbery, J. Richardson, S. Crowder, T. Caslon, T. Longman, B. Law, J. Fuller, J. Coote, and G. Kearsly, London, 1759.

Kenneth Watkin, "Warriors Without Rights? Combatants, Unprivileged Belligerents, and the Struggle Over Legitimacy", Program on Humanitarian Policy and Conflict Research, Harvard University Occasional Paper Series, number 2, vol. 2, 2005.

Heather Wilson, *International Law and the Use of Force by National Liberation Movements*, Clarendon Press, Oxford, 1988.

Official Documents etc

Final Agreement to End the Armed Conflict and Build a Stable and Lasting Peace, 24 November 2016, http://especiales.presidencia.gov.co/Documents/20170620-dejacion-armas/acuerdos/acuerdo-final-ingles.pdf (accessed 15 November 2017).

Final record of the diplomatic conference of Geneva of 1949 convened by the Swiss federal Council for the establishment of international conventions for the protection of war victims and held at Geneva from April 21st to August 12th, 1949, ICRC Library, https://library.icrc.org/library/Default.aspx (accessed 15 April 2018) [Final Record].

Letter of Dr Toni Pfanner, Head of the Legal Division, ICRC Headquarters, to the Department of Law at the University of California of 15 April 1997.

Official Records of the 1974–1977 Diplomatic Conference, available at Official Records of the Diplomatic Conference on the Reaffirmation and Development of International Humanitarian Law Applicable in Armed Conflicts, Library of Congress, www.loc.gov/rr/frd/Military_Law/RC-dipl-conference-records.html and available at ICRC Library, https://library.icrc.org/library/Default.aspx (accessed 15 April 2018), Vols. IV, VII, VII [Official Records].

"Practice Relating to Rule 159. Amnesty", ICRC IHL Database Customary IHL, https://ihl-databases.icrc.org/customary-ihl/eng/docs/v2_rul_rule159 (accessed 15 November 2017).

Report on the work of the Conference of Red Cross Experts on the Reaffirmation and Development of International Humanitarian Law Applicable in Armed Conflicts, Vienna 20 March-24 March, 1972 [1972 Report A].

Report on the Work of the Conference, Conference of Government Experts on the Reaffirmation and Development of International Humanitarian Law Applicable in Armed Conflicts, Second Session, 3 May -3 June 1972, ICRC, 1972 [1972 Report B].

US Supreme Court, Williams v. Bruffy (1877), 96 US 176.

Part II

6 Evolution of rules and concepts in international humanitarian law

Navigating through legal gaps and fault lines

Mark Klamberg

6.1 Introduction

This part concerns specific rules and concepts in the field of international humanitarian law (IHL). Some argue that IHL in its modern juridical-technocratic version is a rather anti-theoretical and at times even anti-intellectual discipline.[1] All modern theories of jurisprudence arguably need to include an understanding of or theory on change.[2] The next sections present different ways of observing and analysing change. It is a spectrum ranging from internal and agency-based to external and structural explanations and perspectives. At the end of this introduction, an attempt will be made to describe how IHL as a system allows room of manoeuvre for states and other actors, including exploitation due to legal gaps and fault lines.

6.2 Internal and external modes of theorizing

The turn to history in international law is intertwined with the understanding that there is no universal natural law. When Robert Plummer Ward set out to write a treatise on diplomatic law of universal application, he discovered the following after having collected the material:

> men had the most opposite opinions of their duties towards one another, if not in the great outline and first principles of those duties, yet most certainly in the application of them; and that this was occasioned by the varieties of religion and the moral system which governed them, operated upon also by important local circumstances which are often of such consequence in their direction.[3]

Consequently, he did not write a treatise on the universal application of diplomatic law, instead he wrote a history of the law of the nations of Europe. His

1 Mégret, 2016, p. 762.
2 Hovencamp, 1985.
3 Ward, 1795, pp. 11–12.

turn to history was not a consequence of scepticism towards natural law. It was rather his historical inquiry that led him to understand the unrealistic pretensions of natural law.[4] With a historical perspective, it is also clear that the laws of war are tied to a secular tradition of thinking about the justness of war. Mégret suggests two predominant modes of theorizing, one "internal," and the other "external." Among internal theories such as theories of essence, possibility, operation and implementation, one could with a historical perspective consider theories of evolution,[5] a cyclical theory of history[6] and discontinuity in history.[7]

Among the external theories, one may find those who challenge the continued relevance of the "war" model that assumes wars are between sovereigns on a battlefield with clearly defined geographical and temporal boundaries. Modern conflicts increasingly occur globally (the "war" on terror) or virtually (computer network attacks). War in its traditional sense has begun to disappear and thus the perceived need to regulate war is pointless.[8]

6.3 Structure versus agency

As indicated above, theories and approaches to the development of concepts and rules in IHL may place different emphasis on structure versus agency. This is a key question across social sciences, to what extent explanation should be couched in terms of autonomous actions of individuals or seen as a product of context or structure in which the individuals operate and over which they have no control.[9] This structure/agency debate may be nuanced. Hay argues that

> structure and agency logically entail one another – a social or political structure only exists by virtue of the constraints on, or opportunities for, agency that it effects. Thus it makes no sense to conceive of structure without at least hypothetically positing some notion of agency which might be effected (constrained or enabled).[10]

Ideas of structure and agency are arguably central to any notion of power because power ultimately concerns the victory of the *agent* or *subject* over its other – *structure* or *object*.[11] This relationship between *agency* and *structure* raises at

4 Craven, 2016, p. 24.
5 Mégret, 2016, pp. 762–769.
6 Schlesinger Sr., 1939.
7 Foucault (1989), by contrast, argues that one should seek to reconstitute not large "periods" or "centuries" but "phenomena of rupture, of discontinuity". Grewe (2000, p. 9)

> the assumption of an uninterrupted continuity of the international legal order must be limited … The continuity of cultural historical development from Antiquity to the Middle Ages is not necessarily equivalent to the continuity of specific legal principles and conceptions.

8 Mégret, 2016, p. 771.
9 Stoker, 1995, p. 16.
10 Hay, 1995, p. 189.
11 Ibid, p. 191.

least two issues. First, we have to contextualize agency and second, when we choose to describe structures we choose to describe them either as resources (enabling action) or constraints (limiting opportunities for action).[12]

Moreover, the analysis of the historicizing of IHL may be done at three levels with focus on (i) individual actors – a single person, an organization or a state; (ii) the interaction between two or several actors or (iii) the system as a whole, a global perspective that involves the economical, societal and technological context.[13] It is rather material factors that do the explanation.[14] A system may in abstract terms be defined as a body of components that interact. The pattern of interaction constitutes the system.[15] At the system level, one may examine whether there is a hegemon, if it is bipolar, multipolar or anarchic and whether the system is stable or subject to change. As indicated earlier, these three levels are not necessarily mutually exclusive.

Some of the theories and approaches to the development of IHL place greater emphasis on structure, especially when there is an emphasis on technology and interdependency. Other theories based on moral and conceptual ideas open up more space for agency. It is also possible to take into account both structure and agency as illustrated by Sutton's chapter on the principle of distinction. She takes a relational approach on how rules, norms and behavioural ideals are disseminated and shaped by humanitarian actors.[16] Similarly, Evangelidi analyses the concept and idea of restraint in terms of reciprocity between the belligerent parties.[17]

6.4 Theories of evolution

An evolutionary approach to law may be traced back to Savigny.[18] Theories of evolution accept that IHL is not static. Laws of war are created and adapt to changing circumstances and challenges, which may be of practical, political, technological and moral nature. Tendencies include (i) greater humanitarianism in the sense that IHL has gradually tried to cover more groups; (ii) that IHL has become more intrusive and less governed by the classical Westphalian framework in which inter-state armed conflicts dominate; now they rather evolve towards covering all kinds of conflicts; (iii) greater support against the idea of "total war" and notions that military necessity justify any attack, even on civilians; (iv) modification of IHL as a result of interaction with human

12 Ibid, p. 205.
13 Jönsson, 1992, p. 14.
14 Kratochwil, 2008, p. 95.
15 Jönsson, Elgström and Jerneck, 1992, p. 163.
16 Chapter 9 of this book. For reviewer: We have not yet decided about the numbering of chapters.
17 Chapter 10 of this book.
18 Savigny, 1892, pp. 8–9:

> In recent times, the view has become common that in the beginning all societies lived in an animalistic state, and from there have come to a tolerable existence through gradual evolution, and finally to the heights upon which we now stand

Translation in Elliott, 1985, pp. 40–41. See also Clark, 1980–1981, p. 1241.

rights. This humanization has led to structural changes of IHL, moving away from a view that IHL is transactional and reciprocal between states. Instead, the idea is that the laws of war are owed to the combatants and non-combatants as such.[19]

In addition to observing changes in a chronological order and in terms of tendencies, the evolution of concepts and rules within IHL may also be analysed and theorized in relation to three components: variation, selection and retention. The *theory of variation* describes the mechanism by which potential new legal concepts are generated.[20] In the context of IHL, this may include states, scholars and organizations such as the International Committee of the Red Cross (ICRC) that continuously "invent" new legal solutions to problems. In the words of Sinclair, the *theory of selection* "describes how, from the variations generated, the successful are selected, and the unsuccessful rejected."[21] In a legal context, this is the account of the selection when an applicable legal norm is replaced by a new norm.[22] For example, why did the 1907 Hague Convention IV on the Laws and Customs of War on Land replace the 1899 Hague Convention II with Respect to the Laws and Customs of War on Land? The *theory of retention* asks, why does a legal norm remain in place when conditions for selection change?[23] For example, the distinction between international armed conflict and non-international armed conflict has arguably over time become increasingly anachronistic. Theories on legal evolution tend to focus more on legal concepts than on specific legal rules.[24] In the context of this part of the book, the focus on concepts may be illustrated by Sutton's chapter on the principle of distinction and Evangelidi's analysis of the concept and idea of restraint.[25]

Evolution does not have to be logical in the sense that all changes progress toward a goal. As Nietzsche states, "[t]he evolution of a thing, a custom, an organ is not a *progressus* towards a goal, let alone the most logical and shortest *progressus*, requiring the least energy and expenditure."[26] Thus, reasonable caution is warranted when determining and describing whether a certain legal concept follows a certain evolutionary trajectory.

6.5 Legal gaps and fault Lines

One could also discuss the understanding of specific rules in terms of legal gaps and fault lines.[27] As argued earlier, IHL as a system allows room of manoeuvre

19 Mégret, 2016, pp. 768–769.
20 Sinclair, 1986–1987, p. 454; van der Sluijs, 2015–2016, pp. 90–91.
21 Sinclair, 1986–1987, p. 454.
22 van der Sluijs, 2015–2016, pp. 90–91.
23 Sinclair, 1986–1987, p. 455; van der Sluijs, 2015–2016, p. 91.
24 van der Sluijs, 2015–2016, p. 92.
25 Chapters 9 and 10 of this book.
26 Nietzsche, 1956, Second Essay, XII, p. 210; See also Wrange, 2007, p. 83.
27 Klamberg, 2017.

for states and other actors, where some actions are permissible and other actions are prohibited. Between the two areas, legal gaps and fault lines will create a grey area of uncertainty whether a particular course of action is permitted, a condition which may be exploited. These gaps and fault lines are subject to continuous tensions between structure and agency and as such they can be subject to change in the sense that the law becomes solidified in an area which was previously in a state of flux or uncertainty. Changes in the structure may also cause new gaps and fault lines to emerge.

IHL, as most other fields of law, attempts to categorize different situations, which subsequently determine the applicable rules. Such categories may at certain points of time appear logical, coherent and able to cover all potential situations. However, evolution in a technological, societal and economical context may reveal gaps between these categories or push different legal rules, principles and regimes in conflict with each other, causing legal fault lines. Legal gaps and fault lines will cause a need to re-evaluate the existing rules and in some cases create new. Piatkowski's study on aerial bombardment during the Second World War concerns the applicability of existing law and in some cases the need for evolution, in relation to new technologies.[28] Technological changes force us to discuss the applicable law for computer network attacks, drone warfare and whether new weapons need to have special rules. Psychological operations (psyops, sometimes also referred to as influence operations) have arguably always been part of conflicts; however, their character has changed partly because of technological changes. With mass media, international communications, internet and social media, states as well as non-state actors are confronted with new possibilities, threats and means of waging conflicts of interests. Societal and economical changes have arguably made states interdependent and thus less likely to engage in inter-state conflicts. Rather conflicts are between states and non-state actors or between various non-state actors. States may also use non-state actors for proxy warfare in other states. This forces us to re-evaluate traditional thresholds for characterizing conflicts, dichotomies between international armed conflict on one hand and non-international armed conflict on the other. Old concepts such as combatants may appear less relevant in the age of "war" against terrorism. The actors involved in a conflict may seek to exploit these legal gaps and fault lines. The use of computer network attacks, psychological operations, irregular and/or non-state groups, "peacekeeping" forces and expulsion of populations may keep a situation at the lower end, that is, as internal disturbances and tensions or as a non-international armed conflict.[29]

The following chapters examine the evolution of specific IHL concepts and rules in the context of legal gaps and fault lines.

28 Chapters 10 and 11 of this book.
29 Klamberg, 2017, p. 201.

References

Robert C. Clark, "The Interdisciplinary Study of Legal Evolution", *Yale Law Journal*, vol. 90, no. 5, 1980–1981, pp. 1238–1274.

Matthew Craven, "Theorizing the Turn to History in International Law", in Anne Orford, Florian Hoffmann and Martin Clark (Eds.), *The Oxford Handbook of the Theory of International Law*, Oxford University Press, Oxford, 2016, pp. 21–37.

Donald E. Elliott, "The Evolutionary Tradition in Jurisprudence", *Columbia Law Review*, vol. 85, no. 1, 1985, pp. 38–94.

Michel Foucault, *The Archaeology of Knowledge*, Routledge, London, 1989.

Wilhelm G. Grewe, *The Epochs of International Law* (Transl. and rev. Michael Byers), De Gruyter, Berlin, 2000.

Colin Hay, "Structure and Agency", in David Marsh and Gerry Stoker (Eds.), *Theory and Method in Political Science*, Macmillan Press, Basingstoke, 1995, pp. 460–479.

Herbert Hovencamp, "Evolutionary Models in Jurisprudence", *Texas Law Review*, vol. 64, no. 4, 1985, pp. 651–685.

Christer Jönsson, Ole Elgström and Magnus Jerneck, *Internationell Politik*, Studentlitteratur, Lund, 1992.

Mark Klamberg, "Exploiting Legal Thresholds, Fault-Lines and Gaps in the Context of Remote Warfare", in Jens David Ohlin (Ed.), *Research Handbook on Remote Warfare*, Edward Elgar Publishing, Cheltenham, 2017.

Friedrich Kratochwil, "Constructivism: What It Is (Not) and How It Matters", Donatella della Porta and Michael Keating (Eds.), *Approaches and Methodologies in the Social Sciences A Pluralist Perspective*, Cambridge University Press, Cambridge, 2008, pp. 80–98.

Frédéric Mégret, "Theorizing the Laws of War", in Anne Orford, Florian Hoffmann and Martin Clark (Eds.), *The Oxford Handbook of the Theory of International Law*, Oxford University Press, Oxford, 2016, pp. 762–778.

Friedrich Nietzsche, *The Genealogy of Morals* (1887) (Francis Golffing transl.), Anchor Books, New York, 1956.

Friedrich Carl von Savigny, *Vom Beruf unserer Zeit für Gesetzgebung und Rechtswissenschaft* (1840) (3rd ed.), Mohr, Freiburg, 1892.

Arthur Meier Schlesinger Sr., "Tides of National Politics", *Yale Review*, vol. 29, 1939, pp. 217–238.

Michael B.W. Sinclair, "The Use of Evolution Theory in Law", *University of Detroit Law Review*, vol. 64, no. 3, 1986–1987, pp. 451–477.

Gerry Stoker, "Introduction", in David Marsh and Gerry Stoker (Eds.), *Theory and Method in Political Science*, Macmillan Press, London, 1995, pp. 1–19.

Jessika van der Sluijs, "Trajectories – rättens rörelseriktning som relevant bedömningsinstrument", *Juridisk Tidskrift*, vol. 27, no. 1. 2015–2016, pp. 88–119.

Robert Plumer Ward, *An Enquiry into the Foundation and History of the Law of Nations in Europe*, Butterworth, London, 1795.

Pål Wrange, *Impartial or Uninvolved? The Anatomy of 20th Century Doctrine on the Law of Neutrality*, Elanders, Visby, 2007.

7 A hidden fault line

How international actors engage with IHL's principle of distinction

Rebecca Sutton

7.1 Introduction

International peacekeeping missions, in particular those espousing a comprehensive or integrated approach, are sites where international humanitarian, political, peacekeeping, and military actors struggle to delineate their relationships with each other. This chapter scrutinizes the interactions of international actors who work in and around UN, NATO, and EU comprehensive and integrated missions, exploring how issues of "distinction" arise in their encounters with each other.

Under international humanitarian law (IHL), the principle of distinction requires parties to the conflict to distinguish between the civilian population and combatants as well as between civilian objects and military objectives.[1] This rule receives pride of place as Rule 1 in the International Committee of the Red Cross (ICRC) customary IHL study,[2] and the International Court of Justice has called it an "intransgressible" principle of international customary law as well as a "cardinal principle" of IHL.[3] While its central importance to the body of law that regulates the conduct of hostilities is beyond dispute, scholars are increasingly drawing attention to the fragility and contested nature of this vaunted legal tenet.[4]

While IHL's principle of distinction is organized around a civilian-combatant binary, this chapter attends to an important fault line[5] that is obscured by that binary arrangement—this hidden fault line exists within the civilian category. As will be discussed here, among the diverse international actors who engage in international interventions today, there are marked civilian-civilian tensions.

1 Protocol Additional to the Geneva Conventions of 12 August 1949, and Relating to the Protection of Victims of International Armed Conflicts, 8 June 1977, 1125 UNTS 3, Can TS 1991 No. 1 (AP I), Article 48.

2 Rule 1, ICRC Customary Law Study, Volume 1. Available at: www.icrc.org/eng/assets/files/other/customary-international-humanitarian-law-i-icrc-eng.pdf.

3 Advisory Opinion on the Legality of the Threat or Use of Nuclear Weapons, ICJ Reports 226, 8 July 1996, paras. 78–79.

4 Kinsella, 2011, p. 3.

5 Klamberg, 2017.

This chapter suggests, in particular, that international humanitarian actors are constructing themselves as a special civilian category, distinguished both from combatants and also from other civilians. To illuminate these dynamics, this chapter draws on original empirical findings from field research conducted at civil-military trainings in Sweden, Germany, and Italy.

7.2 "Distinction" in the context of integrated missions

This section will briefly outline the nature of comprehensive international missions and explain the relevance of "distinction" in these intervention contexts. It must be acknowledged at the outset that struggles over distinction are not unique to comprehensive interventions. There is value in focusing the empirical lens on comprehensive interventions, however, because they constitute sites where struggles over "distinction" happen overtly and where the lines drawn around the humanitarian category are hotly contested.[6]

Under the aegis of global institutions such as the EU, the UN, and NATO, the international community has undergone a steady—if fraught—move toward coherent, integrated, and multidimensional interventions. In the context of such missions, diverse international actors are called upon to work closely together, often toward the (ostensibly) shared aim of peace.[7] Such arrangements have proven to be a flashpoint of tension, particularly between international humanitarian actors and the other international actors operating in their midst.[8] The UN is one of many institutions that moved toward some form of coherence or integration at the end of the 20th century.[9] Integration as a general concept gained momentum in subsequent years, with explicit linkage of development and security by the mid-2000s[10] and increasing conceptualization of a relief-development continuum.[11]

Today, there is a lingering debate about where humanitarian action should fit in relation to the political and military aspects of integrated missions. While this debate plays out in connection with NATO and EU interventions in similar ways, this discussion will focus on UN missions as the relevant literature is comparatively more robust. Proponents of a closer relationship between humanitarian action and other components of UN integrated missions emphasize the

6 ICRC, *2013 Annual Report*, p. 51. Available at: www.icrc.org/eng/assets/files/annual-report/icrc-annual-report-2013.pdf (accessed 22 April 2018).

7 Stockton, 2003.

8 Metcalfe et al., 2011.

9 MacRae and Leader define integration as a particular, extreme, variant of coherence. Macrae and Leader, 2000, p. 9. For more on the NATO variant, see Paddon and Owen, 2012, p. 271.

10 UN High-Level Panel on Threats, Challenges, and Change, *A More Secure World: Our Shared Responsibility* (New York: United Nations, 2004), p. viii; UN Report of the Panel on United Nations Peace Operations, UN Report A/55/305 – S/2000/809, August 21 2000, pp. 34–37.

11 UN Report of the Secretary-General's High Level Panel: Delivering as One, 2006, available at: www.un.org/events/panel/resources/pdfs/HLP-SWC-FinalReport.pdf (accessed 22 April 2018).

importance of the overall aim of attaining peace.[12] They believe that improved coordination between the diverse actors will enhance prospects for peace and that the need for unified action should eclipse the preferences of any single actor.[13] Opponents of such a close relationship insist that integration undermines the ability of humanitarian actors to access beneficiaries, increases threats to aid worker security, subordinates humanitarian action to political agendas, and leads to a dilution of humanitarian leadership.[14] Of particular relevance here are concerns voiced about the blurring of humanitarian spheres of action with other types of activity. These broader anxieties translate into a more specific concern related to targeting, namely the fear that integration policies blur the distinction between civilians and military targets under IHL.[15] A study of the UN integrated mission in Liberia (UNMIL) found, for example, that it is too difficult to distinguish between UNMIL's civilian and military components; it attributes this to the fact that both are driven by integration policies to meet military and developmental aims.[16]

Having noted that the issue of targeting is in play, a specific question for international legal scholars here is how IHL's principle of distinction applies to the international actors engaged in these integrated missions. The simplest answer is that this rule applies in the same way it does in other contexts. From a strict doctrinal perspective, humanitarian actors, UN civilian actors, and other political and diplomatic civilian actors will have protected status under IHL's civilian category. International military forces, and some peacekeeping actors, will fall on the other side of the civilian-combatant binary and be treated as combatants. It follows that actors with civilian status are shielded from direct attack—as long as one does not directly participate in hostilities—while those actors with combatant status are deemed legitimate military targets. Accordingly, when the observers cited earlier highlight fears about targeting, they are not referring to formal IHL rules so much as the perceptions of other (armed) actors in their midst. As the empirical findings below suggest, concerns about perceptions indeed play a pivotal role in shaping the relationships of these international actors.

Turning specifically to international humanitarian actors, as mentioned, civilian humanitarian actors will be protected under IHL by virtue of falling into the civilian category. Humanitarian actors are legally classified as civilians in Geneva Convention (GC) IV and Additional Protocol (AP) I. Article 71(2) of AP I provides that in International Armed Conflicts (IACs), those engaged in war fighting are required to respect and to protect humanitarian actors "as

12 Philpott and Powers (Eds.), *Strategies of Peace: Transforming Conflict in a Violent World*, Oxford University Press, Oxford, 2010, n. 38. See also Beauchamp, 2012, p. 207.

13 Philpott and Powers (Eds.), 2010, n. 36.

14 Antonio Donini, "Between a Rock and a Hard Place: Integration or Independence of Humanitarian Action", International Review of the Red Cross, 92, No. 880, 2010, p. 52. See also Glad, 2011, p. 5.

15 Schirch, 2014.

16 Hull, 2008.

civilians."[17] Additionally, some humanitarian actors may also have recourse to additional protections, rights, and obligations under IHL. There is a division among humanitarian studies scholars on the question of whether, as a doctrinal matter, IHL has in fact given humanitarian actors something *more* than civilian protection. Durham and Wynn-Pope assert that the IHL obligation to "respect and protect" humanitarian actors provides the latter with "more substantial footing and a specific status" under IHL than what they had previously under the GCs.[18] Furthermore, they submit that this additional protection is merited because humanitarian actors often face greater risk to their personnel, supplies and facilities than the general civilian population.[19] Others counter that humanitarian actors are protected as civilians, highlighting the "as civilians" language of Article 71(2) of AP I and noting that the "respect and protect" language also extends similarly to all non-combatants in the APs.[20] This chapter does not seek to resolve this important doctrinal dispute. It turns instead to the practices of the international actors themselves to discern what they treat as the most important fault line(s) in their relationships. This will be revisited in detail below.

If one is interested in the tensions between different international actors, a helpful starting point is the literature on (humanitarian) civil-military relations (CMR). This scholarship illuminates that while civilian actors might struggle with military notions of command and control, it can be equally hard for hierarchically organized and command-based military actors to navigate the diversity of the civilian humanitarian community and to make sense of the complex landscape of international civilian actors. As Weir finds, "While understanding of the humanitarian principles is generally limited, the standards, objectives, and capabilities of the humanitarian community – let alone the individual agencies – are often a mystery to the military actors that operate alongside them."[21] Slim submits that humanitarians, fundamentally, disagree more with the military than vice versa and this goes beyond operational issues to concerns of ethics, values, and identity.[22] The khaki uniforms of the military make humanitarian actors uneasy, he argues, and "the reds, blues and whites of their own organizational plumage have deliberately evolved to set themselves strikingly apart from the colours of the military."[23] Rieff, for his part, believes that blockages in humanitarian-military interactions stem from the military side. Although humanitarian and military actors might outwardly express mutual respect for

17 Article 71(2) of AP I. Rome Statute, supra; Statute of the Special Court for Sierra Leone, 2178 UNTS 138, 145; 97 AJIL 295; UN Doc. S/2002/246, Appendix II. There is no equivalent rule in NIACs, but this chapter sources the protection in customary law, following Mackintosh, 2007, p. 118.

18 Ibid.

19 Ibid. pp. 334, 329, 339.

20 Barrat, 2014, p. 323. Fast, 2014, p. 197.

21 Weir, "Conflict and Compromise: UN Integrated Missions and the Humanitarian Imperative", KAIPTC Monograph No. 4, 2006, p. 41.

22 Slim, 1996, p. 125.

23 Ibid.

each other, Rieff wagers that soldiers who are competent enough to fight the Taliban are "not going to do what relief workers want. Rather, they will expect relief workers to listen to them."[24]

For the purposes of this chapter, a significant limitation of the CMR literature is that it organizes relationships along civilian-combatant lines. While this is unsurprising, it has the effect of setting up the civilian-combatant binary as the most important fault line in operation. Some scholars have expressed frustration with this tendency and proposed other potential formulations for the specific context of comprehensive missions.[25] Practitioners have noted this too. As one humanitarian policy actor proposes, the civil-military is currently applied to international comprehensive or integrated missions for the simple reason that "we don't have a better one."[26] Another humanitarian policy actor suggests that it might be more appropriate to speak instead of humanitarian and development agencies, on one hand, and political and military actors, on the other.[27] She suggests linking the political and military realms in order to reflect critiques by humanitarian actors of the politicized nature of certain UN missions.[28]

Beyond expressing dissatisfaction with the application of the civil-military framework to comprehensive missions, scholars have also drawn attention to a related but slightly different problem. This is the evident lack of academic engagement with the internal boundaries of international missions, as a more general matter.[29] Such observations serve as the jumping off point for the investigation that is the subject of this chapter. With the aim of peering deeper inside the community of international actors, the author of this chapter traveled to three global civil-military training sites. The research methodology that was employed in connection with the empirical research will now be discussed.

7.3 Methodology

In terms of epistemology, this chapter is closer to the interpretive end of the positivist-interpretivist spectrum. The empirical aspects of this chapter are underpinned by subjectivist ontology. In attending to the perceptions of diverse international actors, it is less concerned about whether a particular perception is objectively correct than if such a perception exists and has concrete implications.[30] This chapter takes a relational approach, drawing on and building upon emerging scholarship that focuses on relationships between actors.[31] In the field

24 Rieff, 2002, p. 119.
25 Goodhand, 2013, p. 288.
26 Interview, 2016.
27 Interview, 2016.
28 Interview, 2016.
29 Goodhand, 2013, p. 288; Carrayanis, 2016.
30 See Thomas, 1966 [1931]), pp. 289–305.
31 Fast, 2014, p. 8; Roth, 2015, p. 91; Desmond, 2014.

of humanitarian studies,[32] Fast defines a relational approach as bringing attention to the relationships that humanitarian actors forge with others, as well as those that they neglect.[33] This approach dovetails nicely with Kinsella's entreaty to treat IHL's principle of distinction itself as a relationship.[34]

This discussion is informed by field research conducted by the author at civil-military trainings in Sweden, Italy, and Germany in 2015 and 2016. The three sites studied are as follows: a Civil-Military Cooperation (CIMIC) training by NATO in Italy, a CMR training by the Swedish Armed Forces in Sweden, and a Comprehensive Approaches to Multi-Dimensional Peace Operations (CAMPO) training delivered by the German Center for International Peace Operations (Zif), Germany. Each of these three civil-military trainings aims to prepare diverse international actors to work inside of, or in connection with EU, NATO, and UN missions. Across the three training sites, the author engaged in a total of 200 hours of participant observation at formal training sessions and events and conducted formal interviews with 38 trainers and trainees. While interviews and focus group discussions are important tools for situations where the researcher seeks specific information, participant observation serves as a helpful technique when a researcher seeks to make sense of complex social relationships or patterns of interaction.[35]

While one might assume that struggles over "distinction" do not arise at the training sites, so obviously, as they would in the operational field context, it will be demonstrated that *"distinction" is in fact in play at these training sites.* First, the bulk of actors observed and interviewed in the selected training sites are the very same actors who also find themselves at the coalface of international interventions. They are the frontline workers who work in conflict zones and confront other actors daily as a matter of happenstance. Their firsthand accounts of their experiences thus offer granular, thick descriptions of, for example, how humanitarian actors perform "distinction" in the operational context and how others respond to it. Second, trainings serve as sites where relevant rules, norms, and behavioral ideals are disseminated and shaped. This renders them particularly fascinating as sites for research on the operational reality of a vaunted IHL principle.

7.4 Empirical findings at civil-military trainings

The empirical findings discussed here suggest that an important contest is going on within the civilian category. Specifically, the findings demonstrate that international humanitarian actors are employing "distinction" to separate or distance themselves not just from military actors but also from other types of civilian actors with whom they do not wish to be affiliated. Through their practices of

32 Barnett, 2013, p. 393, designating humanitarian studies as a field.
33 Fast, 2014, p. 8.
34 Kinsella, 2011, p. 6.
35 Bryman, 1984, p. 81.

line drawing, humanitarian actors employ the idea of "distinction" to erect a boundary around themselves. Other international actors linked with international interventions, both combatant and civilian, are consequently pushed to the other side of this line. To elucidate these processes of distinction and how other international actors respond, brief vignettes from each of the training sites will now be discussed.

7.4.1 A CMR training at Swedish Armed Forces International Centre

The Swedish Armed Forces offer a two-week training on CMR at the Swedish Armed Forces International Centre (SWEDINT), outside of Stockholm. The primary aim of this course is to impart to international civilian, military, and police actors the necessary skills for cooperating and coordinating with each other in international peace support operations led by the UN, the EU, or NATO. This training responds to the fact that international military forces play an increasingly prominent role in crisis response and peace support operations in contemporary armed conflicts. In an effort to help trainees learn the requisite skills, the training also involves innovative virtual reality (VR) simulation exercises.

The entanglement and enmeshment of diverse international actors is captured vividly in a "mixed reality"[36] simulation that takes place at the SWEDINT training. This simulation begins in a dedicated VR exercise room at SWEDINT, where trainees embark on a joint assessment mission. The team, which encompasses international humanitarian and military actors as well as UN civilians, is tasked with carrying out an assessment of local needs in a fictional conflict zone. As part of the exercise, the virtual UN vehicle on the screen travels to the headquarters of a local humanitarian NGO named H.E.L.P. After the international assessment team virtually encounters the representative for the NGO, the trainees are instructed to relocate to a separate training room where a live actor, serving as the representative of H.E.L.P, awaits them.

At the outset of this simulated in-person meeting, a (real) UN civilian is put in charge of speaking for the (simulated) mission and handling the interaction with the (real but played by an actor) H.E.L.P representative. He introduces himself as being from the UN mission, quickly adding, "but we are civilian." Trying to ingratiate himself with the NGO representative, he emphasizes, "I am with the civilian UN, so we can work together." Then, gesturing to his military counterparts, he proceeds, "but I know you are allergic to the uniforms beside me." The NGO representative nods, replying that she must indeed keep her independence. She goes on to say, however, this will also require separation from him, the UN civilian, as well. As a humanitarian NGO actor, she in fact views the entire UN

36 'Mixed Reality' joins virtual reality exercises with other forms of simulation, such as role play. See a discussion at: https://theconversation.com/military-needs-a-more-realistic-approach-to-virtual-reality-58552 (accessed 22 April 2018).

as "a military of sorts." While the UN civilian representative bristles at this, he attempts to salvage the meeting and keep the conversation going. He promises her that next time, he will leave behind his military and police colleagues before coming to meet with the NGO. This, unsurprisingly, attracts the ire of one of the military actors who is participating in the simulated assessment mission. Sitting one row behind the UN civilian representative, she leans forward and interjects angrily, "Don't apologize for the military, we are part of the team!" Her fellow military colleague backs her up, adopting a tone of resignation, "If we continue to put up the boundaries between us, we are never going to function together."

Reflecting on how the simulation exercise played out, a SWEDINT military trainee expresses his wish that humanitarian actors would understand, "We are not the enemy." Another proposes that the uniform military actors wear is simply "a piece of cloth." One of the trainers, who has worked extensively in humanitarian-military coordination, warns that humanitarian actors are right to be skeptical of such advances. As he cautions, "You need to know what game you're playing in." He expands upon this: "…[T]he moment you get too close to the military, you are sort of lost… You have to be really cautious and tell them, 'The military is likely to open their arms and invite you to everything, and these are the people you need distance from.'" He offers a story from Darfur where a humanitarian NGO asked the UN Mission (UNAMID) for help recovering the NGO's broken vehicle. The UN Office for the Coordination of Humanitarian Affairs (OCHA) recommended to this NGO to refrain from direct communication with UNAMID and also—due to concerns of local perceptions—to remove the NGO's logo sticker from the broken vehicle so it would not be visible. The NGO, however, failed to heed this advice and as a result local onlookers saw UNAMID driving a convoy with a broken NGO car on top of it. What is noteworthy here is how his initial warning to humanitarian actors to keep their distance from military forces expands to include the specter of affiliation with the larger UN mission.

In both the VR exercise and discussions with participants at SWEDINT, one detects the operation of a civilian-civilian fault line. While this line is apparently of pivotal importance to the actors who employ it, it is easily obscured when the civilian-combatant divide is assumed to be the most significant "distinction" in operation.

7.5 A NATO CIMIC training

The NATO training discussed here is a Multi-National Civil-Military Cooperation Group (MNCG) training that takes place in Motta di Livenza, Italy. The week-long Functional Specialist CIMIC Course has the stated goal of providing Functional Specialists with a basic understanding of NATO CIMIC policies, principles, and tasks.[37] Each NATO Functional Specialist has a civilian area of

37 NATO MNCG Functional Specialist Course, available at: www.cimicgroup.org/Cimic%20Courses/cimic_courses/cimic_functional_specialist_course_cfsc (accessed 22 April 2018).

expertise—such as veterinary medicine or psychology. Serving as "CIMIC personnel" in NATO missions, their role is to bridge the gap between military institutions and civilian organizations.

The civil-military specialists who attend the NATO CIMIC training are confronted by humanitarian trainers who implore them keep their distance out of respect for "distinction." During a training session on the humanitarian principles, a trainer from Medicins Sans Frontieres (MSF) explains to participants that to protect their security, humanitarian NGOs also rely on neutrality and separation from combatants. "It is a matter of perception; the military is part of the conflict and NGOs will be in danger if seen this way." She describes the humanitarian principles as both a legal obligation and "moral and operational necessity," which humanitarian actors rely on for access. She gives the example of how MSF has been able to operate in insurgent-controlled parts of Afghanistan "where even NATO wasn't able to go." She also asks the trainees whether a military commander can sit with MSF at a table and order, "You do a hospital here, change that convoy time." When the trainees tentatively answer in the negative, the trainer responds emphatically: "MSF will never sit at [a] table with military partners." Noting that the MSF trainer "got everyone going" in her session, one trainee later offers, "It's good for these guys in uniform to see someone like her talk about what it would be like on the other side, how they understand the humanitarian principles."

At the outset of another training session, a trainer from the ICRC describes the relationship between the military and the ICRC as historic, as both types of actors have long been present in conflict spaces. Having emphasized the importance of maintaining a dialog, he explains that the ICRC must stay outside of NATO's comprehensive approach, which includes all CIMIC work. He expands on this:

> It's beautiful, fantastic, but we are not part of it. We are not part of the end state, our job is not to have peace and security. This is your job, and [the job] of politicians and governments. Our job is to take care of victims of armed conflict. We're in the picture, but not contributing.

He notes that in operational contexts, military actors tend to respond to such pronouncements by saying "Great to have you on board. Are you not here? You *are* here! So great to have you as part of the comprehensive approach." He tells the trainees, "They have the right to have this perception... But in the end the issue is this perceived neutrality: we are not going to plan, analyze, deploy together. As far as this is understood, life is beautiful, and everything is happy." A trainer from OCHA reiterates this, stating,[38] "We say to NATO, do not include us under your umbrella because we are nearby and maybe working in the same environment or doing the same things. We are not part of this comprehensive

38 This session is delivered via Skype rather than in person.

approach." She also explains that humanitarian actors are troubled by "the association, mobilization, and utilization of humanitarian assistance to achieve other objectives." When military actors engage directly in so-called humanitarian activities, she contends, this leads to confusion. The problem is, "The goal is different. Is the population understanding that? Do you think I will still have access to the Taliban side?" The risk of confusion, she explains, is heightened by *a priori* ideas of locals that all foreigners are the same. Both humanitarian and military actors are foreign, have means, operate in times of crisis, and say they're "here to help." Military forces, and peacekeepers in particular, further fuel this confusion when they perceive their own tasks as complementary for humanitarian actors.

While the above pronouncements focus mostly on the relationship between humanitarian and military actors, many NATO actors are quick to point out that they believe humanitarian actors are in competition with other civilian actors. One of the military trainers proposes that the "bigger battle" is not along humanitarian-military fault lines but rather among international civilian actors. She cites tensions between humanitarian actors and civilian political actors such as the US State Department. In casual conversation, she also refers to "our civilian and humanitarian colleagues." When asked why she differentiated between "humanitarian" and "civilian" actors in this way, she explains that it was just an impulse as she thinks of them as two separate groups. Another military trainer describes UN civilian actors and non-UN humanitarian actors as being in a "very competitive" relationship. A trainee submits that when humanitarian actors put distance between themselves and other civilian actors such as human rights actors, "This divides the civilian population into castes." In his view, "UN, NGOs…everyone should be the same." Contemplating who is civilian among international actors, one NATO trainer concludes, "It is very simple. You're civilian if you are not carrying a weapon and you're not participating in hostilities." When asked how this translates to the context of comprehensive missions, he ponders, "Now that is interesting…This is so hard, this is the nub edge of it. It's about perceptions."

What is particularly interesting about these exchanges at the NATO CIMIC training is that, even though humanitarian actors are trying to advocate for their protection as civilians along a civilian-combatant divide, military forces perceive them as drawing lines within the category and asking for special treatment. Military misgivings about these civilian-civilian tensions seem to seep into the way they think about the civilian-combatant divide and appear to make them less receptive to humanitarian entreaties for "distinction." These dynamics come to the fore during a heated exchange in the classroom regarding the then-recent U.S. bombing of MSF's hospital in Kunduz Afghanistan. In a subsequent discussion of the MSF trainer's plea to the soldiers in the room to respect such hospital facilities, one trainee wonders aloud: "What makes that an MSF hospital, as opposed to other hospitals they don't call MSF hospital? It would still be civilian…."

7.5.1 A training in comprehensive approaches at Zif

The final site for discussion is the CAMPO training that is run by the German Centre for International Peace Operations (Zif).[39] This week-long training takes place at the Akademie Schmöckwitz outside Berlin. It is facilitated by training staff from Zif, the Command and Staff College of the German Armed Forces in Hamburg and involves guest lectures by high-level UN actors. The stated aim of the CAMPO training is to prepare trainees to follow a comprehensive approach to multidimensional peacekeeping operations in the operational contexts in which they are deployed. The training participants include both civilian and military actors, almost all of whom are presently engaged in EU, NATO, or UN missions.

In the training at Zif, CAMPO trainees learn about the difficulty of defining and describing civilians. One training slide introduces different "categories" of civilians that international actors must be familiar with. Noting the myriad groups, which range from the judiciary to education actors to international NGOs, the trainer concludes, "It's very rough to say 'civilians.'" Highlighting the existence of a plethora of military actors, a trainer says the civilian is "not that easy to describe either." This trainer proposes that there are "different kinds of civilians. Within the civilians, we have humanitarians." The latter, it is noted, have a different "time horizon" than those civilian actors who do long-term development work. Referring to the various actors who fall within the civilian category, another trainer instructs that you "have to understand and distinguish the different things." Nodding to diversity within the humanitarian category as well, one trainer adds, "There is not one humanitarian community with the same interests," and there are "an enormous number of humanitarian organizations."

One military trainer also refers to humanitarian actors as "*civilian* civilians." From a UN military perspective, she proposes, "civilian" simply refers to the police. Another military trainer sees it differently, countering that in law, "humanitarians are just civilians. There is no other kind of civilian." If humanitarian actors are saying otherwise, then "this must be something special the humanitarians have created for themselves, because that's not the law." Furthermore, at the CAMPO training, humanitarian NGOs are also portrayed as belonging to the wider category of non-state actors. Interestingly, this framing situates humanitarian actors alongside armed actors. As one trainer puts it, "On the nice side we have NGOs. On the not-too-nice side, we have armed actors and privatization of violence."

The haziness around the civilian category is further reflected in two different simulation exercises at CAMPO. In the first, participants engage in a simulated intervention to a fictional land with a local population called the "Batari" people. As part of the exercise, trainees are required to identify which actors in the fictional environment are civilian. Trainees struggle to come to a consensus:

39 In German: Zentrum fur Internationale Friedenseinsatz (Zif). See: www.zif-berlin.org/en/training/zif-training-courses/specialization-courses/campo.html (accessed 22 April 2018).

is it only the Batari local civilians? Is it also the non-Batari population in the area? And what about the Batari Liberation Army fighters who are not carrying weapons? To cope with this complexity, one trainee group elects to break open the category of civilians and to split it up into different "kinds" of civilian actors.

In the second simulation exercise at CAMPO, trainees are broken into the four following groups: (1) humanitarian/development; (2) civilian; (3) military; and (4) police. Previously, trainees had been placed in mixed groupings—for example, police actors were placed together with military actors. As they form their new groups, the trainer jokes, "these are single ethnicities now...you can return to your ethnicity." It is noteworthy that humanitarian actors are given their own category (with development actors) apart from other international civilian actors. Additionally, the fact that humanitarian actors *are* also civilians is tacitly recognized as well. At the close of a presentation by Group #1, a military trainer signals that it is the turn of Group #2, saying, "OK, now it's the civilians, since we are already in that sector." Group #2, the "civilian" group, is framed as including "political and diplomatic and everything." One UN civilian trainee who is placed in Group #2 explains that, in operational field contexts, international military actors often confuse Groups #1 and #2. "For them, I am humanitarian, just because I am civilian. Human Rights, Child Protection, Civil Affairs – they think we are humanitarian."[40] The difference, from this trainee's perspective, is "I don't deliver anything to anybody. We facilitate, we do Protection of Civilians with the mission...." She alludes to further tensions within the civilian side of the UN mission as well, proposing that each civilian group elaborates "a specific nationalism. Within the mission, can you imagine? This is mine, this is yours. Everybody wants the lead."

One CAMPO military trainer proposes that if the concern is about meeting the needs of war-affected populations, it is the relationships between civilian actors that is decisive. Contemplating the relationship between international humanitarian actors and other international civilian actors, one civilian trainee submits:

> They have their own personality. Humanitarians think they are superior to everybody else – military, police, but even amongst civilians...UN programs and funds are looked on by MSF and hardcore humanitarians as the people who don't do anything. Down at the bottom is the military... any peacekeeper will have a political agenda, and they maintain they have a humanitarian agenda.

A UN civilian trainee who works as a national staff member in his own country, South Sudan, says of humanitarian actors: "They don't like to be coordinated. They will talk to you as friends, but when you come to work they will freeze you. They are just separate." Another UN civilian trainee reports that sometimes they "write me off as a member of the mission, driving in a mission vehicle." She

40 These are all examples of different civilian sections within a UN mission.

feels that because they don't like the mission, "they don't like me…as a person." Another UN civilian trainee offers constructive suggestions for handling encounters with humanitarian actors:[41]

> In meetings with humanitarians, I might not defend my own organization. I have this feeling that I want to get sympathy from the humanitarians and get close to them, so I can do that by separating myself from [my] institution…but you have to be careful, if you want to stay in your organization. So I'll criticize [the UN mission] while giving an option of collaboration.

She proceeds to say of humanitarian actors, "You can change them, if you are open and you give them information about the mission." She notes that there is also a marked tendency for UN actors to believe that everyone inside the UN mission is "good" while everyone outside of it is "bad." She reports that her UN colleagues see humanitarian actors as a "threat" and that they "just don't like them." She thus does not take it too seriously when these colleagues say to her, "Be careful with the humanitarians." When these UN actors complain that humanitarian actors do not know what they are doing, or that they fail to coordinate with others, she gets the sense that they are unwilling to cope with the complexities. They take the stance that "we are '[the UN Mission]' and this unifies them against others.…We look for a common enemy, there is no logic behind it, it's all the humanitarians."

The simulated exercises and other exchanges at CAMPO hint at the complex dynamics that characterize the relationships of international actors working in comprehensive missions. While trainees struggle to come up with satisfying definitions of the "civilian," they also acknowledge and take an interest in fraught interactions among and between civilian actors. Although some of the commentary above may appear on the surface to have little to do with law, perceptions of civilian-civilian divisions in fact say much about the legal realm—but one example is the characterization of humanitarian actors as "*civilian* civilian actors."

7.6 Conclusion

Drawing on original empirical field research conducted at global civil-military trainings, this chapter has examined the tensions that exist among the international actors who work in or around comprehensive and integrated missions. While IHL's principle of distinction organizes relationships along a civilian-combatant binary, the practices of international actors point to the existence of another fault line that is crucial but typically obscured. This is the civilian-civilian fault line. This chapter focused in particular on how international humanitarian actors activate a "distinction" not only between themselves and combatants but also between themselves and other civilian actors.

41 Interview CAMPO participant FGD—location withheld for reasons of confidentiality.

References

Michael N. Barnett, "Humanitarian Governance", *Annual Review of Political Science*, vol. 16, 2013, pp. 379–398.

Claudie Barrat, *Status of NGOs in International Humanitarian Law*, Brill Nijhoff, Leiden, 2014.

Sylvain Beauchamp, "Humanitarian Space in Search of a New Home", Benjamin Perrin (Ed.), *Modern Warfare: Armed Groups, Private Militaries, Humanitarian Organizations, and the Law*, UBC Press, Vancouver, 2012, pp. 199–234.

Alan Bryman, "The Debate about Quantitative and Qualitative Research: A Question of Method or Epistemology", *The British Journal of Sociology*, vol. 35, no. 1, 1984, pp. 75–92.

Tatiana Carrayanis, "Review: Peaceland by Severine Autessere", *Cambridge Review of International Affairs*, vol. 29, no. 1, 2016, pp. 337–341.

Antonio Donini, "Between a Rock and a Hard Place: Integration or Independence of Humanitarian Action", *International Review of the Red Cross*, no. 880, 2010.

Matthew Desmond, "Relational Ethnography", *Theory and Society*, vol. 43, no. 5, 2014, pp. 547–579.

Larissa Fast, *Aid in Danger: The Perils and Promise of Humanitarianism*, University of Pennsylvania Press, Philadelphia, PA 2014.

Marit Glad, *A Partnership at Risk? The UN-NGO Relationship in Light of Integration*, Norwegian Refugee Council, Oslo, 2011.

Jonathan Goodhand, "Contested Boundaries: NGOs and Civil-Military Relations in Afghanistan", *Central Asian Survey*, vol. 32, no. 3, 2013, pp. 287–305.

Cecilia Hull, *Integrated Missions: A Liberia Case Study*, Division of Defence Analysis, Swedish Defence Research Agency, Stockholm, 2008.

Helen Kinsella, *The Image Before the Weapon: A Critical History of the Distinction between Combatant and Civilian*, Ithaca and London, Cornell University Press, 2011.

Mark Klamberg, "Exploiting Legal Thresholds, Fault-Lines and Gaps in the Context of Remote Warfare", in Jens David Ohlin (Ed.), *Research Handbook on Remote Warfare*, Cheltenham, Edward Elgar Publishing, 2017, pp. 186–210.

Kate Mackintosh, "Beyond the Red Cross: the Protection of Independent Humanitarian Organizations and their Staff in International Humanitarian Law", *International Review of the Red Cross*, no. 865, pp. 113–130.

Joanna Macrae and Nicholas Leader, *Shifting Sands: The Search for 'Coherence' Between Political and Humanitarian Responses to Complex Emergencies*, Overseas Development Institute, Humanitarian Policy Group Report, no. 8, London, 2000.

Metcalfe et al., UN Integration and Humanitarian Space: An Independent Study Commissioned by the UN Integration Steering Group, Stimson and Overseas Development Institute, London and Washington, 2011.

Emily Paddon and Taylor Owen, "Whither Humanitarian Space? The Costs of Integrated Peacebuilding in Afghanistan", in Benjamin Perrin (Ed.), *Modern Warfare: Armed Groups, Private Militaries, Humanitarian Organizations, and the Law*, UBC Press, Vancouver, 2012, pp. 267–286.

Daniel Philpott and Gerard Powers (Eds.), *Strategies of Peace: Transforming Conflict in a Violent World*, Oxford University Press, Oxford, 2010.

David Rieff, "Humanitarianism in Crisis", *Foreign Affairs*, vol. 81, no. 6, 2002, pp. 111–121.

Silke Roth, *The Paradoxes of Aid Word: Passionate Professionals*, Routledge Humanitarian Studies, London, 2015.

Lisa Schirch, *Research Gaps on Civil-Military Policy Trends*, Overseas Development Institute, Humanitarian Practice Network, London, 2014. Available at: www.odihpn.org/humanitarian-exchange-magazine/issue-61/research-gaps-on-civil–military-policy-trends (accessed 22 April 2018).

Hugo Slim, "The Stretcher and the Drum: Civil-Military Relations in Peace Support Operations", *Journal of International Peacekeeping*, vol. 3, no. 2, 1996, pp. 123–140.

Nicholas Stockton, *Humanitarianism Bound: Coherence and Catastrophe in the Congo, 1998–2002*, Unpublished study, Centre for Humanitarian Dialogue, Geneva, 2003.

William I. Thomas, "The Relation of Research to the Social Process", Morris Janowitz (Ed.), *W.I. Thomas on Social Organization and Social Personality,* University of Chicago Press, Chicago, 1966 [1931]), pp. 289–305.

Erin Weir, *Conflict and Compromise: UN Integrated Missions and the Humanitarian Imperative*, KAIPTC Monograph, no. 4, Accra, 2006.

8 Restraint *in bello*

Some thoughts on reciprocity and humanity

Anna Evangelidi

8.1 Introduction

War has always been thought of as "the province of danger," as Clausewitz described it, entailing very real and severe consequences for the human being on all warring sides. Exposed to mutual danger, those who practised warfare, warriors and soldiers, friends and enemies alike, were an integral part of the physical and normative reality of war. War as a reciprocal armed interaction captures mutual danger and vulnerability between the adversaries as the pragmatic raison d'être for restraint in bello. Hence, the efforts to keep war within legal and ethical bounds with a view to containing the consequences of destructive warfare violence have been inevitably grounded in an element of mutuality. This is also reflected in the current law of armed conflict (LOAC) which seeks to alleviate human suffering by regulating, through prohibitions and restrictions, the conduct of hostilities in armed conflicts between combatants who face the reciprocal risk of harm. Proceeding from this premise, the chapter offers some thoughts on how restraint in war has been pursued through considerations of reciprocity and humanity. It first looks at how reciprocity, in the sense of the adversaries' reciprocal commitment to the law, hopes to provide a more or less reassuring, manageable or predictable basis for mutually restrained violence by presuming shared perspectives on and understandings about the importance of restraint in the conduct of war. It then turns to humanity as an enduring hidden necessity for respect for the enemy as human being and looks at how it can or should continue to work towards restraint even when the expectation of reciprocity is belied or when there is little hope for reciprocal behaviour. Finally, it briefly discusses reciprocity and humanity in warfare waged by unmanned aerial vehicles (UAVs) and questions whether they could play a role in supporting restraint in this kind of war, which departs from the paradigm of a reciprocal armed interaction.

8.2 Reciprocity

The pragmatism and the anxieties that have traditionally surrounded reciprocity as an incentive for and guarantee of restraint *in bello* is aptly captured by

Sir Hersch Lauterpacht: "it is impossible to visualize the conduct of hostilities in which one side would be bound by rules of warfare without benefiting from them and the other side would benefit from rules of warfare without being bound by them."[1] Restraint has long been a matter of mutually beneficial reciprocity. It was deemed a realistic prospect among adversaries that were expected to appreciate the advantages of commitment to the accepted rules of conduct, and be able and willing to reciprocate. As such, it was parsed through values and attributes[2] which at different points in history manufactured affinities, forged ties and conferred a certain shared identity, which seemed to reflect commonly felt understandings about limits of warfare and provide "a vital framework of expectations concerning the conduct of others."[3] One's behaviour towards the adversary was thus entangled in various perceptions (or prejudices) of who the enemy was, which often revealed rigid dichotomies between the (normatively superior) self and the others, that is, "us" as opposed to "them." This meant that, in seeking to achieve a level of trust and a degree of common shared ground between the adversaries, reciprocity ran the risk of ending up shrinking the scope and reach of restraint in the sense that "... the force of 'us' is, typically, contrastive ... it contrasts with a 'they' which is also made up of human beings ..."[4]

In the codified law of war of the mid-19th and early 20th centuries, in which the current law is rooted, restraint continued to build on mutual expectations of reciprocity, originating in *inter partes* paired with *inter nos* ideas, and the threat (and fear) of reprisals.[5] Structured around the realities of a state-centric international system, characterised by its reverence to sovereignty as a source of equality in the world,[6] the law embraced restraint as a manifestation of the value base and the standards of states as sovereign equals and "civilised" nations infused with their own versions of normative ethos *in bello*. In the Saint Petersburg Declaration of 1868,[7] which sought to outlaw the use of arms which "uselessly aggravate the sufferings of disabled men, or render their death inevitable," the reach of the obligations agreed was clearly limited to the belligerent relations between the contracting "civilized nations." Later on, in the 1899 Hague Convention II and the 1907 Hague Convention IV on the Laws and Customs of War on Land, the inclusion of the *clausula si omnes* restricted the application and the binding effect of the provisions thereof solely to conflicts to which all belligerents involved were also parties to the treaties.[8] The (in)famous *si omnes*

1 Lauterpacht, 1953, p. 212.

2 These included, for example, professional custom and martial values, religion, culture, justice, civilisation, sovereignty, etc., see e.g. Stacey, 1994, p. 36; Johnson, 1981; Mégret, 2006.

3 Parker, 1994, p. 42.

4 Rorty, 1989, p. 190.

5 See e.g. Meron, 2006, pp. 1–2.

6 See e.g. Neff, 2005, pp. 186–188.

7 Roberts and Guelff, 2000, p. 53.

8 See e.g. ICRC, 2016 Geneva Convention (GC) I Commentary, para. 194 ("an obstacle to the effective application of humanitarian law to inter-State armed violence"); Best, 1994, p. 46.

reciprocity, which proved to undercut restraint, was abandoned in later codifications of the law of war.[9] While the unduly contractual character of wartime obligations gradually faded away into the growing emphasis on the humanitarian dimension of the law,[10] the anticipation of reciprocation of restraint continued to reverberate through the legal regulation of warfare.[11]

In the Geneva Conventions of 1949 (and later in the 1977 Additional Protocol I (API) on international armed conflicts), the contracting parties undertook the obligation to "respect" as well as to "ensure respect for" the law "in all circumstances."[12] In so doing, they reaffirmed the principle that *pacta sunt servanda*, resisting the pressures of war, and pointed to the dwindling fortunes of at least a negative notion of reciprocity. Hereby, breaches and violations could be met in kind, allowing for normative deviation and reneging on commitment to restraint in the face of the frustration of the expectation of reciprocity.[13] Linked with this aspect of reciprocity are reprisals[14] as a mechanism to enforce the law through recourse to acts, otherwise contrary to the law, in response to a violation by the adversary. Although their aim is to put an end to the initial breach of a still-binding norm, induce a return to compliance and deter future violations of the law,[15] reprisals are crudely based on an idea of seeking to right a wrong by means of a wrong, as it were. As they dangerously make space for an escalating spiral of death and destruction, and provide a pretext, an opportunity or excuse for unlawful violence,[16] reprisals render a disservice to restraint. Albeit not outlawed *in toto*, reprisals are prohibited against specific classes of individuals and objects, and to the extent they are permitted they are subject to certain stringent requirements recognised as customary.[17] But even so, reprisals remain

9 1929 Convention relative to the Treatment of Prisoners of War (Art 82); 1929 Convention for the Amelioration of the Condition of the Wounded and Sick in Armies in the Field (Art 25); 1949 GCI-IV (Common Art 2); Additional Protocol (AP) I (Art 96).

10 See e.g. Meron, 2006.

11 See e.g. Provost, 2002, pt II; Sivakumaran, 2012, pp. 245–246; Watts, 2009.

12 Common Art 1 GCI-IV; Art 1(1) API. ICRC, Customary IHL, 2009, p. 498 (Rule 140: "The obligation to respect and ensure respect for international humanitarian law does not depend on reciprocity"). See e.g. Provost, 2002, p. 137; Watts, 2009, p. 412; Meron, 2006, pp. 10–11; Best, 1994, p. 146.

13 ICRC, 1952 GCI Commentary, pp. 25–26; See also ICRC, 1986 API Commentary, pp. 37–38 ("... reciprocity invoked as an argument not to fulfil the obligations of humanitarian law is prohibited," which is to be distinguished from a "positive" type of reciprocity "by which the Parties mutually encourage each other to go beyond what is laid down by humanitarian law"); See also Watts, 2009, pp. 426–427; and Art 60(5) Vienna Convention on the Law of Treaties.

14 Schwarzenberger, 1968, p. 453; Cassese, 2001, p. 229.

15 See especially Kalshoven, 1971.

16 Stowell, 1942, p. 649; Best, 1994, p. 146; Draper, 1958, pp. 98–99; Kalshoven, 1971, pp. 367, 377.

17 See Dinstein, 2016, pp. 289–296; ICRC, Customary IHL, 2009, pp. 513–515 (Rule 145: "Where not prohibited by international law, belligerent reprisals are subject to stringent conditions"); also *Kupreskić et al*, ICTY T. Ch., 14 January 2000, paras 531–536 and *Martić*, ICTY T. Ch., 12 June 2007, paras 465–467 (confirmed in *Martić*, ICTY, App. Ch., 8 October 2008, paras 263–267).

paradoxical in that they resort to "inhumanity as a means of enforcing the law of armed conflict, that is, in the interests of humanity."[18]

Nevertheless, the "respect for the human person" was invoked by Jean Pictet, in the 1952 International Committee of the Red Cross (ICRC) Commentary on the Conventions, to underscore the move away from the synallagmatic character of the law, that is, "as contracts on a basis of reciprocity concluded in the national interest of each of the parties," towards humanitarian obligations undertaken "as solemn affirmations of principles respected for their own sake" and as "a series of unconditional" and "unilateral engagements solemnly contracted before the world as represented by the other Contracting Parties."[19] Echoing this understanding, the 2016 ICRC Commentary placed the "human person" at the heart of the system of protection established by the (universally ratified) Conventions to emphasise parties' duty to ensure "universal respect" of the provisions, indicating that the Conventions "create *erga omnes partes* obligations."[20] But traces of the contractual aspects of restraint could still be detected in the law *vis-à-vis* states which were not parties to the treaties.[21] However, the Conventions and API remained applicable and the states parties bound by them so long as states non-parties recognised the value of mutual restraint and reciprocated (*de facto* application),[22] thus "creat[ing] incentives for non-parties to embrace humanitarian norms in practice."[23] Notwithstanding its reciprocal nature, the LOAC has tried to evolve away from reciprocity. In that direction, it is argued, also points the progressive narrowing of the scope of targets of reprisals.[24] However, the expectation of reciprocal behaviour does not cease to be relevant to the pursuit of restraint in the law in so far as it can play a positive role in encouraging or convincing the adversary to similarly respect the law, leading to adherence to or compliance with obligations.

An important step within (rather than beyond) the confines of a legal system monopolised by states as sovereign equals and shaped by the experiences of war as an inter-state affair was the inclusion of Article 3 common to the 1949 Geneva Conventions which provided for the automatic application of a minimum of humanitarian norms to non-international armed conflicts without any expectation of reciprocity.[25] Article 3 has been referred to as "an almost miraculous

18 Kalshoven, 1971, p. xi. But see "humanity" as customary limitation to recourse to reprisals: e.g. *Martić* Trial (n. 17) para. 467 (alluding to the Martens clause, the ICTY held that reprisals "must respect the 'laws of humanity and dictates of public conscience'").

19 ICRC, 1952 GCI Commentary, pp. 28–29, 25.

20 ICRC, 2016 GCI Commentary, para. 119.

21 Art 2 GCI-IV; Art 96(2) API.

22 Arts 2(3) GCI-IV and 96(2) API; ICRC, 1952 GCI Commentary, pp. 35–37 and ICRC, 2016 GCI Commentary, paras 324, 348–350 (also noting its "reduced importance in practice today" in view of GCs' universal ratification); ICRC 1986 API Commentary, pp. 1087–1088; Provost, 2002, pp.153–156; Watts, 2009, pp. 413–414. But see Arts 1(4) GCI-IV and 96(3) API in relation to wars of national liberation.

23 Osiel, 2009, p. 69.

24 See e.g. Dinstein, 2016, pp. 295; Roberts, 2008, p. 944; Meron, 2006, p. 15.

25 See e.g. *Hadzihasanovic*, ICTY, App. Ch., 16 July 2003, para. 19 ("... internal armed conflict is now the concern of international law without any question of reciprocity"); also Fleck, 2008, p. 632; Provost, 2002, pp. 156–158, 160–163.

self-imposed entrenchment on deeply felt concerns regarding incursions on sovereignty ..."[26] and "remarkable as an international legal commitment to"[27] restraint *vis-à-vis* non-state actors. As it did not intend to "affect the legal status" of non-state parties to a conflict, Article 3 seemed to inch towards the understanding that restraint, at least in the form of "elementary considerations of humanity,"[28] was a *sine qua non* of the battlefield, even if the adversary was not formally "one of us" – albeit one that, at least functionally, looks like "us." It has been suggested that there still exists a role for reciprocity in a *de facto* form, which is linked to the criteria constituting the threshold of applicability (and the existence of an armed conflict).[29] In addition, in paragraph 3, article 3 further "encourages" or "exhorts" the parties to conclude special agreements, whereby they could bring into force part or all of the Geneva Conventions.[30] As René Provost observes, this introduces "a model of symmetrical reciprocity" which seems to discourage the parties from commitment to the law in view of the disparities in military might, political power and weapons technology, and the corollary differing capabilities for compliance.[31] If the realities and idiosyncrasies of such conflicts are not taken into account, there could hardly be a valued place for reciprocity in internal conflicts in the sense of a "shared understanding" about the mutual benefit of compliance.[32]

8.3 Humanity

In the face of disappointments of expectations of reciprocal behaviour, humanity continues to be the unassailable nucleus of restraint. Humanity is a thread running through the codifications of the law of war and never ceased to inform

26 Elder, 1979, p. 38.

27 Watts, 2009, p. 410.

28 *Nicaragua*, ICJ, 28 June 1986, p. 114.

29 Moir, 2002, pp. 85–86, 107–108; See the organisational characteristics of non-state actors (relating also to the ability to carry out their obligations): e g. Art 3GCI-IV, ICRC, 1952 GCI Commentary, pp. 49–50; ICRC, 2016 GCI Commentary, paras 421 ff; Art 1 APII (where *de jure* reciprocity is absent) and the higher threshold for application), ICRC, 1987 APII Commentary, p. 1353; Provost, 2002, p. 157 ("Rejection of reciprocity in the context of internal conflicts may sometimes adversely affect the chances that the state concerned will acknowledge the existence of hostilities intense enough to warrant application of Article 3 or Protocol II").

30 Art 3(4) GCI-IV ("... the Parties should further endeavour..."); ICRC, 2016 GCI Commentary, para. 848 ("encouraging" "more than merely pointing out the possibility," noting also the "pressing nature of this exhortation") and ICRC, 1952 GCI Commentary, pp. 59–60 ("The provision does not merely offer a convenient possibility, but makes an urgent request, points out a duty...").

31 Provost, 2012, p. 34.

32 Provost, 2012, pp. 36 ("... reciprocity and asymmetry are not mutually inconsistent concepts") and 32–34; Sivakumaran, 2012, p. 246 ("... the idea of *de facto* reciprocity is not incompatible with an asymmetrical conflict"); See also White, 2014, p. 103 ("... the greatest problem besetting the law of armed conflict is the fact that reciprocity is largely absent from modern conflict").

the rules that reify restraint.[33] Humanity is, Larry May writes, "a value and an ideal. Humanity is often referred to as a kind of principle, where … all humans are deserving of respect because of the dignity that is found in each member of humanity."[34] For Yoram Dinstein, however, humanity is "not an obligation" in positive law or an "overarching, binding, norm", but rather "[w]hat we actually encounter are humanitarian considerations, which pave the road to the creation of legal norms and thus explain the evolution of IHL."[35]

From the early stages of international law, there can be found direct references to "humanity," albeit within the context of (*de jure*) reciprocity and the arguably more restrictive standard of "civilisation."[36] Addressing the concerns concomitant with the development of military technology, the Saint Petersburg Declaration of 1868[37] importantly linked the ban on the use of explosive and/or inflammable light projectiles to "the laws of humanity."[38] Also, the later 1899 and 1907 Hague Conventions included in their Preamble the so-called Martens clause[39] which affirmed that belligerents' obligations were not to be exhausted to *lex scripta* and tied the idea of restraint to "the principles of the law of nations as they result from the usages established among civilized peoples, from the laws of humanity, and the dictates of the public conscience." Not only did the clause recognise customary law as part and parcel of international law but also, importantly, it left room for inroads of humanity on positive law by "approach[ing] the question of the laws of humanity for the first time not as a *moral* issue but from a *positivist* (or, to put it more accurately, from an *apparently positivist*) perspective."[40] The Martens clause (or versions thereof) has made its way in the denunciation provisions in the 1949 Geneva Conventions,[41] as well as in Article 1(2) API, which replaced, amongst others, the "*laws* of humanity" with

33 Draper, 1973, p. 131 ("… the content of these rules, and the emphasis in their rationale, was dominantly humanitarian, a new form of secular morality based on the merit and value of the individual human being as such"); Lauterpacht, 1952, p. 379; Gill, 2013, pp. 40–41 (referring to humanity as "the need and objective to limit the suffering and devastation caused by war and provide protection to those most vulnerable …"). See also *Corfu Channel*, ICJ 9 April 1949, p. 22 ("… certain general and well-recognized principles, namely: elementary considerations of humanity, …"); *Nicaragua* (n. 28) p. 112; *Legality of the Threat or Use of Nuclear Weapons*, ICJ, 8 July 1996, p. 257. See also *Kupreskić* (n. 17) paras 525–526; *Martić*, ICTY T. Ch., 8 March 1996, para. 13.

34 May, 2017, p. 78.

35 Dinstein, 2012, p. 73.

36 See e.g. Johnson, 1981; Kinsella, 2017, p. 210.

37 The Declaration considers that "the progress of civilization should have the effect of alleviating as much as possible the calamities of war." See also the (not legally binding) 1880 Oxford Manual (referring to "the rights of humanity" in the Preface and "the laws of humanity and morality" in Art 86 on reprisals), Schindler and Toman, 1988, p. 36.

38 Boothby, 2016, p. 47 (thus "asserting the customary status of that rule …").

39 Roberts and Guelff, 2000, p. 69.

40 Cassese, 2000, p. 188 (emphasis in original). But see also Koskenniemi, 2001, p. 87.

41 Articles 63/62/142/158 GCI-IV; See also references to "humanity" in Art 108 GCIII; Art 5 (Derogations) GCIV.

"*principles* of humanity." In the "emasculated version of the clause"[42] included in the Preamble of Additional Protocol II (APII) on non-international armed conflicts, reference is made only to "the principles of humanity and the dictates of the public conscience" while the Protocol "recalls" that the human person remains the direct beneficiary of the protections thereof.[43]

As the LOAC seeks to set bounds to the conduct of hostilities between individuals who are implicated as opponents by violent claims upon each other's life and (physical and emotional) integrity, the appeal to humanity has been (and still is) not only pertinent but also urgent. And, arguably, the mutual exposure to danger which has been regarded as a core component of the ethical reality of war is perhaps to serve as a normative reminder of the humanity of the adversary and a vestigial sense of what is essentially a human (albeit hostile) relationship.[44] The law acknowledges that the enemy in armed conflict does not lose their human hypostasis.[45] In a normative regime premised on the implicit assumptions within which a human armed interaction is embedded, humanity is manifested in considerations of fairness, which capture a broader normative dynamic, whereby all participants have "a reasonable chance to survive."[46] The law does not give belligerents free rein to practise hostilities and use lethal force in the course of conflict at will, in whatever way they see fit.[47] Humanity speaks to one's responsibility over violence *vis-à-vis* the adversary, rather than a right to it, so to speak. Through prohibitions, which reflect long-standing and well-established rules that impose constraints on the conduct of hostilities,[48] the law aims at guiding behaviour towards one's adversary. In this sense, the law is to be thought of as a fundamentally "other-directed" regime. This suggests that one's (human) adversary is to "benefit" from one's appropriate behaviour in line with the law's prescriptions and proscriptions relating to the use of force.[49] If humanity is to serve as the motivating force for restraint and have a mitigating influence on violence, then it should require the kind of wartime behaviour that is ethically demanded or expected towards the enemy as human being primarily. This requires one to acknowledge, beyond legal obligations, the humanity of the

42 Meron, 2000, p. 81.
43 Cassese, 2000, p. 209.
44 See e.g. Kahn, 2002, p. 4; Ignatieff, 2000, p. 161.
45 See e.g. Rodin, 2006, p. 159 (referring to "the intrinsic moral value of soldiers and civilians as human beings that is the proper focus of the rules of war"); Meron, 2006, p. 5; Luban, 2013, p. 316.
46 Shue, 2016, p. 43.
47 See the fundamental principle that limits the freedom of choice of means and methods of warfare (Article 35(1) API).
48 These rules include the prohibition of superfluous injury or unnecessary suffering (Art 35(2) API), the prohibition of attack against individuals *hors de* combat (Art 41 API), the prohibition of denial of quarter (Art 40 API). See also ICRC, Interpretive Guidance, p. 82 ("Restraints on the use of force in direct attack," referring to basic notions of humanity). See also Haque, 2017, Ch. 4.
49 Lauterpacht, 1953, p. 212.

adversary.[50] Humanity should not be entrapped in the contingencies and vagaries of traditional reciprocity. The enemy need not be "one of us" to be deemed worthy of restrained violence; otherwise, the binary thinking and the mire of divisions, in which reciprocity has traditionally operated, would be perpetuated, thus curtailing the purview of humanity or even rationalising inhumanity. The denial of the humanity of the adversary, that is, behaving as if enemies were the "wrong sort of human beings,"[51] runs the risk of backfiring on "us." In other words, to paraphrase Jonathan Shay, enemy soldiers can become extremely dangerous because they are human just like us.[52] In that respect, Adil Ahmad Haque suggests that "… if it can be shown that the law provides combatants with sound moral guidance, then combatants may be more willing to obey the law even when their adversaries do not."[53] Be it a matter of principle or policy, or even as a grudging concession, humanity is a duty that one owes to the adversary and no less to oneself. As such it should not be contingent on the law-abiding tendencies of the enemy. Geoffrey Best speaks tellingly of the coexistence of reciprocity and humanity to which we turn for restraint: "… the whole IHL enterprise is objectively paradoxical …: war on the one hand, human nature on the other. Yet the enterprise is not abandoned. … And just as some life and credibility is kept in it at one end of the scale by the purposeful prudence which works with calculations of reciprocity and consequences, so at the other end does it depend on the potentially imprudent principles of humanity and honour which decline to believe in the total, unrecognizable alienness, the nonhumanity of the enemy, …"[54]

Humanity is an abiding element in the law and suggests the human constant. It refers to the human, which is the unquestionable continuity amidst changes in bello, and offers a compelling argument for restraint.

8.4 Restraint and UAVs

UAVs or drones introduce a model of violence which fundamentally disrupts the factual and normative conditions of war/armed conflict which the LOAC contemplates as a reciprocal armed interaction.[55] Unmanned warfare is not only an asymmetrical but also an "absolutely unilateral" violent enterprise.[56] As drone operators are physically absent and out of reach and the target is subjected to overwhelming lethal violence and left with no realistic option of resistance, defence or escape, unmanned warfare seems to preclude *ab initio* any expectation

50 See e.g. May, 2017, pp. 78–90. See also Best, 1994, p. 290.

51 Rorty, 1989, p. 190.

52 Shay, 1994, p. 203.

53 Haque, 2017, p. 3. See also e.g. *Kupreskić* (n. 17) paras 511 ("The defining characteristic of modern international humanitarian law is … the obligation to uphold key tenets of this body of law regardless of the conduct of enemy combatants") and 517–518.

54 Best, 1994, p. 291.

55 See Mégret, 2013, p. 1310.

56 Chamayou, 2013, p. 13.

of reciprocity. This is true independently of whether the targeted side is one that violates systematically the law (or is presumed to do so) or one that is inclined to honour humanitarian obligations.[57] In either case, unmanned violence is equally problematic and does not seem to provide an incentive for adherence or compliance. Looking at how drone warfare "affect[s] the ability and willingness of the other side to engage with the laws of war," Frédéric Mégret observes that "[t]here is, symbolically, an extraordinarily dehumanizing aspect to drone warfare in that it deprives its targets from ever even being able to engage in a humanitarian gesture that would manifest their good will ..."[58] Indeed, arguably, a technologically weaker party, for all its willingness to comply, may even be pushed into unlawful acts and violations in an attempt to overcome the radical asymmetry imposed by disparities in technological capability.[59] From a different perspective, Kenneth Anderson claims that drones are a manifestation of "the move to robotics [which] is driven in part by concerns about the loss of behavioural means to affect the behaviour of parties on the other side who do not follow the rules of war."[60] As such, he observes, UAVs seem to have emerged as "technological counters," compensating for the "loss of reprisal to enforce behaviour" (and the "loss of reciprocity exploited by the other side").[61] It may be argued that drones could hardly represent a kind of wartime behaviour in the interests of restraint, let alone serve to motivate for restraint and induce respect for the law.[62]

Be that as it may, as the targets on the receiving side of UAVs do not cease to be human beings, it is worth rehearsing Michael Ignatieff's words:

> We owe them [i.e. the enemy] nothing other than the mercy that all human life has a right to claim. But we owe ourselves much more. We retain obligations in combat even when those we fight do not reciprocate. The obligations we owe are to ourselves alone, ...[63]

If humanity is the irreducible core of restraint, what is profoundly unsettling in unmanned warfare is that it fails to acknowledge the ethical standing that the law "grants" or "recognises" to the adversary as human and excludes the target from the protections that the law provides for opponents. UAV violence makes it virtually impossible for the target to have "a reasonable chance to survive."[64] Drones bring about a reality of warfare where the elimination of risk

57 Mégret, 2013, p. 1312. See also Moyn, 2013.
58 Mégret, 2013, p. 1312.
59 Ibid; White, 2014, pp. 89, 103.
60 Anderson, 2009, p. 345.
61 Ibid, pp. 344–345. But see Beard, 2009, pp. 442–443.
62 See e.g. O'Connell, 2016 arguing that, "[j]udging by the situations in Libya, Yemen, Somalia, and to some extent Pakistan today, drone strikes have helped create far more dangerous situations than prior to their use".
63 Ignatieff, 2001.
64 See Shue, 2016, p. 43. Targets have the opportunity for surrender or capture provided in the law closed off, see n. 48.

is exclusively reserved for oneself in disregard for the humanity of the adversary. Indeed, unmanned warfare is not a far cry from an enterprise strewn with the inhumanity of unilateral "annihilating" force,[65] which is reminiscent of "a putting-to-death."[66] The point about UAVs thus is that they cannot be deemed an advance in restraint *in bello.*

8.5 Conclusion

If restraint as an objective of the legal regulation of warfare is to serve the overarching goal of peace,[67] even in the sense of "peace as a kind of wary modus vivendi … [which] could … ripen into something fuller and more harmonious,"[68] then the warring sides "have, one and all, a common interest" in committing themselves to (self-)restraint and contributing to a climate which does not sustain inhumanity. If we are to achieve less loss of life, less harm and less suffering in a moment of most intense human controversy, humanity needs to be reinstated so that it enables us to reclaim the idea of restraint essentially as a matter of respect for the adversary as human being. There is still much to work for.

References

Kenneth Anderson, "The Rise of International Criminal Law: Intended and Unintended Consequences", *The European Journal of International Law*, vol. 20, no. 2, 2009, pp. 331–358.

Jack M. Beard, "Law and War in the Virtual Era", *American Journal of International Law*, vol. 103, no. 409, 2009, pp. 409–445.

Geoffrey Best, *War and Law Since 1945*, Clarendon Press, Oxford, 1994.

Gabriella Blum and David Luban, "Unsatisfying Wars: Degrees of Risk and the Jus ex Bello", *Ethics*, vol. 125, no. 3, 2015, pp. 751–780.

William H. Boothby, *Weapons and the Law of Armed Conflict* (2nd ed.), Oxford University Press, Oxford, 2016.

Antonio Cassese, *International Law*, Oxford University Press, Oxford, 2001.

Antonio Cassese, "The Martens Clause: Half a Loaf or Simply Pie in the Sky?", *European Journal of International Law*, vol. 11, no. 1, 2000, pp. 187–216.

Grégoire Chamayou, *A Theory of the Drone* (transl. Janet Llloyd), The New Press, New York, 2013.

Yoram Dinstein, *The Conduct of Hostilities under the Law of International Armed Conflict* (3rd ed.), Cambridge University Press, Cambridge, 2016.

Yoram Dinstein, "The Principle of Proportionality", in Kjetil Mujezinović Larsen, Camilla Guldahl Cooper and Gro Nystuen (Eds.), *Searching for a 'Principle of Humanity' in International Humanitarian Law*, Cambridge University Press, Cambridge, 2012.

Gerald Irving A. Dare Draper, *The Red Cross Conventions,* Praeger, Santa Barbara, 1958.

65 Gusterson, 2016, p. 40 (describing the dehumanising and extensive nature of injuries inflicted).

66 Chamayou, 2013, p. 162. Kahn, 2013, p. 200.

67 ICRC, 1987 API Commentary, p. 27.

68 Blum and Luban, 2015, p. 754. See also Howard, 1979, p. 14.

Gerald Irving A. Dare Draper, "Military Necessity and Humanitarian Imperatives", *Revue du droit pénal militaire et du droit de la guerre*, vol. 12, no. 2, 1973, pp. 129–151.

David A. Elder, "The Historical Background of Common Article 3 of The Geneva Convention of 1949", *Case Western Reserve Journal of International Law*, vol. 11, no. 1, 1979, pp. 37–69.

Dieter Fleck, "The Law of Non-International Armed Conflicts", in Dieter Fleck (Ed.), *The Handbook of Humanitarian Law in Armed Conflicts* (2nd ed.), Oxford University Press, Oxford, 2008, pp. 581–610.

Terry Gill, "Chivalry, A Principle of the Law of Armed Conflict?", in Marcel Brus and Brigit Toebes (Eds.), *Armed Conflict and International Law: In search of the Human Face: Liber Amicorum in Memory of Avril McDonald*, Asser Press, Hague, 2013.

Hugh Gusterson, *Drone: Remote Control Warfare*, MIT Press, Cambridge MA, 2016.

Adil Ahmad Haque, *Law and Morality at War*, Oxford University Press, Oxford, 2017.

Michael Howard, "Temperamenta Belli: Can War Be Controlled?", in Michael Howard (Ed.), *Restraints on War: Studies in the Limitation of Armed Conflict*, Oxford University Press, Oxford, 1979.

ICRC, *Customary International Humanitarian Law* (Vol. 1: Rules), in Jean-Marie Henckaerts and Louise Doswald-Beck (Eds.), Cambridge University Press, Cambridge, 2009.

ICRC, *Interpretive Guidance on the Notion of Direct Participation in Hostilities under International Humanitarian Law*, in Nils Melzer (Ed.), ICRC, Geneva, 2009.

Michael Ignatieff, *Virtual War: Kosovo and Beyond*, Chatto & Windus, London, 2000.

Michael Ignatieff, "It's war – but it doesn't have to be dirty", *The Guardian*, 1 October 2001 available at: www.theguardian.com/world/2001/oct/01/afghanistan.terrorism9 (accessed 22 April 2018).

James Tumer Johnson, *Just War Tradition and the Restraint of War: A Moral and Historical Inquiry*, Princeton University Press, Princeton, 1981.

Paul W. Kahn, "Imagining Warfare", *European Journal of International Law*, vol. 24, no. 1, 2013, pp. 199–226.

Paul W. Kahn, "The Paradox of Riskless Warfare", *Philosophy and Public Policy Quarterly*, vol. 22, no. 3, 2002, pp. 2–8.

Frits Kalshoven, *Belligerent Reprisals*, Sijthoff, Amsterdam, 1971.

Helen M. Kinsella, "Superfluous Injury and Unnecessary Suffering: National Liberation and the Laws of War", in Tarak Barkawi and George Lawson (Ed.), *International Origins of Social and Political Theory*, (Political Power and Social Theory, Vol. 32), Emerald Publishing Limited, Bingley, 2017, pp. 205–231.

Martti Koskenniemi, *The Gentle Civilizer of Nations: The Rise and Fall of International Law, 1870–1960*, Cambridge University Press, Cambridge, 2001.

Hersch Lauterpacht, "The Problem of the Revision of the Law of War", *British Yearbook of International Law*, vol. 29, 1952, pp. 360–382.

Hersch Lauterpacht, "The Limits of the Operation of the Law of War", *British Yearbook of International Law*, vol. 30, 1953, pp. 206–243.

David Luban, "Military Necessity and the Cultures of Military Law", *Leiden Journal of International Law*, vol. 26, no. 2, 2013, pp. 315–349.

Larry May, "Humanity, Necessity, and the Rights of Soldiers", in Jens David Ohlin, Larry May and Claire Finkelstein (Eds.), *Weighing Lives in War*, Oxford University Press, Oxford, 2017.

Frédéric Mégret, "From 'Savages' to 'Unlawful Combatants': A Postcolonial Look at International Law's 'Other'", in Anne Orford (Ed.), *International Law and Its Others*, Cambridge University Press, Cambridge, 2006, pp. 265–317.

Frédéric Mégret, "The Humanitarian Problem with Drones", *Utah Law Review*, vol. 2013, no. 5, 2013, pp. 1283–1319.

Theodor Meron, "The Martens Clause, Principles of Humanity, and Dictates of Public Conscience", *American Journal of International Law*, vol. 94, no. 1, 2000, pp. 78–89.

Theodor Meron, *The Humanization of International Law*, The Hague Academy of International Law, Martinus Nijhoff Publishers, Leiden, 2006.

Lindsay Moir, *The Law of Internal Armed Conflict*, Cambridge University Press, Cambridge, 2002.

Samuel Moyn, "Drones and Imagination: A Response to Paul Kahn", *European Journal of International Law*, vol. 24, no, 1, 2013, pp. 227–233.

Stephen C. Neff, *War and the Law of Nations: A General History*, Cambridge University Press, Cambridge, 2005.

Mary Ellen O'Connell, "The Future of Peace, Weapons, and War", Frans van Hasselt lecture 2015: The Future of Peace, Weapons and War, TU Delft, 6 September 2016, available at: https://sg.tudelft.nl/2016/09/06/frans-van-hasselt-lecture-2015-the-future-of-peace-weapons-and-war/ (accessed 22 April 2018).

Mark Osiel, *The End of Reciprocity: Terror, Torture, and the Law of War*, Cambridge University Press, Cambridge, 2009.

Geoffrey Parker, "Early Modern Europe", in Michael Howard, George J. Andreopoulos and Mark R. Shulman (Eds.), *The Laws of War: Constraints on Warfare in the Western World*, Yale University Press, New Haven, CT 1994.

René Provost, *International Human Rights and Humanitarian Law*, Cambridge University Press, Cambridge, 2002.

René Provost, "Asymmetrical Reciprocity and Compliance with the Laws of War", in Benjamin Perrin (Ed.), *Modern Warfare: Armed Groups, Private Militaries, Humanitarian Organizations, and the Law*, University of British Columbia Press, Vancouver, 2012, pp. 12–42.

Adam Roberts and Richard Guelff, *Documents on the Laws of War* (3rd ed.), Oxford University Press, Oxford, 2000.

Adam Roberts, "The Equal Application of the Laws of War: A Principle under Pressure", *International Review of the Red Cross*, vol. 90, no. 872, 2008, pp. 931–962.

David Rodin, "The Ethics of Asymmetric War", in Richard Sorabji and David Rodin (Eds.), *The Ethics of War: Shared Problems in Different Traditions*, Ashgate, Farnham, 2006.

Richard Rorty, *Contingency, Irony, and Solidarity*, Cambridge University Press, Cambridge, 1989.

Dietrich Schindler and Jiří Toman, *The Laws of Armed Conflicts: A Collection of Conventions, Resolutions, and Other Documents* (3rd ed.), Martinus Nijhoff, Leiden, 1988.

Georg Schwarzenberger, *International Law as Applied by International Courts and Tribunals: The Law of Armed Conflict*, Sweet & Maxwell, London, 1968.

Jonathan Shay, *Achilles in Vietnam: Combat Trauma and the Undoing of Character*, Atheneum, New York, 1994.

Henry Shue, *Fighting Hurt: Rule and Exception in Torture and War*, Oxford University Press, Oxford, 2016.

Sandesh Sivakumaran, *The Law of Non-International Armed Conflict*, Oxford University Press, Oxford, 2012.

Robert C. Stacey, "The Age of Chivalry", in Michael Howard, George J. Andreopoulos and Mark R. Shulman (Eds.), *The Laws of War: Constraints on Warfare in the Western World*, Yale University Press, New Haven, CT 1994.

Ellery C. Stowell, "Military Reprisals and the Sanctions of the Laws of War", *The American Journal of International Law*, vol. 36, no. 4, 1942, pp. 643–650.

Sean Watts, "Reciprocity and the Law of War", *Harvard International Law Journal*, vol. 50, no. 2, 2009, pp. 365–434.

Nigel D. White, *Advanced Introduction to International Conflict and Security Law*, Edward Elgar Publishing, Cheltenham, 2014.

Case Law

ICJ

Military and Paramilitary Activities in and against Nicaragua case (*Nicaragua* v *USA*), ICJ, Merits, Judgment, 28 June 1986 [1986] ICJ Rep 14.

Corfu Channel case (*United Kingdom of Great Britain and Northern Ireland v Albania*), ICJ, Merits, Judgment, 9 April 1949 [1949] ICJ Rep 4.

Legality of the Threat or Use of Nuclear Weapons, Advisory Opinion, 8 July 1996, ICJ [1996] Rep 226.

ICTY

ICTY, *Prosecutor v Kupreskić et al.* (Case No IT-95–16), ICTY T. Ch., Trial Judgment, 14 January 2000.

ICTY, *Prosecutor v Hadzihasanovic* (Case No IT-01–47-AR72), ICTY App. Ch., Interlocutory Appeal on Decision Challenging Jurisdiction in Relation to Command Responsibility, 16 July 2003.

ICTY, *Prosecutor v Martić* (Case No IT-95–11–R61), ICTY T. Ch., Decision, 8 March 1996.

ICTY, *Prosecutor v Martić* (Case No IT-95-11-T), ICTY T. Ch., Judgement, 12 June 2007.

ICTY, *Prosecutor v Martić* (Case No IT-95-11-A), ICTY, App. Ch., Judgement, 8 October 2008.

Conventions

1868 St, Petersburg Declaration Renouncing the Use, in Time of War, of Explosive Projectiles under 400 Grammes Weight, November 29/December 11, 1868.

Hague Convention (II) with Respect to the Laws and Customs of War on Land, July 29, 1899 (entered into force September 4, 1900).

Hague Convention (IV) Respecting the Laws and Customs of War on Land, October 18, 1907 (entered into force January 26, 1910).

Convention relative to the Treatment of Prisoners of War, Geneva, July 27, 1929 (entered into force June 19, 1931).

Convention for the Amelioration of the Condition of the Wounded and Sick in Armies in the Field, Geneva, July 27, 1929 (entered into force June 19, 1931).

Geneva Convention (I) for the Amelioration of the Condition of the Wounded and Sick in Armed Forces in the Field, August 12, 1949 (entered into force October 21, 1950).

Geneva Convention (II) for the Amelioration of the Wounded, Sick and Shipwrecked Members of Armed Forces at Sea, August 12, 1949 (entered into force October 21, 1950).

Geneva Convention (III) Relative to the Treatment of Prisoners of War, August 12, 1949 (entered into force October 21, 1950).
Geneva Convention (IV) Relative to the Protection of Civilian Persons in Time of War, August 12, 1949 (entered into force October 21, 1950).
Protocol Additional to the Geneva Conventions of August 12, 1949, and relating to the Protection of Victims of International Armed Conflicts (Protocol I), June 8, 1977 (entered into force December 7, 1978).
Protocol Additional to the Geneva Conventions of 12 August 1949, and relating to the Protection of Victims of Non-International Armed Conflicts (Protocol II), June 8, 1977 (entered into force December 7, 1978).
The Laws of War on Land, 9 September 1880 (Institute of International Law) (Oxford Manual).
Vienna Convention on the Law of Treaties, May 23, 1969 (entered into force January 27, 1980).

Commentaries

ICRC, Commentary on the Geneva Convention I for the Amelioration of the Condition of the Wounded and Sick in Armed Forces in the Field (ICRC 2016) https://ihl-databases.icrc.org/ihl/full/GCI-commentary.
ICRC, Commentary on the Geneva Convention I for the Amelioration of the Condition of the Wounded and Sick in Armed Forces in the Field (ed Jean S. Pictet) (ICRC 1952).
ICRC, Commentary on the Additional Protocols of 8 June 1977 to the Geneva Conventions of 12 August 1949 (eds Yves Sandoz et al.) (ICRC 1987).

9 Judging the past – international humanitarian law and the Luftwaffe aerial operations during the invasion of Poland in 1939

Mateusz Piątkowski

9.1 Introduction

International humanitarian law (or the laws of war) is considered as the most fragile part of international law. The area that is governed by this set of rules and customs is inherently interfering with core aspects of state sovereignty. It tends to limit the inflexible right of every state to wage war. This creates a potential area of disagreement among the nations. At the same time, the weaponry used in war is increasingly efficient, and the humanitarian perspective of warfare is undermined. The arrival of new means and methods of combat is always a clear challenge for the existing legal framework. Such mechanisms reappeared in the beginning of the 20th century when the first military aircrafts were deployed in combat roles, and unfortunately, it is still topical in the contemporary world with the introduction of the lethal autonomous devices. The source of the issue is related to reluctance of states to adopt an acceptable level of limitation of the course of warfare. Another problem arises from technical argumentation, which is usually on an early stage of its development, indicating no concrete yardstick.

Those considerations fit perfectly in the picture of the law of aerial warfare during the 20th century. The bombings of Warsaw, Rotterdam, London, Hamburg, Tokyo and Dresden are still subject to a long-lasting discussion, attracting attention from the legal and historical fields. In such a legal landscape, I decided to dedicate my research to both contemporary and historical aspects of aerial warfare in the light of the relevant *ius in bello* provisions. This case study, which concerns the Second World War bombardments, is substantially important to better understand the blurred connections between law, technology and international relationships. In this respect, the presented background of the bombing of the Polish town Wieluń in September 1939 is particularly significant, as it was among the first acts of this war, awakening the need of detailed examination from the perspectives of history and law.

Without warning, without appeals or an official declaration of war, and accompanied by the thunder from guns from the border, between 4.40 and 5.40 a.m. on the 1st of September 1939, a formation of 30 Ju-87 Junkers dive bombers began a deadly run above the provincial town close to the German-Polish border. The locality burned in the flame of incendiary bombs, which would become a prelude for a new type of warfare. The discussion about the legality of air bombardments during the Second War World has not mentioned the tragedy of this city, or the serious international humanitarian law issues of the first organized air operation in the Second World War. The point of this article is to consider the existence and the role of the rules covering aerial warfare at the time and to find the answer to the question how international law protected or could have protected the inhabitants of Wieluń at the dawn of 1st September 1939. Then, the chapter will turn to the aspect of post-war fact-finding challenges. It will be summarized by questions concerning international criminal law.

9.2 The law: the development of aircraft as a war machine

Aviation was introduced as a method of warfare with the deployment of the Montpelier balloons during the French Revolutionary Wars in the late 18th century.[1] During the next age, the aerostats were constantly upgrading, offering the belligerents new possibilities of long-range reconnaissance, transportation and commutation. This evolution also included the legal aspects of airspace travels both in time of peace and war. During the Franco-Prussian war 1870–1871, the German authorities treated and captured a French balloonist as a spy.[2] This brought the status of the air crew to the agenda of the Brussels Conference in 1874 and it reappeared during the plenary meetings of the Institute of International Law.[3] The well-known first international regulation concerning the problems of air bombardment was a declaration at the Hague peace conference in 1899, which banned projectiles and explosives as armaments of the balloons.[4] The Declaration was ratified by all major powers and valid for the following five years. During the next peace conference in Hague in 1907, the countries accepted to extend the power of declaration until the next peace conference, which was never summoned.[5] From a legal point of view, the declaration is still binding. However, it has been considered to fall into *desuetude*.[6]

The First World War catalysed the development of the aircraft industry. From a technical newbie, the plane became a full war machine with decisive influence on the modern battlefield. The bombing of London in 1914 showed to the world the global problem of an indiscriminate attack on civilians.[7] After the war, in-

1 Haydon, 2000, pp. 8–9.
2 van Wijk, 1982, pp. 309–313.
3 Lycklama à Nijeholt, p. 1.
4 Declaration (IV, 1), to Prohibit, for the Term of Five Years, the Launching of Projectiles and Explosives from Balloons, and Other Methods of Similar Nature. The Hague, 29 July 1899. www.icrc.org/ihl.nsf/FULL/160?OpenDocument (accessed 17 September 2017).
5 Declaration (XIV) Prohibiting the Discharge of Projectiles and Explosives from Balloons. The Hague, 18 October 1907. www.icrc.org/ihl.nsf/FULL/245?OpenDocument (accessed 17 September 2017).
6 Bierzanek, 1988, p. 396; Garner, 1932, p. 103; Hanski, 1992, p. 59.
7 Biddle, 2002, p. 20–23.

ternational legal experts faced a serious issue, trying to find a solution for rules covering the new means of fighting such as chemical weapons, unrestricted submarine warfare and aircraft operations.

9.2.1 Article 25 of the IV Hague Convention

The article 25 of the IV Hague Convention was meant to be the relevant regulation for air bombardments.[8] The scope of the provision was to protect *undefended places* against attacks made by *whatever means.* The Second Peace Hague Conference records provided that the intended applicability of the article would also be found active in case of aerial bombardment. In 1911, the Madrid Institute of International Law upheld that "the rules established by the Hague Conventions of 18th October 1907, relative to Sieges and Bombardments by Land or Naval Forces, are applicable to aerial war."[9] That conclusion and the lack of dedicated definition for air warfare rules led the pre-war judicial bodies to conclude that the article 25 of the IV Hague Convention applied to the air warfare by analogy.[10]

The responsibility of the German side which was held liable for repaying the damages made by air attacks on Bucharest and Salonica (*Coenca Brothers case* and *Kiriadolou case)* was based on the violation of the warning requirement as laid down in article 26 of the Hague Convention.[11] A strong connection between those two articles (25 and 26) led the judges to the conclusion that the Hague regulations covering land warfare are applicable to air warfare as well.[12] This notion, which was generally accepted by scholars, quickly sparked an intense academic discussion. After a detailed consideration from the viewpoint of *ius in bello* rules and battlefield practice, some authors strongly opposed the applicability of article 25 for air warfare. James W. Garner noticed that the provision of the Hague regulation is *illogical and impractical.*[13] The literal interpretation of the meaning of article 25 would lead the reader to a paradoxical conclusion. What does the word *undefended* mean in air warfare? Richard F. Wymann gives an example of a hypothetical situation based on the correct application of that article.[14] In a strictly narrow meaning, an undefended tank factory will be considered as a non-legitimate target. On the other hand, a city with inhabitants defended from the air attack by a single machine gun will be a lawful military objective.

Another important issue is differences in the definition of the word *undefended.* That phrase could be interpreted differently in land, naval and air operations.

8 Convention (IV) respecting the Laws and Customs of War on Land and its annex: regulations concerning the Laws and Customs of War on Land. The Hague, 18 October 1907.

9 Goda, 1996, p. 96.

10 Rogers, 2006, p. 91.

11 Post, 2006, p. 160 (Greco-German Mixed Arbitral Tribunal).

12 Johnson, 1965, pp. 31–32.

13 Garner, 1924, p. 57.

14 Wymann, 1984.

Most commonly, according to the Hague regulation, a city is "undefended" when it can be conquered without any resistance.[15] But for the air forces, this definition must be built from a different basis to become an acceptable standard for belligerents. For instance, it is highly doubtful if a single machine gun would be sufficient to defend the area against air attacks. A relevant practical problem was presented by W. Hays Parks: During the bombing of London in the First World War, the British air defence HQ was unable to decide whether building an anti-aircraft establishment would allow German forces to legalize the shelling of the city according to article 25.[16]

These requirements have rapidly lost their significance in the jet engine and missile era, where it is impossible to distinguish between *undefended* and *defended* areas from the point of view of article 25 of the IV Hague convention. Remigiusz Bierzanek concluded that provision was exceptionally inadequate in the conditions of modern air warfare and even more contrary to national practices.[17] A much more acceptable analogy to air operations is laid down in the IX Hague Convention, covering sea bombardment. The article 2 of the Convention allows to target military structures such as "military works, military or naval establishments, depots of arms (…)" irrespective of their location.[18] However, due to a mixture of wrongful judicial decisions and the lack of good will among states, the international practice denied the applicability of the IX Hague Convention to aerial warfare.

9.2.2 Hague Rules of Aerial Warfare

In 1922 in Washington, D.C., the victorious powers tried to determine the acceptable limitation concerning the after-war arms race. In addition, the delegates were ready to deal with the question related to the international humanitarian law that reappeared during the Great War (e.g., unrestricted submarine warfare and the use of poisonous gases). This included the question of aerial warfare. The countries decided to establish a joint commission, the so-called Jurist Commission.[19] The Commission would represent lawyers and military advisors from six countries (United States, United Kingdom, France, Japan, Italy and the Netherlands) under the leadership of the US Supreme Court judge Joseph B. Moore.[20] Their work began after authorization from Conference participants in December 1922.[21] Article 22 of the Rules strictly forbids bombing aimed to

15 See Piątkowski, 2017.

16 Parks, 1990, p. 15.

17 Bierzanek, 1988, p. 406.

18 Convention (IX) concerning Bombardment by Naval Forces in Time of War. The Hague, 18 October 1907.

19 In 1920, the International Red Cross appeal to League of Nations for urgent intervention which solved the matter of unregulated aerial warfare. Gomez, 1998.

20 Toman and Schindler, 2004, p. 25.

21 Hanke, 1993, p. 15.

shatter the civilian morale (so-called terror bombing).[22] Article 24 was the most discussed provision during the Commission's meetings, but thanks to the effort of its chairman it was unanimously agreed upon and adopted as a part of draft.[23] The solutions contained in the provision definitely outran its times. First of all, it is known to be one of the first international humanitarian law document that constructs the definition of "military advantage" in the modern aspect.[24] It proposed the introduction of the term *military objective* and presented a closed catalogue of military targets (with the word "exclusively").[25] The third and fourth paragraphs contain instructions addressed to air operation planners. To fulfil the obligations arising from The Hague Rules, the attacker must abstain from bombardment when the military targets cannot be engaged without harming the civilian population. The fourth paragraph entailed the proportionality rule (for the first time in written form) and demands from the commander to evaluate the risk of indiscriminate bombing of the civilian population and the anticipated military advantage.[26] The Hague Rules from 1923 are praised by experts of international humanitarian law. Heinz M. Hanke emphasized that the regulations were finally dismissing the requirement of *defended locality*.[27] J. M. Garner pointed out that the test of military advantage included in article 24 of the Hague Rules was logical and coherent.[28] A more critical approach was represented by Parks, who noticed that the state practice refused and forgot the idea of the Hague Rules of 1923.[29] Nevertheless, the impact and significance of the rules cannot be denied.[30] Remigiusz Bierzanek noticed that the Air Warfare Rules had a "persuasive power."[31] Lawrence Oppenheim concluded that the regulation from 1923 was a base for a further codification of laws and customs covering air warfare.[32] In 1928, the British Royal Air Force Chief of Staff wrote that "although the code then drawn up has not been officially adopted, it is likely to represent the practice which will be regarded as lawful in any future war."[33] Indeed, the Air Warfare Rules were never adopted by any country as a binding convention or a multinational treaty. However, they were recognized by the air forces' legal advisers around the world, and implemented in military manuals and orders.[34] This activity will open a new

22 Rules concerning the Control of Wireless Telegraphy in Time of War and Air Warfare. Drafted by a Commission of Jurists at the Hague, December 1922–February 1923, available at: https://ihl-databases.icrc.org/ihl/INTRO/275?OpenDocument (accessed 17 September 2017).
23 Rogers, 1982, p. 297.
24 Piątkowski, 2015, p. 185. Cf. especially Article 52 of Additional Protocol I from 1977.
25 Kalshoven, 2016, p. 41.
26 Hensel, 2007, p. 53.
27 Hanke, 1993, p. 21.
28 Garner, 1924, p. 70.
29 Parks, 1990, p. 32.
30 Gardam, 2009, p. 55.
31 Bierzanek, 1982, p. 301.
32 Oppenheim and Lauterpacht, 1952, p. 519.
33 Goda, 1996, p. 99.
34 Bierzanek and Hanke give multiple examples of domestic military manuals and instruction issued by the air forces of United States, United Kingdom, Japan, Italy, Poland or Germany (order

discussion about the influence of the Hague Rules from 1923 and their binding power as a customary international humanitarian law, as it was underlined in the *Shimoda v. State* Tokyo District Court judgement in 1963.[35]

9.3 The Bombing

9.3.1 Wieluń as a military objective in the light of belligerent plans

Wieluń, a town in the Province of Łódź, over 200 km southwest of Warsaw, in 1939 was a small urban border area with 16,000 inhabitants. It was home to the local authorities of the region, a major city of the Wieluń County and a centre of local cultural and economic life.[36] After the Treaty of Versailles, Wieluń was located only 20 km from the Polish-Germany border.[37] Expecting the war, in March 1939, the Polish Supreme Command formed the Łódź Army, operationally responsible for defending the area of Łódź, including Wieluń.[38] The army units were deployed to secure the region from German invasion and to protect the communication links to Warsaw. To complete that mission, in the summer 1939, the army engineers' corps began a field fortification programme, using the natural terrain obstacles like the valley of rivers Warta and Widawka. Those plans left a town of Wieluń out of the scope of preparations, due to the proximity to the frontier. These circumstances were investigated by the Łódź branch of the Institute of National Remembrance – Commission for the Prosecution of Crimes against the Polish Nation (Instytut Pamięci Narodowej, IPN) in 2011.[39] According to the Commission, the town was not held by the Polish military forces before

---

from 22 July 1939 addressed to field units and martial courts): Hanke, 1993, p. 35; Bierzanek, 1988, pp. 396–408; Rotocki, 1970, pp. 143–170.

35 *Ryuichi Shimoda, et al v.* The State, Japanese Annual of International Law, No. 8, 1964.

36 For further reading about the city and its role in the region, see generally Olejnik, 2009 with a speech of the President of the Republic of Poland Lech Kaczynski (in English): http://wbi.d2.pl/wtn/00/album39popr.pdf (accessed 25/02/2018); *J. v. Mattern, H. M Kloth:* "Stukas über Wielun", *Der Spiegel* 26 August 2009: http://einestages.spiegel.de/static/topicalbumbackground/4821/stukas_ueber_wielun.html (accessed 25 February 2018); A. Hreczuk: "Flugzeuge, Papa, Flugzeuge!", *Der Tagesspiegel* 30 August 2009: www.tagesspiegel.de/zeitung/weltkriegsbeginn-flugzeuge-papa-flugzeuge/1590804.html) (accessed 28 February 2018).

37 N. Davis, "We must not forget the real causes of the war" *The Independent*, 29 August 2009: www.independent.co.uk/voices/commentators/we-must-not-forget-the-real-causes-of-the-war-1778973.html: (accessed 28 February 2018). For a better understanding of the location of the city, see the original Polish military chart from 1938 on the website: www.mapywig.org/m/wig100k/P44_S27_WIELUN.jpg (accessed 25 February 2018).

38 See generally Koskodan, 2011; the Łódź Army was commanded by general Rómmel (not to mistake for the German Feldmarschal) and contained five infantry divisions (2, 10, 22, 28 and 30) and two cavalry brigades (Wolynska and Kresowa), but due to the late mobilization only three divisions (10, 28 and 30) and one cavalry brigade were ready for action on the 1st September 1939. Porwitt, 1983.

39 The Institute of National Remembrance – Commission for the Prosecution of Crimes against the Polish Nation (IPN) was established by the Polish parliament in 1998.

and during the time of the attack. Nevertheless, to fully understand the value of Wieluń as a military target is it important to get acquainted with the Wehrmacht invasion plan in that area. According to the "Fall Weiss" operation, the area of Łódź was the primary target of Group Army South, and its two armies, the 8th Army and the 10th Army. The Wieluń region was under the operational jurisdiction of the 10th Army. The planned assault breakpoint was localized nearby Częstochowa, about 60 km southeast of Wieluń, where the Polish defence preparation level was at the lowest, due to lack of coordination between the Army Łódź and its southern neighbour the Cracow Army. The 8th Army had been selected to storm the north flank of the Łódź Army, near the town of Sieradz (ca. 50 km from Wieluń).[40] This short historical background of German military plans shows that the role of Wieluń in the *Fall Weiss* plan was marginal, and proves the theory about a very low military value for the whole region, and the town itself.

9.3.2 Undeclared strike

The first air strike on Wieluń was carried out by *I Gruppe, 76 Sturmgeschwader* (Dive Bombers Regiment) from the Nieder-Ellghut airfield (nowadays Ligota Dolna) under the command of *Hauptmann* Walther Siegel. The unit was affiliated to a special dive bombers formation, under the command of general Wolfram von Richthofen, the Guernica air raid commander. Von Richthofen was the head of all dive bomber regiments in *4. Luftflotte* (4th Air Fleet) commanded by Alexander Lohr.[41] The first air strike was performed under complete surprise at 5.40 am. For a long time, it was suggested that the Wieluń bombing occurred a few minutes earlier than the shelling of Westerplatte in Danzig/Gdansk and that the act of bombing would thus hold the status of first act of the Second World War. The famous Stuka dive bombers started their dive run from around 2,000 meters above the ground. For the first time in the history of the Second World War, the citizens of Wieluń heard the horrible and terrifying sound of the *Udet-system.*[42] After reaching 800 meters on their altimeters, the bombers released a deathly package consisting of 112 demolition bombs and 29 heavy projectiles.[43] The results of the bombing were dramatic. The first bombs hit a local hospital, killing 32 people. The building in the town market, the church and the synagogue were also destroyed. About 75% of all urban area was burned or demolished; at least 127 civilians were killed.[44]

40 Kennedy, 1956, pp. 83–85.

41 J. Trenkner, "Ziel vernichtet", Die Zeit 2003/07: www.zeit.de/2003/07/A-Wielun (accessed 25 February 2018).

42 So-called *Jerichontrompeten*, the Udetsystem, was a special mechanism in the gear of Ju-87, which used the air flow to create a characteristic sound from the diving Stukas after reaching a 60 degrees attack angle.

43 A photocopy of the official report by Walther Siegel from the Wielún bombing is available at: www.historiawielunia.uni.lodz.pl/cel_zniszczony.pdf (accessed 17 September 2017).

44 More often the total number of 1,300 killed is excerpting in official publications. But in summary, it was impossible to confirm such a death toll; the Commission's investigation confirmed

9.4 Legal opinion on the Luftwaffe bombing of the town

In the case of bombing of urban areas, it is possible to find certain discrete legal viewpoints held by different authorities. The first one is represented in the investigation conducted by the Commission for the Prosecution of Crimes against the Polish Nation, Łódź Detachment. The second is an opinion of the German District Prosecutor in Munich.

9.4.1 The Commission for the Prosecution of Crimes against the Polish Nation, Łódź Detachment[45]

The investigation was conducted by the Commission under the Decree of 31 August 1944, "On the Punishment of Nazi Criminals Guilty of Murder and Torture Inflicted upon Civilians and Prisoners and for Traitors of the Polish Nation," which had been issued by the communist government of Poland. As a result, the Commission stated that the bombing of a town was a violation of article 1 of the 1944 Decree. In factual justification, the Commission remarked that:

a the town of Wieluń was treated as one, single target, without any distinction between civilian and military objectives;
b the town was not hit as a result of poor intelligence data, or a factual mistake. This conclusion was derived from the fact that the attack consisted of subsequent waves of bombers at 12.00 am and 2.00 pm on 1st September 1939;
c it has been proved beyond doubt that the city was "undefended."

In conclusion, the Commission upheld that the Luftwaffe bombing had violated the following laws and customs of the international humanitarian law:

a article 25 of IV Hague Convention (Wieluń was an "undefended" place in the scope of that provision). In fact, due to specific circumstances of the attack, the town was bombarded under the condition of undeclared war, eliminating the possibility from the Polish side to counterattack or intercept the incoming bomber raid;
b article 26 of the above-mentioned regulation (failure in the warning requirement) and article 27 (protection of heritage) and the

without doubts 127 killed during the air strike on Wielun. The number of 1,300 killed is most likely the total sum of all killed inhabitants of the town of Wielún and the district of Wielún during the whole of September 1939.

45 Based on investigation files, the decision of remission of the investigation from 9th June 2011, OKL S/10/04/Zn, chart file no. 1140. The reprint is kept by the author. File signature S/10/04/Zn.

c breach of article 6 of the International Military Tribunal London Charter (wanton destruction of cities, towns or villages, or devastation not justified by military necessity).[46]

9.4.2 The German investigation

In 1978, the Commission issued an official application to German prosecution authorities, demanding them to begin proceedings concerning the Wieluń bombing and the possible indictment of the perpetrators that were still alive. The motion was examined by the Prosecutors office in Deggendorf.[47] The German side dismissed that point of view due to the lack of evidence and contested the legal basis for the application (without any further justification). The Office of the prosecutor in Deggendorf admitted that the bombing of the hospital of Wieluń had been a breach of article 26 of the IV Hague Convention, but it had been qualified as an ordinary killing, so at the date of the application applied to statutory limitations.

Under the chairmanship of Witold Kulesza, during the 1990s, the Commission submitted a request for a renewal of the investigation. The legal qualification of the crime was an important part of the Commission's application. The crime was qualified as a ***murder***, which is a separate violation from ***killing*** in the view of German criminal law. The § 211 of the German Criminal Code describes a murder as a killing for "pleasure, for sexual gratification, out of greed or otherwise base motives, by stealth or cruelly or by means that pose a danger to the public or in order to facilitate or to cover up another offence."[48] The § 78 (2) of the German Criminal Code lays down that the felony committed under the conditions of § 211 *is not subject to a statute of limitations*. This provision is especially significant in the light of the fact that the Federal Republic of Germany is not a party to the Convention on the Non-Applicability of Statutory Limitations to War Crimes and Crimes Against Humanity, of 26 November 1968 and the European Convention on the Non-Applicability of Statutory Limitation to Crimes against Humanity and War Crimes.[49] Kulesza expressed that in the view of the Commission's argumentation, the bombing of Wieluń was (a) *cruel* (in the meaning of § 211 of the German Criminal Code) – the death occurred in flames caused by incendiary bombs; (b) by *stealth* – the air operation occurred under the conditions of an undeclared war.[50] Nevertheless, no official proceedings were resumed.

46 Charter of International Military Tribunal, London 8th of August 1945, *Journal of Laws of the Polish Republic*, 1947, no. 63, item 367.

47 Vermerk 320 uJs 203766/78 (1 uJs 1316/78 StA Deggendorf) "Tötung einer unbekannten Vielzahl von polnischen Staatsangehörigen in Wielun, Regierungsbezirk Lodz."

48 Criminal Code in the version promulgated on 13 November 1998, Federal Law Gazette [*Bundesgesetzblatt*] I p. 3322, last amended by Article 3 of the Law of 2 October 2009, Federal Law Gazette I p. 3214.

49 List of state parties: http://treaties.un.org/pages/ViewDetails.aspx?src=TREATY&mtdsg_no=IV-6&chapter=4&lang=en_(accessed 25 February 2018); http://conventions.coe.int/Treaty/Commun/ChercheSig.asp?NT=082&CM=1&DF=&CL=ENG (accessed 25 February 2018).

50 Interview with Witold Kulesza about war crimes conducted by German Armed Forces in September 1939, *Pierwszy był Wieluń* (Wielún was first), *Rzeczpospolita* 9 September 1999: http://archiwum.rp.pl/artykul/241734.html (accessed 25 February 2018).

9.4.3 The bombing of Wieluń and international criminal law

Two authors, who analyse the case of urban bombing, strongly advocate the theory that the tragedy of Wieluń was caused by an unfortunate mistake made by the German intelligence, rather than being an intentional terror action against the town and its inhabitants.[51] According to them, the Luftwaffe actions were primarily directed against military objectives – a unit from a cavalry brigade (which was wrongly recognized). Generally, in criminal law, the mistake of fact excludes the criminal responsibility for crimes, which could be committed wilfully.[52] Examples of such actions could be following: bombing a civilian bunker believing it is a military target; or soldiers shooting at a military object that turns out to be civilian.[53] International criminal law recognizes this defence according to Nuremberg case law, especially as it is presented in the Rendulic case. The so-called *Rendulic rule* refers to the reasonable commander standard constructed in the Hostage Case conducted as one of the American Subsequent Nuremberg trials.[54] The court examined the circumstances of issuing the order with instructed Wehrmacht to destroy the northern areas of Norway to slow down the advancing Soviet forces in 1944. The Soviet offensive did not occur, since the intelligence data were faulty, so *post factum* the destruction of the Norway northern territories was unjustified by the military situation and thus constituted a violation of article 6 sec (b) of the International Military Tribunal (IMT) Charter. The court considered all factors and possibilities relevant at the time of Rendulic' decisions and acquitted the defendant on the charge of a breach of the Fourth Hague Convention.[55] In conclusion, the court laid down that revoking the *mistake of law* defence is successful in conditions of *reasonable and honest error of judgement rather than ignoring obvious facts.*[56] It is important to note that the Nuremberg court suggested that the bad weather in the fall of 1944, the severe conditions that were present for a few months, was a justified circumstance in the view of the *error in fact.* Referring back to the Wieluń case, during the International Tribunal in Nuremberg, High Commander of Luftwaffe, Herman Goering, in his testimony stated that German Air Forces sent photos from

51 Bębnik, 2009, p. 55; Emmerling, 2007, p. 21.

52 See article 28 of the Polish Penal Code: Whoever commits an act while being in error as to a circumstance constituting a feature of a prohibited act, shall not be seen as intentionally committing an offense.

53 See generally van Sliedregt, 2003; Cryer et al., 2010, p. 414.

54 Martin et al., 2006, pp. 536; Piątkowski, 2013, pp. 69–84.

55 "If the facts were such as would justify the action by the exercise of judgment, after giving consideration to all the factors and existing possibilities, even though the conclusion reached may have been faulty, it cannot be said to be criminal. After giving careful consideration to all the evidence on the subject, we are convinced that the defendant cannot be held criminally responsible although when viewed in retrospect, the danger did not exist." *Hostage Case,* Trial of War Criminals Before The Nuremberg Military Tribunal, Vol. IX. Nuremberg 1946–1949, p. 1296.

56 *Draft code of crimes against the peace and security of mankind (Part II) – including the draft statute for an international criminal court,* Extract from the *Yearbook of the International Law Commission* 1996, vol. (II) p. 41, para. 12.

reconnaissance missions before and after the planned air operation.[57] Marcus Emmerling has pointed out that around 20 minutes before the action, the 76th Dive Bomber Regiment deployed two reconnaissance bombers Dornier Do 17 to gather the latest information about the target. These planes failed to find Wieluń due to morning fog.[58] Despite the lack of reconnaissance data, the HQ of 76st *Sturmgeschwader* decided to deploy all available Ju-87 Stuka bombers against the town.

9.5 Conclusion

The tragedy of the Polish border town illustrates the problem of the effectiveness of international law during the Second World War. The only relevant provision – article 25 of the Fourth Hague Convention – illuminated its incorrectness and inability to protect the civilian population against the dangers arising from unrestricted aerial warfare. On the other hand, the circumstances of the attack are significantly unusual due to the time of the attack and the overall characteristic of *status mixtus* – a time between war and peace.[59] This highlights the possibility of qualifying the strike as the only example of the Hague regulations concerning aerial bombardment violation during the Second World War. The status of the aforementioned Hague Rules of Aerial Warfare as customary international law is controversial. Even if the operation was based on the intelligence data that reported Polish units from a cavalry brigade nearby the town, such circumstances are not sufficient conditions to exculpate the perpetrators of the bombing from criminal responsibility in the light of IMT case law. It could even be suggested that Wieluń was a live training ground for newly deployed Junkers Ju-87 Stuka dive bombers, which was conducted to measure the target efficiency against urban areas. In that case, rumours about the Polish military activity in the town would only have served as a method of excuse, which undercover the main reasons of Luftwaffe action against Wieluń. Bombing was an entrance for a new type of total global war, which indiscriminately hit civilians' objects, expressing the disrespect for any international obligations and rules *ius in bellum*.

References

Grzegorz Bębnik, *Wieluń, 1 września 1939r.*, in Janusz Wróbel (Eds.) *Wieluń był pierwszy. Bombardowania lotnicze miast regionu łódzkiego we wrześniu 1939r.*, Instytut Pamięci Narodowej, Łódź, 2009.

Remigiusz Bierzanek, *Wojna a prawo międzynarodowe*, Ministerstwo Obrony Narodowej, Warsaw, 1982.

57 *Hostage Case*, Proceedings 8 March–23 March 1946, Trial of War Criminals before the Nuremberg Military Tribunal, vol. IX. Nuremberg 1946–1949, p. 562.

58 Emmerling, 2007, p. 20.

59 Green, 1993, pp. 67–68.

Remigiusz Bierzanek, "1923 Hague Rules for the Control of Radio in Time of War. Commentary", in Natalino Ronzitti (Ed.), *The Law of Naval Warfare: A Collection of Agreements and Documents With Commentaries*, Martinus Nijhoff Publishers, Dordrecht, 1988, pp. 396–408.

Tami Davis Biddle, *Rhetoric Reality in Air Warfare: The Evolution of British and American Ideas about Strategic*, Princeton University Press, Princeton, 2002.

Robert Cryer, Håkan Friman, Darryl Robinson and Elizabeth Wilmshurst, *An Introduction to International Criminal Law and Procedure*, Cambridge University Press, Cambridge, 2010.

Marcus Emmerling, *Luftwaffe nad Polską 1939*, cz. III: *Stukaflieger*, Armagedon, Gdynia, 2007.

Fredrick Stansbury Haydon, *Military Ballooning During the Early Civil War*, John Hopkins University Press, Baltimore, 2000.

Judith Gardam, *Necessity, Proportionality and the Use of Force by States*, Cambridge University Press, Cambridge, 2009.

James Garner, "Proposal Rules for the Regulation of Aerial Warfare", *The American Journal of International Law*, vol. 18, no. 1, 1924, pp. 56–81.

James Garner, "International Regulation of Air Warfare", *Air Law Review*, vol. 3, no. 2, 1932, pp. 130–126.

Paul Goda, "The Protection of Civilians from Bombardment by Aircraft: The Ineffectiveness of the International Law of War", *Military Law Review*, vol. 93, no. 31, 1996, pp. 98–100.

Francisco Gomez, "The Law of Air Warfare", *International Review of Red Cross*, vol. 38, no. 323, 1998, pp. 347–362.

Leslie Green, *The Contemporary Law of Armed Conflict*, Manchester University Press, Manchester, 1993.

Heinz Hanke, "The 1923 Hague Rules of Air Warfare – A Contribution to the Development of International Law Protecting Civilians from Air Attack", *International Red Cross Review*, vol. 33, no. 292, 1993, pp. 12–44.

Raija Hanski, "The Second World War. Means and Methods of Combat", in Lauri Hannikainen, Raija Hanski and Alan Rosas (Eds.), *Implementing Humanitarian Law Applicable in Armed Conflicts: The Case of Finland*, Martinus Nijhoff, Dordrecht, 1992.

Howard M. Hensel, "The Protection of Cultural Objects During Armed Conflicts", in Howard M. Hensel (Ed.), *The Law of Armed Conflict: Constraints on the Contemporary Use of Military Force*, Ashgate Publishing Company, Aldershot/Burlington, 2007, pp. 39–104.

David Johnson, *Rights in Air Space*, Manchester University Press, Manchester, 1965.

Fritz Kalshoven, "The History of International Humanitarian Law Treaty-Making", in Rain Liivoja and Tim McCormack (Eds.), *Routledge Handbook of the Law of Armed Conflict*, Routledge, New York/London, 2016, pp. 33–49.

Robert Kennedy, *The German Campaign in Poland* (1939), Department of the Army, Merriam Press, Hoosick Falls, 1956.

Kenneth Koskodan, *No Greater Ally: The Untold Story of Poland's Forces in World War II*, Osprey Publishing, Oxford, 2011.

Francisco Forest Martin, Stephen Schnalby, Richard Wislon, Jonathan Simon and Mark Tushnet, *International Human Rights and Humanitarian Law: Treaties, Cases and Analysis*, Cambridge University Press, Cambridge, 2006.

Jenny Lycklama a Nijeholt, *Air Sovereignty*, Martinus Nijhoff, The Hague, 1910.

Tadeusz Olejnik, *Wieluń – polska Guernica* (Wielun – The Polish Guernica) Wieluń – Kielce 2009 with speech of the President of the Republic of Poland Lech Kaczynski (in English), available at: http://wbi.d2.pl/wtn/00/album39popr.pdf (accessed 25 February 2018).

Lassa Oppenheim and Hersch Lauterpacht, *International Law*, Longmans, London, 1952.

William Parks, "Air Law and the Law of War", *The Air Force Law Review*, vol. 32, no. 1, 1990, pp. 1–225.

Mateusz Piątkowski, "The Rendulic Rule and the Law of Aerial Warfare", *Polish Review of International and European Law*, vol. 2, no. 3, 2013, pp. 69–84.

Mateusz Piątkowski, *Security of the Civilian Population From the Consequences of Aerial Warfare in the Light of the Hague Rules of Aerial Warfare of 1923*, Vilnius University Faculty of Law, Vilnius, 2015.

Mateusz Piątkowski, *A Brief History of the Law of Aerial Warfare*, Lambert Academic Publishing, Saarbrücken, 2017.

Marian Porwitt, *Komentarze do historii polskich działań obronnych 1939 r.*, Wydawnictwo Oborny Narodowej, Warszawa, 1983.

Harry Post, "War Crimes in Air Warfare", in Natalino Ronzitti and Gabriella Venturini (Eds.), *The Law of Air Warfare: Contemporary Issues*, Eleven Publisher, Utrecht, 2006, pp. 157–177.

Anthony Rogers, "Conduct of Combatant and Risk Run by the Civilian Population", *Military Law and Law of Wars Review*, vol. 21, 1982, pp. 293–318.

Anthony Rogers, *Law on the Battlefield*, Manchester University Press, Manchester, 2006.

Zbigniew Rotocki, "Polish Directives of 1939 Concerning Aerial Bombardment in the Light of International Rules of Air Warfare", *Polish Yearbook of International Law*, no. 3, 1970, pp. 143–170.

Elies van Sliedregt, *The Criminal Responsibility of Individuals for Violations of International Humanitarian Law*, TMC Asser Press, Hague, 2003.

Jiri Toman and Dieter Schindler, *The Laws of Armed Conflict* (4th Ed.), Martinus Nijhoff Publisher, Dordrecht, 2004.

Aart van Wijk, "The Legal Status of the Aircraft Commander – Ups and Downs for a Controversial Personality in International Law", in Arnold Kean (Ed.), *Essays in Air Law*, Martinus Nijhoff Publishers, Hague, 1982, pp. 309–313.

Richard Wymann, "The First Rules of Air Warfare", *Air University Review*, vol. 35, no. 3, 1984, pp. 94–102.

Part III

10 Emotions and the law

Mats Deland

10.1 Introduction

It is impossible to speak about emotions from a historical perspective, and in connection to the development of Law (and state building in general), without mentioning the seminal work of Norbert Elias – or of Lucien Febvre or Philippe Ariès. We know preciously little about how human beings have felt during the ages – or, for that matter, how they have talked about their feelings.[1] However, we know this much: emotions have varied. Elias is correct in pointing out that the control of aggressive impulses has a relation to the monopolization of violence in the absolutist and constitutional states, Febvre has a point in stressing the internal development of the Renaissance men and Ariès is helpful in showing how the relation between parents and children has grown warmer over the years.[2] These are all classics, old histories, discussed, and partly refuted decades ago, but what they have in common is that they make clear that when we talk about human emotions – feelings, passions, and aggressions – we are not talking about constants. Emotions vary, probably widely (and probably not as widely as sometimes presumed), over time and space. So does law. When we talk about law and emotions, we are talking about the relation between two categories that are not in any way stable.

This also means that the analysis runs the risks of two forms of anachronism – about the law (e.g., by interpreting it as a forerunner to later legal arrangements) and about how humans felt at the time. It is all too easy to fall back into familiar interpretation matrices, whether they are grounded in everyday experiences or psychological theories. This is also why this research is so important.[3] Analytical science has to work with simplifications, with ideal types, working hypotheses, and *ceteris paribus*, the risk however lies in reification, in believing that conceptions created for analytical reasons also represent reality outside the points made in the current discussion.

1 On the later subject, a complimentary science called emotionology, see Stearns and Stearns, 1985, pp. 813–836.

2 Cf, Burke, 1990; Elias, 1939; Febvre, 1941; Ariès, 1975.

3 Bandes, 2016.

10.2 Psychology and civilization

Just as neoclassical economic theory uses the abstraction of *Homo Oeconomicus* to illustrate the subject of rational choice, legal scholars sometimes talk of *Homo Juridicus.* Both have their origin in contract theory, or more specifically the Will Theory, which stipulates a consensus between the contractors (rather than the influence of power relations). There are different theories of the origin of this figure, where one tradition locates in the Christian tradition (*Imago Dei*) while Marxists following the Russian scholar Evgeny B. Pashukanis see the origin rather in the development of (capitalist) contract relations.[4] Regardless, these figures are abstractions and just as in economics, there have been many attempts to use social or psychological theories to arrive at a more realistic understanding of human action. For instance, American legal realism in the tradition of Karl Llewellyn largely relied on behaviorism while Scandinavian legal realism in the tradition of Axel Hägerström relied on neo-Kantian philosophical psychologism.[5] Recent attempts to arrive at some sort of adjusted model of rationality also include cultural cognition theory, which acknowledges emotions as part of the mental setup for considered decisions.[6] However, law and emotions is not only a way to come to terms with influences that shape law and adjudication, the causal direction also goes the other way around: Law produces emotions through a number of social mechanisms.[7]

However, given that the issue of law and emotions is basically a way to acknowledge the limits of analytical abstractions and rational choice models, just as institutional economics serves as way to put neoclassical economic theory into brackets, it is important to see the historical baggage of these terms. If we return to Norbert Elias' seminal work, one of the motives behind the investigation was the (by then already faded) habit of dividing states according to stages of civilization and barring those that were not considered as civilized enough from full access to the protection of international law (i.e., to sovereignty). Naturally, there is a substantial distance between the court rules investigated by Elias and the legal differences that were addressed in the legal discourse of stages of civilization, but as Andrew Linklater has argued, one cannot be understood without the other. There was also a direct link since experiences from colonial expeditions and attacks were used as mirroring images in the formulation of civilizational instructions.[8] At the same time, although the rules for international relations have changed after the Second World War and decolonization, the idea of detachment and repression of emotions lingers, for instance, in criminal and police law, where criminal activity can be understood as lack of civilization, or even de-civilization.[9] This illustrates the tight connection between law and ideas of rational choice, however limited.

4 See Supiot, 2017; Pashukanis, 2003; Miéville, 2005.
5 Fuller, 1934; Pattara, 2014, p. 290.
6 See for instance, Arkush, 2008.
7 West, 2016.
8 Linklater, 2011, pp. 1–26; 2016. Cf, Gong, 1984.
9 Fletcher, 1995; Shelden and Vasiliev, 2017, p. 59.

10.3 The influence of emotions on law

The politics of emotions has recently been theorized in a post-political context as politics of conduct, or ethopolitics, in political science also understood as the GAL-TAN scale.[10] It may be argued that emotions have played an important role in political events such as the British Brexit referendum and the presidential election in the USA, as well as the nativist upsurge in the EU countries.[11] The political science of emotions is an expanding field and fills a gap that too long was left by rational choice abstractions and overemphasizing of a politics of interest.[12] In another unsettled time, when Friedrich Nietzsche spoke of Law's origins in resentment, Sigmund Freud of its origins in oedipal family relations and feelings of guilt, Walter Benjamin about its origins in violence, Axel Hägerström about origins in revenge and Carl Schmitt about the total abandonment of law in the state of exception, all of them thus questioning the value of law, Hans Kelsen and Hans J. Morgenthau instead chose to modernize a realist legal theory – in different directions – with the help of Freudian psychoanalytic theory.[13] While both the legal and psychological theories involved are dated at this point, this example shows how legal theory benefits from and develops through the encounter with the best and most groundbreaking theories of each period of time. While an understanding of emotions shows one of the limits of law, it also points to directions in which it can be amended.

10.4 This section

The chapters that are included in this section are excellent examples of this. In the first chapter, Nele Verlinden gives three examples of how the laws of war are developed through and for emotions. The first example draws attention to the spectacular public relations campaign of Henry Dunant, the founder of the Red Cross movement, in the early 1860s. The laws of war themselves, however, are rather aiming to deactivate emotions. When human soldiers in some armies are replaced by remote controlled or automatic weapons, the already existing asymmetry of warfare is exacerbated in ways that are hard to foresee. Another aspect that is not really accounted for in existing law is the mental suffering of civilians through warfare. As Verlinden shows, this lacuna urgently needs to be addressed.

In the second chapter, Ka Lok Yip addresses the underlying understandings of how the laws of war are supposed to influence the actual behavior on and around the battlefield. Starting from a debate about an ICRC-funded study, she contrasts a sociological understanding of law creating automated reactions among the actors in combat, to an agential understanding that presupposes morally independent actors making rational choices. As Kip shows, this kind of

10 Rose, 2000, pp. 1395–1411; Hooghe, Marks and Wilson, 2002, pp. 965–989.

11 Rydgren, 2005.

12 Demertzis, 2006, pp. 103–122.

13 Schuett, 2007; Rolnik, 2003.

philosophical underpinnings is very important when issuing battle instructions, but as she notes, one must be careful not to expect too much ability to moral choices in the dense and intensive mental environment of deadly combat.

In the third chapter, Alexandra Hofer discusses the emotionally laden issue of national identities, from the background of the conflict between Israel and Palestine. As she points out, international law lends itself to be used both for political discourses and for the identity building that relates to nationalist politics. In that way, certain legal interpretations – and, in this case, even adjudications (by the International Court of Justice [ICJ]) – become deeply contested parts of the conflict itself, rather than cooling it off, even less solving it. Indeed, nationalism is an important example of when laws are both shaped by emotions and shaping them.

References

Philippe Ariès, *L'Enfant et la vie familiale sous l'Ancien Régime* (1960), Seuil, Paris, 1975.

David J. Arkush, "Situating Emotion: A Critical Realist View of Emotion and Nonconscious Cognitive Processes for Law and Legal Theory", *BYU Law Review*, vol. 5, no. 1, 2008, pp. 1277–1366.

Susan A. Bandes, "What roles do emotions play in law?", *Emotion Researcher*, October 2016, available at: www.susanbandes.com/wp-content/uploads/2017/03/emotionresearcher.com-What-Roles-Do-Emotions-Play-in-the-Law.pdf (accessed 12 April 2018).

Peter Burke, *The French Historical Revolution, The Annales School 1929–89*, Polity Press, Cambridge, 1990.

Nicolas Demertzis, "Emotions and Populism", in Simon Clarke, Paul Hoggett and Simon Thompson (Eds.), *Emotion, Politics and Society*, Palgrave Macmillan, Hampshire, 2006, pp. 103–122.

Norbert Elias, *Über den Prozeß der Zivilisation. Soziogenetische und psychogenetische Untersuchungen. Erster Band. Wandlungen des Verhaltens in den weltlichen Oberschichten des Abendlandes; Zweiter Band. Wandlungen der Gesellschaft. Entwurf einer Theorie der Zivilisation*, Verlag Haus zum Falken, Basel, 1939.

Lucien Febvre, "La sensibilité et l'histoire. Comment reconstituer la vie affective d'autrefois?", *Annales d'histoire sociale*, vol. 3, no. 1–2, 1941, pp. 5–20.

Jonathan Fletcher, "Towards a Theory of Decivilizing Processes", *Amsterdams Sociologisch Tijdschrift*, vol. 22, no. 2, 1995, pp. 283–296.

Lon L. Fuller, "American Legal Realism", *University of Pennsylvania Law Review*, vol. 82, no. 5, 1934, pp. 439–462.

Gerrit W. Gong, *The Standard of 'Civilization' in International Society*, Clarendon Press, Oxford, 1984.

Liesbet Hooghe, Gary Marks and Carole J. Wilson, "Does Left/Right Structure Party Positions on European Integration?", *Comparative Political Studies*, vol. 35, no. 8, 2002, pp. 965–989.

Andrew Linklater, "International Society and the Civilizing Process", *Ritsumeikan International Affairs*, vol. 9, 2011, pp. 1–26.

Andrew Linklater, "The 'Standard of Civilization' in World Politics", *Human Figurations, Long-Term Perspectives on the Human Condition*, vol. 5, no. 2, 2016, pp. 700–719.

China Miéville, *Between Equal Rights. A Marxist Theory of International Law*, Haymarket Books, Chicago, IL, 2005.

Evgeny B. Pashukanis, *The General Theory of Law and Marxism* (1924) (transl. 1978 Barbara Einhorn), Transaction Publishers, New Brunswick, NJ, 2003.

Enrico Pattara, "Hägerström's Philosophy of Right", in Sven Eliaeson, Patricia Mindus and Stephen P. Turner (Eds.), *Axel Hägerström and Modern Social Thought*, The Bardwell Press, Oxford, 2014.

Eran J. Rolnik, "A brush with the law: The encounter between Hans Kelsen and Sigmund Freud", Paper read at the international conference 'Trauma and Memory: Subjective & Collective Experiences: Legal, Medical and Cultural Perspectives. Bar Ilan University. Israel, December 2003.

Nikolas Rose, "Community, Citizenship and the Third Way", *American Behavioral Scientist*, vol. 43, no. 9, 2000, pp. 1395–1411.

Jens Rydgren, "Is Extreme Right-Wing Populism Contagious? Explaining the Emergence of a New Party Family", *European Journal of Political Research*, vol. 44, no. 3, 2005, pp. 413–437.

Robert Schuett, "Freudian Roots of Political Realism: The Importance of Sigmund Freud to Hans J. Morgenthau's Theory of International Power Politics", *History of the Human Sciences*, vol. 20, no. 4, 2007, pp. 53–78.

Randall G. Shelden and Pavel V. Vasiliev, *Controlling the Dangerous Classes: A History of Criminal Justice in America* (3rd ed.), Waveland Press, Long Grove, IL, 2017, p. 59.

Peter N. Stearns and Carol Z. Stearns, "Clarifying the History of Emotions and Emotional Standards", *The American Historical Review*, vol. 90, no. 4, 1985, pp. 813–836.

Alain Supiot, *Homo Juridicus. On the Anthropological Function of the Law* (2007) (transl. Saskia Brown), Verso, London, 2017.

Robin West, "Law's Emotions", *Richmond Journal of Law and the Public Interest*, vol. 19, no. 4, 2016, pp. 339–361.

11 To feel or not to feel? Emotions and international humanitarian law

Nele Verlinden

11.1 Introduction: the relationship between international humanitarian law and emotions

Emotions are an intrinsic element of warfare: pride and patriotism may motivate soldiers to fight, the hope for independence may lead armed groups to violent resistance, and victory may lead to joy and relief, while the loss of lives definitely causes tremendous suffering among victims. Law, on the other hand, attempts to offer objective rules to regulate human interaction, including warfare.[1] International humanitarian law (IHL), a body of international law aimed at reducing the suffering of victims of armed conflict, is often used as an illustration of how emotions have impacted on the development of new international law treaties.[2] While this is undoubtedly true, this chapter will show that the relationship between emotions and IHL is more complex. Three main points of contact between IHL and emotions will be addressed: the perspective of the lawmakers (II), the fighting parties (III), and the victims of armed conflict (IV), before concluding (V).

By way of preliminary remark, it should be noted that this chapter approaches the topic "emotions and IHL" solely from a legal perspective. It does not aspire to pronounce on emotions and warfare from any other point of view – for example, from a psychological, social, ethical, or philosophical perspective[3] – however interesting such approaches may be. Hence, "emotions" in the context of this chapter should be broadly understood as any "state of feeling,"[4] positive or negative, a human can have. In other words, for the purpose of this chapter, emotions mean the antipode of *ratio*, reason.

11.2 The lawmaker: indignation and compassion as origins of IHL

Any IHL specialist is familiar with the story of Henry Dunant (1828–1910), a Swiss businessman who passed by the Italian town Solferino, in June 1859,

1 A more nuanced discussion on the aims of "law" can be found, for example, in Hart, 2012.
2 See for instance Popovski, 2016, pp. 192–194.
3 See for instance Miller, 2001, pp. 241–264; Ross, 2014.
4 Merriam-Webster Dictionary, www.merriam-webster.com/.

where a battle was taking place between the Austrians and the Franco-Sardinians. Dunant, stationed in Castiglione della Pieve nearby Solferino, saw the many casualties of the battle of 24 June arriving in the town while the military medical services were insufficiently prepared to offer adequate medical care. Upon his return to Geneva, Dunant wrote his famous book *A memory of Solferino*, describing what he had witnessed during his trip. With an award-winning degree for drama and detail – a style not uncommon for writings of the 19th century – Dunant describes the Solferino battle and suffering of that day.[5] He addresses the lack of medical care for the wounded after the battle[6] and poetically portrays how he felt witnessing all this suffering:

> The *feeling* one has of one's own utter inadequacy in such extraordinary and solemn circumstances is unspeakable. It is, indeed, *excessively distressing* to realize that you can never do more than help those who are just before you ....[7]
>
> The *moral sense* of the importance of human life; the humane *desire* to lighten a little the torments of all these poor wretches, or restore their shattered courage; the *furious and relentless activity* which a man summons up at such moments: all these combine to create a kind of energy which gives one a positive craving to relieve as many as one can. [...] But then you feel sometimes that your *heart is suddenly breaking* – it is as if you were stricken all at once with a *sense of bitter and irresistible sadness*, because of some simple incident, some isolated happening, some small unexpected detail which strikes closer to the soul, seizing on our sympathies and *shaking all the most sensitive fibres of our being.*[8]

Dunant subsequently proposed two solutions that would trigger the creation of National Red Cross Societies, the International Red Cross Committee, and the adoption of IHL conventions.[9] The Geneva Convention for the Amelioration of the Condition of the Wounded in Armies in the Field was adopted by 12 States on 22 August 1864.[10] The combination of Dunant's emotional writings with his excellent network of high-level friends across Europe offered a momentum for the codification of IHL rules. Dunant's emotional account of

5 For instance, "Here is a hand-to-hand struggle in all its horror and frightfulness; Austrian and Allies trampling each other under foot, killing one another on piles of bleeding corpses, felling their enemies with their rifle butts, crushing skulls, ripping bellies open with sabre and bayonet. No quarter is given; it is a sheer butchery; a struggle between savage beasts, maddened with blood and fury. Even the wounded fight to the last gasp. When they have no weapon left, they seize their enemies by the throat and tear them with their teeth." Dunant, 1862/1959, pp. 19–20.

6 Ibid., p. 38, pp. 41 and 53–54.

7 Ibid., pp. 72–73.

8 Ibid., pp. 73–74.

9 Ibid., p. 115 and 126.

10 By 1907, the Convention had 57 State parties. See ICRC, IHL Treaty database, available at: https://ihl-databases.icrc.org/applic/ihl/ihl.nsf/vwTreatiesHistoricalByDate.xsp (accessed 22 April 2018).

the Solferino battle was "an exhilarating experience for this young man who had come without warning from obscurity to touch the heart and stir the conscience of Europe."[11] He managed to pass on his emotions to influential figures, leading to a legislative translation of a fundamentally emotional reaction to suffering of war. After Dunant's initiative, States took the lead in organizing diplomatic conferences which would lead to the adoption of other IHL treaties.[12]

The adoption of the four Geneva Conventions in 1949 marked a second crucial moment in the codification of IHL. States no longer needed a Henry Dunant to be triggered to create new rules – the horrible facts of the Second World War spoke for themselves. The Second World War was followed by years of civil wars around the globe. Many of those conflicts were not covered by the existing IHL framework, which focused on classic inter-State wars or international armed conflicts (IACs).[13] During the negotiations of the Additional Protocols to the Geneva Conventions, States nevertheless refused to adopt a new treaty that would have regulated NIACs in the same way as international conflicts. An International Committee of the Red Cross (ICRC) proposal in that regard was rejected because it did not provide "sufficient guarantees for respect due to national sovereignty and for non-interference with internal affairs."[14] Hence, the 1977 Additional Protocols show that the feeling of compassion for the victims had its limits, defined by an increasing sense of sovereign protectionism and skepticism about obligations imposed by international law.[15]

In the decades after the adoption of the Protocols, it became clear that traditional treaty making, based on a consensus between all States, proved no longer effective. Rather, the consensual method served as a "triple victory" for those States who were against new IHL rules: they could slow down the negotiation process, they could water down the text, and eventually they refused to sign or ratify the treaty anyway.[16] Instead, NGO campaigns started to serve as modern "Henry Dunants" using testimonies of victims and constructing an emotional story to convince State leaders to adopt new treaties. This method proved successful for the 1997 Ottawa Convention on anti-personnel mines,[17] the 1998 Rome Statute,[18] the 2006 Dublin Convention on Cluster Munitions, and the 2014 Arms Trade Treaty.

It seems that States' willingness to act out of a particular emotion triggered by certain events has decreased in comparison with the previous century.[19] States

11 Dunant, 1862/1959, p. 9.

12 For example, The Hague Conventions of 1899 and 1907 or the Geneva Convention for the Amelioration of the Condition of the Wounded and Sick in Armies in the Field of 1906.

13 Except, of course, for common Art. 3 of the Geneva Conventions 1949.

14 See Sandoz et al., 1986, para. 4412.

15 See also Bugnion, 2003, p. 191.

16 Sandoz, 1999, p. 241.

17 See Part I of Cameron, Tomlin and Lawson, 1998.

18 Boyle and Chinkin, 2007, pp. 71–74.

19 In this regard, see also an analysis of States' willingness to prosecute war crimes in the course of history: Bass, 2000.

think twice before supporting the adoption of new international obligations. A stagnation in the codification of international law does of course not mean that international law cannot develop further: the steady development of customary IHL,[20] as well as the adoption of best practices and soft law documents,[21] shows that the need for IHL rules that are adapted to the current type of warfare can be fulfilled in other ways. Nevertheless, it is regrettable that civil society organizations have to put so much effort in convincing States to set aside their own national interests for the sake of a better protection of victims of armed conflict.

11.3 The fighting parties: deactivation of emotions

Paradoxically, while emotions triggered the creation of IHL, the same body of law tries to "deactivate" the emotions of fighting soldiers.[22] Indeed, IHL imposes obligations on fighting parties to protect certain persons, despite the (negative) feelings the soldiers on the ground might have *vis-à-vis* those persons. It is a given fact that belonging to a certain group, whether it is an official State army or a non-State armed group, makes the killing of a person belonging to another group easier to accept.[23] In other words, "social identity," which can be defined as "that part of an individual's self-concept which derives from his knowledge of his membership of a group together with the value and *emotional significance* attached to the membership,"[24] facilitates the killing of persons who do not belong to that identity.[25] Hence, one of the underlying goals of IHL rules is that they prohibit behavior combatants might otherwise because they belong to a group, be inclined to exercise against their victims.

This mechanism of "deactivation of emotions" can be found in numerous IHL provisions. For instance, while a soldier would prefer to kill prisoners of war out of revenge, this is clearly prohibited by article 13 of the Third Geneva Convention of 1949 (GC III). Similarly, soldiers, who surrender or who are *hors de combat*, may not be killed (article 41 AP I) and the bulk of rules enshrined in the Fourth Geneva Convention (GC IV) envisages the protection of "enemy civilians."[26] However, reality reveals that international rules prohibiting certain conduct cannot prevent that conduct from being committed. After all, fighting persons are human beings with feelings of anxiety, anger, and revenge, which can influence their behavior during an armed conflict. This raises the question

20 See Henckaerts and Doswald-Beck, 2005.

21 For example, the Montreux Document on pertinent international legal obligations and good practices for States related to operations of private military and security companies during armed conflict of 2009.

22 In this regard, see also the contribution by Anna Evangelidi in this book.

23 For a full study of this phenomenon, see Castano, Leidner and Slatuwa, 2008, pp. 259–271.

24 Ibid., pp. 259–260.

25 See for instance Cox and Wood, 2016, pp. 112–129.

26 Art. 4 GC IV imposes a nationality criterion, which has been broadened by case-law to an "allegiance" requirement: *Prosecutor v. Dusko Tadić*, (Case No. IT-94-1-A), ICTY A. Ch., Judgment, 15 July 1999, §166.

whether victims of armed conflict would be better off if faced with a robot, which does not have such feelings – leading us to the highly debated issue of autonomous weapon systems.

There is no internationally agreed definition of autonomous weapon systems. One possible definition defines them as "weapons that can independently select and attack targets," meaning they are autonomous with regard to the "critical functions of acquiring, tracking, selecting and attacking targets."[27] Their development is fairly recent and still ongoing. Already used to a certain extent (e.g., as defensive weapon systems which can attack incoming missiles), their use is expected to grow increasingly in the next years. Fully autonomous weapon systems do not yet exist.[28] Nevertheless, their (possible) use raises a number of very important legal and ethical questions, one of them being the influence of emotions on combatants' behavior and how this aversely – or not – impacts the respect for IHL rules.

Many perpetrators of war crimes are in some way influenced by their emotions at the time of the crime.[29] As Walzer aptly puts it, "[f]ear and hysteria are always latent in combat, often real, and they press us toward fearful measures and criminal behaviour."[30] Since autonomous weapons, as opposed to humans, would not suffer from this "fear and hysteria" which is intrinsic to warfare, the absence of emotions in the case of robots could be advanced as an argument to advocate for their use. Autonomous weapons can be designed without "emotions that cloud their judgment or result in anger and frustration with ongoing battlefield events."[31] In addition, a phenomenon called "scenario fulfillment" would be avoidable when using autonomous systems.[32] This phenomenon entails that humans process incoming behavior in accordance with their pre-existing belief patterns. Hence, a person under stress would have a "tunnel vision," enabling him only to act according the scenario he has in mind. "Robots," according to Arkin, "need not be vulnerable to such patterns of premature cognitive disclosure."[33]

On the other hand, the fact that autonomous weapon systems lack human emotions might not always be in favor of the protection of the victims of armed conflict. According to Human Rights Watch, it would not be possible to "duplicate" the psychological processes that humans use to assess whether an attack is proportionate or not.[34] Therefore, as Schmitt acknowledges, the use of autonomous weapons systems "would need to be limited to cases where the risk to civilians is minimal."[35]

27 ICRC, 2014, p. 5.
28 Ibid., p. 7.
29 See Arkin's list of possible reasons for the commission of IHL violations, Arkin, 2014. p. 33.
30 Walzer, 1978, p. 251.
31 Arkin, 2014, p. 35.
32 Ibid.
33 Ibid.
34 Human Rights Watch, *Losing Humanity: The Case Against Killer Robots,* November 2012, available at: www.hrw.org/report/2012/11/19/losing-humanity/case-against-killer-robots (accessed 13 April 2018).
35 "Background paper", 2014, p. 83.

The debate on the acceptability of autonomous weapon systems is obviously much broader than the single issue whether robots might be a tool to overcome failures caused by human emotions in warfare. Nevertheless, the fact that this *überhaupt* is an issue of debate illustrates the connection between the emotions of those who fight and their respect for IHL rules. As some IHL rules envisage to "deactivate" emotions of combatants, there might indeed be a case for the use of autonomous weapon systems. On the other hand, it is argued that the respect for other IHL rules would precisely require more "human" insight into a particular situation. This brings us to the third perspective on points of contact between emotions and IHL: that of the victims.

11.4 The victims: does their emotional suffering count?

The suffering of victims of armed conflict has always been a core concern of IHL rules. Nevertheless, the concern for emotional suffering is only partially reflected throughout all IHL provisions. While multiple provisions on the protection of persons who find themselves in the power of the enemy take into account possible non-physical suffering, the articles on the conduct of hostilities only occasionally contain specific references to such suffering.

On one hand, at a time where measuring mental well-being was even not yet taken seriously in the medical sphere,[36] the negotiators of the 1949 Geneva Conventions and the 1977 Additional Protocols did think of "emotional suffering"[37] and the psychological well-being of persons in the hands of the enemy during armed conflict – including protective rules both for prisoners of wars and civilians.[38] More generally, this included the many rules prohibiting torture, cruel, or inhuman treatment protect victims of armed conflict from all sorts of severe suffering, including psychological ones.[39]

36 Mental harm as a tangible concept has only been developed in the decades after the adoption of the 1977 Additional Protocols to the 1949 Geneva Conventions. See Lieblich, 2014, p. 203.

37 For the purpose of this paper, emotional, moral, mental, and psychological suffering/injury shall be considered synonymous (even though the Geneva Conventions sometimes refer to moral well-being in a religious rather than an emotional context, see for instance Art. 80 GC III and Art. 103 GC IV, which use "*bien-être moral*" in the French version and "spiritual well-being" in the English version).

38 According to Annex I to GC III, Prisoners of War suffering from a serious mental disease are entitled to immediate repatriation (see Annex I, Part I, A, 2, g and Part II, 2). See also Arts. 30 GC III and 91 GC IV (persons suffering from mental disease), Art. 17 § 3, Art. 99 GC III and Art. 31 GC IV (moral coercion), Art. 11 AP I and Art. 5, 2, e AP II (mental health and integrity of persons), Art. 18 GC III and Art. 97 GC IV (objects with "sentimental value"), Art. 49 GC III (maintaining mental health), Art. 56 GC IV (moral susceptibilities of the occupied population), Art. 100 GC IV (moral victimization), Art. 18 GC I (moral care) and Art. 33 GC IV (prohibition of intimidation or terrorism).

39 See Art. 3 common GCs, Art. 12, § 2 GC I, Art. 12 § 2 GC II, Art. 17 § 4 GC III, Art. 87 § 3 GC III, Art. 89 GC III, Art. 32 GC IV, Art. 75 § 2 AP I, Art. 4 § 2 AP II. While not every provision explicitly mentions "mental suffering," it is unquestioned that torture, cruel, and inhuman treatment include acts which inflict serious or severe mental pain or suffering. See, for

On the other hand, the emotional impact of hostilities is only to a limited extent taken into account by IHL provisions. For instance, article 4, § 2, in AP II prohibits "violence [...] to the mental well-being of persons," but this article is generally understood as not including any conduct of hostilities rules.[40] A clearer prohibition related to the conduct of hostilities can be found in article 51 § 2 AP I and article 13 § 2 AP II, which prohibit "acts or threats of violence the primary purpose of which is to spread terror among the civilian population." This prohibition "can be viewed as the first major provision in IHL to explicitly prohibit acts intended to inflict mental harm."[41] Nevertheless, its scope is limited to terror, which is *intentionally* inflicted upon the civilian population. According to the *travaux préparatoires*, it "excludes terror which was not intended by a belligerent and terror that is merely an incidental effect of acts of warfare which have another primary object and are in all other respects lawful."[42] As a result, psychological trauma as a side effect of attacks is hanging in a "legal limbo."[43]

Nevertheless, the absence of specific references to emotional or psychological damage due to attacks does not mean such damage should automatically be ignored when assessing the legality of a particular attack: Mental suffering definitely is to be included into the evaluation of "superfluous injury or unnecessary suffering" and arguably also in the proportionality test imposed by IHL.

First, even though emotions are not explicitly mentioned in the basic rule which prohibits the employment of weapons, projectiles, and material and methods of warfare of a nature to cause "superfluous injury or unnecessary suffering" (article 35 § 2 AP I), emotional suffering is implicitly included therein. During the negotiations, it was made clear that the notion of "superfluous injury or unnecessary suffering" was the preferred translation for the French notion of *maux superflus*, "which includes both physical and *moral injury*."[44] This broad interpretation is not contested by doctrine. According to Oeter, the "traditional notion of 'unnecessary suffering' means [...] a physical or emotional impairment which cannot be justified by military necessity."[45] Gardam notes that "[t]he

example, *Prosecutor v. Naletilic and Martinovic*, (Case No. IT-98-34-T) ICTY T. Ch., Judgment, 31 March 2003, §246.

40 With the exception, perhaps, of the prohibition of murder. See 2016 ICRC Commentary to the First Geneva Convention, §540.

41 Lieblich, 2014, p. 196.

42 Official Records of the Diplomatic Conference on the Reaffirmation and Development of International Humanitarian Law Applicable in Armed Conflicts, Geneva, 1974–1977, Vol. VX, CDDH/215/Rev.1, p. 274, §51.

43 Lieblich, 2014, p. 186. Remarkably, on one instance during the negotiations of the APs, the emotions of victims were used as an argument *not* to rule out the use of napalm because the "psychological effect both on enemy and friendly troops" was considered an advantage. See ICRC, Report of the Conference of Government Experts on the Use of Certain Conventional Weapons (Lugano, 28 January–26 September 1976), Geneva, 1976, p. 111.

44 Official Records, *supra* note 51, p. 267, § 21 [emphasis added]. For a contrary view, see ICRC, Report of the Conference of Government Experts on the Use of Certain Conventional Weapons (Lucerne 24 September–18 October 1974), Geneva, 1975, p. 8.

45 Oeter, 1995, p. 115.

factors ... to be considered in the equation in terms of suffering or injury encompass both the physical and psychological effects of weapons."[46]

Despite this agreement, the notion of "superfluous injury or unnecessary suffering" remains rather vague and difficult to apply when assessing the legality of weapons. This is why the ICRC undertook the so-called SIrUS project (by reference to the commonly used abbreviation of "serious injury or unnecessary suffering"), the results of which were published in 1997.[47] A group of experts elaborated four objective criteria to determine what constitutes "superfluous injury or unnecessary suffering," and one of them (labelled "Criterion I") includes a reference to mental suffering: It determines that serious injury or unnecessary suffering occurs when a weapon has designed-dependent, foreseeable effects which cause *inter alia* a "specific abnormal psychological state."[48] The authors of the study note that "[w]hilst all weapons produce fear and stress, these reactions are neither specific nor abnormal,"[49] specifying – in overly medical language – that "Criterion I would apply to a weapon designed to disorientate, confuse, induce calm or precipitate seizures or psychosis."[50]

Secondly, there are some good arguments to include mental harm into the IHL proportionality assessment as enshrined in articles 51 § 5, b and 57 § 2, 2 AP I., which prohibit attacks "which may be expected to cause incidental loss of civilian life, injury to civilians, damage to civilian objects, or a combination thereof, which would be excessive in relation to the concrete and direct military advantage anticipated." The proportionality test requires a balancing exercise between two types of information: on one hand, the loss of civilians, injury to civilians, and damage to civilian objects which can reasonably be expected from the attack; and on the other hand, the concrete and military advantage which can be anticipated. Proportionality thus implies a double future-looking assessment.

While the ordinary meaning of "injury to civilians" would be that it only covers physical harm, it has been argued that it is not unreasonable to also extend its meaning to psychological harm.[51] For instance, when defining the notion "cyber attack," the Tallinn Manual explains that

> [w]hile the notion of attack extends to injuries and death caused to individuals, it is, in light of the law of armed conflict's underlying purposes, reasonable to extend the definition to serious illness and severe mental suffering that are tantamount to injury.[52]

46 Gardam, 2004, p. 69.
47 Coupland, 1997, p. 43.
48 Ibid., p. 8.
49 Ibid., p. 23.
50 Ibid.
51 Lieblich, 2014, p. 200.
52 Schmitt, 2013, p. 108.

Thus, by way of teleological interpretation, serious mental suffering as a consequence of an attack should be taken into account when assessing the legality of that attack.[53]

Nevertheless, including mental harm in the proportionality assessment is not an obvious reading of "injury to civilians." State practice on mental suffering in proportionality is scarce. Generally, military manuals and national legislation do not explicitly refer to "mental harm" or any alternative term when discussing the proportionality rule.[54] The occasional use of wider terms – such as by the Canadian Military Manual which refers to "adverse effect upon civilians"[55] – could possibly point at the inclusion of mental harm. In addition, the guidelines adopted in 2005 on the right to a remedy for gross human rights and IHL violations require that "compensation should be provided for any economically assessable damage [...] such as physical or *mental* harm."[56] However, since these rules also concern human rights violations, they do not provide conclusive evidence for mental harm being part of the proportionality rule under IHL.

Even if there would be a customary rule including psychological harm into the proportionality assessment, practical problems might hamper an effective implementation of this wider rule: How can mental harm be measured and foreseen? True, psychologists have over the last decades identified detailed benchmarks to diagnose mental suffering.[57] It is also a fact that it is even for bodily harm difficult to make predictions when planning a certain attack. Nevertheless, it cannot be denied that including mental harm would add a layer of complexity in the obligations that military advisers have to fulfil.

It should also be noted that expanding the proportionality test to mental harm which is not intentionally inflicted would not bring all mental suffering into the IHL picture. Indeed, the so-called "anticipatory anxiety" caused by the use of drones would not fall under the proportionality assessment.[58] More in general, all the emotional problems caused by the simple fact of living in a war zone[59] cannot be avoided by imposing the military to take mental suffering into account when assessing whether the expected civilian injury is excessive to the anticipated military advantage of a specific attack. General emotional suffering

53 See also intervention by Gisel, 2016, p. 120.

54 At least, none of the manuals and national laws included in the practice database of the ICRC Customary Law Study do. See https://ihl-databases.icrc.org/customary-ihl/eng/docs/v2_rul_rule14 (accessed 13 April 2018).

55 Canada, The Law of Armed Conflict at the Operational and Tactical Levels, Office of the Judge Advocate General, 13 August 2001, para. 204.5.

56 Basic Principles and Guidelines on the Right to a Remedy and Reparation for Victims of Gross Violations of International Human Rights Law and Serious Violations of International Humanitarian Law, Adopted and proclaimed by General Assembly resolution 60/147 of 16 December 2005, UN Doc. A/RES/60/147, §20.

57 See Lieblich, 2014, pp. 201–206, who also quite convincingly challenges this "intangibility presumption."

58 See for instance the situation of the Waziris in Pakistan: "Living under Drones", 2012, p. 81.

59 See, for example, Thabet et al., 2002, pp. 1801–1804.

caused by armed conflict is not prohibited by IHL rules. At first sight, this might seem contradictory to the general humanitarian purpose of IHL, which is to alleviate suffering of victims of armed conflict. Nevertheless, one should bear in mind that humanity is only one side of the "IHL medal" and military necessity being the other one. While a universal ban on armed conflicts (international and non-international) would – if respected – indeed avoid mental suffering caused by conflict in general, such a ban is not the purpose of IHL rules, which accept armed conflict as a reality.

In sum, IHL clearly protects the mental well-being of persons who find themselves in the power of the enemy. With regard to the conduct of hostilities, the prohibition to use terror against the civilian population is the only rule which explicitly refers to emotions. Nevertheless, mental suffering is also included in the prohibition to use methods of warfare, which cause superfluous injury or unnecessary suffering. *Incidental* mental suffering, on the other hand, can only be included in the proportionality assessment through a teleological interpretation: Since the goal of IHL rules is to prevent victims from suffering in armed conflict, it would indeed seem advisable to include psychological harm in a proportionality assessment. Unfortunately, however, State practice does not yet take this point of view.

11.5 Conclusion: to feel or not to feel?

As this brief analysis of three different contact points between emotions and IHL shows, the relationship between the two is not straightforward.

From the perspective of IHL lawmakers, the emotions of Henry Dunant served as the triggering point for IHL codification. While States initially had the same humanity-driven codification reflex in reaction to key evolutions in warfare, their willingness to create new IHL obligations has decreased in the last decades. Today, NGOs serve as a modern Henry Dunant, using *inter alia* campaigns based on emotions in an attempt to convince States of the need for additional regulation in warfare.

Emotions play a different role if one looks at the perspective of the fighting parties. From its early codification, IHL contains rules which aim at deactivating negative emotions in favor of the protection of victims of armed conflict. That same deactivation of emotions is now raised both in favor of and against the use of autonomous weapon systems. Emotions, among other factors, play a role in the debate on whether or not such weapon systems should be prohibited – but the issue is far from being settled.

Third, the emotional impact of warfare on victims of armed conflict is not regulated in a consistent manner – even though emotional suffering has gradually gained more attention in IHL rules. While the infliction of serious or severe mental suffering is prohibited by numerous provisions in scenarios whereby a victim is in the power of the enemy, in the conduct of hostilities the only explicit and uncontested prohibition is the use of terror as a method of warfare. If a certain means or method of warfare deliberately inflicts a specific and abnormal psychological state, this would nevertheless be prohibited by the rule, which rules out superfluous injury or unnecessary suffering. In contrast, mental suffering as a side effect of attacks is only prohibited if one interprets the proportionality rule in a teleological way. Mental suffering as a consequence of war in general, however, remains under the IHL radar.

References

Ronald Arkin, "Ethical Restraint of Lethal Autonomous Robotic Systems: Requirements, Research, and Implications", in ICRC, *Autonomous weapon systems: Technical, military, legal and humanitarian aspects, Expert meeting 26–28 March*, Geneva, 2014, pp. 33–38.

"Background paper by the International Committee of the Red Cross", ICRC, *Autonomous weapon systems: Technical, military, legal and humanitarian aspects, Expert meeting 26–28 March*, Geneva, 2014, pp. 57–94.

Gary J. Bass, *Stay the Hand of Vengeance: the Politics of War Crimes Tribunals*, Princeton University Press, Princeton/Oxford, 2000.

Alan Boyle and Christine Chinkin, *The Making of International Law*, Oxford University Press, Oxford, 2007.

François Bugnion, "*Jus Ad Bellum, Jus In Bello* and Non-international Armed Conflicts", *Yearbook of International Humanitarian Law*, vol. 6, 2003, pp. 167–198.

Maxwell A. Cameron, Brain Tomlin and Bob Lawson (Eds.), *To Walk Without Fear: The Global Movement to Ban Landmines*, Oxford University Press, Toronto, 1998.

Emanuele Castano, Berhard Leidner and Patricia Slatuwa, "Social identification Processes, Group Dynamics and the Behaviour of Combatants", *International Review of the Red Cross*, vol. 90, no. 870, 2008, pp. 259–271.

Lloyd Cox and Steve Wood, "Got him: Revenge, emotions and the killing of Osama bin Laden", *Review of International Studies*, vol. 43, part 1, 2016, pp. 112–129.

Robin M. Coupland, *The SIrUS Project: towards a determination of which weapons cause "superfluous injury or unnecessary suffering*, ICRC, Geneva, 1997.

Henri Dunant, *Un souvernir de Solferino*, Genève, 1862/1959, reprinted by the ICRC, *A Memory of Solferino* (translated by volunteers from the District of Columbia chapter of the American Red Cross) available at: www.icrc.org/eng/assets/files/publications/icrc-002-0361.pdf (accessed 13/04/2018).

ICRC, *Report of the ICRC Expert Meeting on "Autonomous weapon systems: technical, military, legal and humanitarian aspects", 26 to 28 March 2014*, Geneva, 2014.

Judith G. Gardam, *Necessity, proportionality, and the use of force by states*, Cambridge studies in international and comparative law, Cambridge University Press, Cambridge, 2004.

Laurent Gisel, ICRC and College of Europe (Eds.), *Proceedings of the 16th Bruges Colloquium Urban Warfare -15–16 October 2015*, Collegium, vol. 46, Geneva. 2016.

Herbert L. A. Hart, *The Concept of Law* (3rd ed.), Oxford University Press, Oxford, 2012.

Jean-Marie Henckaerts and Louise Doswald-Beck (Eds.). *Customary International Humanitarian Law, Vol. I: Rules.* International Committee of the Red Cross and Cambridge University Press, Cambridge, 2005.

Human Rights Watch, *Losing Humanity: The Case Against Killer Robots*, November 2012, available at: www.hrw.org/report/2012/11/19/losing-humanity/case-against-killer-robots (accessed 13/04/2018).

Eliav Lieblich, “Beyond Life and Limb: Exploring Incidental Mental Harm Under International Humanitarian Law”, in Derek Jinks et al. (Eds.), *Applying International Humanitarian Law in Judicial and Quasi-Judicial Bodies*, T.M.C. Asser Press, Hague, 2014, pp. 185–218.

International Human Rights and Conflict Resolution Clinic (Stanford Law School) and Global Justice Clinic (NYU School of Law), *Living under drones: Death, Injury and Trauma to Civilians from US Drone Practices in Pakistan,* 2012, available at http://chrgj.org/wp-content/uploads/2012/10/Living-Under-Drones.pdf (accessed 13 April 2018).

William Ian Miller, “Fear Weak Legs, and Running Away: a Soldier’s Story”, in Susan A. Bandes (Ed.), *The Passions of Law*, New York University Press, New York/London, 2001, pp. 241–263.

Stefan Oeter, “Means and Methods of Warfare”, in Dieter Fleck (Ed.), *The Handbook of Humanitarian Law in Armed Conflicts*, Oxford University Press, Oxford, 1995, pp. 231–333.

Vesselin Popovski, “Emotions and International Law”, in Yohan Ariffin et al. (Eds.), *Emotions in International Politics: Beyond Mainstream International Relations*, Cambridge University Press, Cambridge, 2016, pp. 168–183.

Andrew Ross, *Beyond Fear and Hatred in International Conflict*, Chicago University Press, Chicago, 2014.

Yves Sandoz et al. (Eds.), *Commentary to the Additional Protocols of 8 June 1977 to the Geneva Conventions of 12 August 1949*, ICRC, Martinus Nijhoff Publishers, Geneva, 1986.

Yves Sandoz, “Le demi-siècle des Conventions de Genève”, *International Review of the Red Cross*, vol. 21, no. 834, 1999, pp. 241–263.

Michael N. Schmitt (Ed.), Commentary on the Tallinn Manual on International Law Applicable to Cyber Warfare, Cambridge University Press, Cambridge, 2013.

Abouzeid A. M. Thabet et al., “Emotional Problems in Palestinian Children Living in a War Zone: A Cross-Sectional Study”, *The Lancet*, vol. 359, 2002, pp. 1801–1804.

Michael Walzer, *Just and Unjust Wars. A Moral Argument with Historical Illustrations*, Penguin Books, Harmondsworth, 1978.

12 To kill or not to kill as a social question

Ka Lok Yip

12.1 Introduction

How much freedom do those engaging in warfare have? Marx famously said that men make history but not in circumstances of their own choosing.[1] Despite the changing character of war catalysed by dramatic advancement in military technology and profound transformation of the world's political landscape, the quintessential nature of warfare as duel on an extensive scale[2] perennially produces circumstances definitely not chosen by most people "thrown" into them.[3] Hence, S.L.A. Marshall's findings that only 15% of the US soldiers in the Second World War had actually fired at enemy positions[4] remain probative of arm bearers' struggle with whether or not to kill, which is, on one hand, a personal question offensive to the gut sense "that to harm any part [of humanity] is to harm the whole"[5] and on the other hand a social question amenable to the dialectic between human agency, structure and culture.[6] This chapter focuses on the latter, social question through the prism of a recent debate concerning the strategies for compliance with international humanitarian law (IHL) triggered by the International Committee of the Red Cross (ICRC)-commissioned Study on the Roots of Behaviour in War (the "RBW Study").[7]

The chapter is divided into three substantive parts. The first part introduces the debate on the RBW Study by uncovering the sociological presuppositions held by the RBW Study and its leading critic, Dale Stephens, respectively. It illustrates how the RBW Study's vision of limited human agency in warfare compelled a structurally oriented approach to inducing compliance with IHL while Stephens' opposite vision of self-reflexive individuals acting in their authentic, moral self-identity catalysed an agentially oriented approach to ensuring

1 Marx and Engels, 1968, p. 97.
2 Clausewitz, 2008, p. 1.
3 Heidegger, 2010, pp. 131–132.
4 Marshall, 2000, p. 54.
5 Grossman, 2014, p. 38.
6 See in general Wendt, 1999, ch. 4; Wight, 2006. For alternative sociological approaches, see Giddens, 1979; Archer, 1982.
7 Muñoz-Rojas and Frésard, 2004.

restraint in war. The second part draws on literature on the psychology of social norms and recent empirical cases to assess the practical feasibility and principled merits of Stephens' emphasis on human agency at the expense of structural constraints as a strategy to modify behaviour in warfare. The third part explores how Stephens' objection to emphasising the normativity of IHL because of its association with legal positivism and political liberalism, itself underpinned by political individualism, ends up converting to a sociological form of super-individualism that inflates the power of the individuals and deflates the social process that puts some individuals but not others in power.

12.2 The RBW Study debate

The RBW Study, an interdisciplinary study based on multiple surveys and interviews using a complex methodology, found widespread moral disengagement,[8] depersonalisation[9] and lack of autonomy[10] among individuals engaged in warfare. This finding of severe diminishing of human agency in the battlefield underlies the RBW Study's recommendation for a structurally oriented approach to preventing IHL violations with "influence strategies ... designed not to persuade free individuals of the need to adopt types of conduct in conformity with IHL but to convince more or less structured and hierarchically organized groups to respect these norms."[11]

This approach can be understood as structurally oriented for it emphasises the structural mechanism (both the legal system and the hierarchical military command structure) to cause individuals to comply with IHL norms. While it does not leave the power and propensity of the individuals completely out of account, it is limited to the expectation that they have a certain degree of rationality in choosing to avoid disciplinary actions for IHL violations or disobedience from command and a largely passive capacity to conform to legal norms structurally enforced and culturally diffused within the military establishment. This conformity does not arise out of moral conviction, which would require a degree of autonomous reflexivity that the RBW Study's authors did not concede to exist among "bearers of weapons." Indeed, the RBW Study admitted that "men who are subject to mechanisms of moral disengagement and to an authority that they perceive to be legitimate will, most of the time, carry out orders, even if these are in conflict with their conscience or their values."[12]

This kind of conformity arises out of the individuals' sheer embeddedness in the military "habitus" that produces what Bourdieu called routine, minimally reflexive actions in a "common-sense world"[13] along an "easily identifiable red line"

8 Ibid, pp. 190, 197.
9 Ibid, p. 193.
10 Ibid, p. 194.
11 Ibid, pp. 202, 203, 205.
12 Ibid, p. 205.
13 Bourdieu, 1977, p. 80.

generally followed in their peer group.[14] This passive image of the human in assimilating to external norms resembles the kind featured in the Milgram experiment,[15] also relied on in the RBW Study.[16] In this sense, the RBW Study does accommodate the "internalisation" of legal norms by the individuals but only at a superficial level for the occasion without affecting their deeply held values or self-identity that led to their individuation as unique persons. The RBW Study recognised that "[combatants'] obedience stems from an internal motivation and not just from an external cause" but only by way of an "ideological abdication" to the authority.[17]

This shallow form of internalisation resembles the logic that "to work for a bank is not to be for banking"[18] – just like a banking officer can implement banking operations with great dexterity without necessarily agreeing with capitalism, a military officer can perform military tasks with great "professionalism" without necessarily agreeing with the justice of the cause of the war for which they are fighting. While this schism between one's "professional self" and "authentic self" may provoke deeper reflection in time, most of them stay within the capitalist or the military system, reconciled with the reality in which they find themselves, neither convinced of its rightfulness nor losing their ability to perform the tasks expected of them. This ambivalence of the individuals recalls the vision of Marxist structuralists Althusser and Balibar that "certain relations of production presuppose the existence of a legal-political and ideological *superstructure* as a condition of their peculiar existence"[19] and are "irreducible to any anthropological inter-subjectivity."[20] This is because "the structure of the relations of production determines the *places* and *functions* occupied and adopted by the agents of production, who are never anything more than the occupants of these places, insofar as they are the 'supports' (*Träger*) of these functions."[21] The view of human beings as mere "supports" of "functions" in the context of war is directly connected to the RBW Study's particular choice of expression to refer to the individuals engaged in armed conflicts: "bearers of weapons."[22]

It is therefore not insignificant that this expression always appeared in quotation marks in the critique of the RBW Study made by Dale Stephens,[23] who advocates the opposite, agentially oriented approach to compliance strategies relating to IHL instruction and practice. Indeed, at the end of his article, Stephens even introduced the alternative expression "warrior" and lamented the negative public reactions towards a European military force's suggestion to reintroduce its use.[24]

14 Muñoz-Rojas and Frésard, 2004, p. 203 (n. 7).
15 Milgram, 2009.
16 Frésard and Muñoz-Rojas, 2004, p. 195.
17 Ibid.
18 Kennedy, 1994, p. 335.
19 Althusser and Balibar, 1979, p. 177.
20 Ibid, p. 180.
21 Ibid.
22 See e.g. Frésard and Muñoz-Rojas, p. 189 (n. 7).
23 Stephens, 2014, p. 752.
24 Ibid, p. 772.

Stephens' approach can be understood as agentially oriented for it emphasises the role of the individuals, through their own ethical and moral enquiry and identification with the values underlying IHL, rather than the law as a social structure, to ameliorate violence. Stephens saw an "inevitable loss" in marginalising deep passions from the targeting decision process.[25] He argues that the "juridification of the battlespace" brings with it a sense of misplaced hope that wartime violence is acceptably corralled because of the liberal belief that legitimate decision and law may be made on the basis of commonly shared public reasons and justifications and the legal positivist focus on "rules-talk."[26] But since the law is in reality highly uncertain and often interpreted in a free-wheeling and unpredictable way, marginalising moral, social and emotional considerations in interpretation surrenders enormous authority to lawyers and legal process.[27] Particularly, Stephens argued that if emotions are the basis for moral reasoning, then it follows that the legal requirement of marginalising emotion runs counter to good decision-making.[28] The practical feasibility and principled merits of this agentially oriented approach will be further examined in the next section.

12.3 Human agency versus structural constraints in changing behaviour in war

Stephens proposed that we rely more on the individuals' own agency to change behaviour in war – can we? Should we?

12.3.1 Practical feasibility of emphasising human agency at the expense of structural constraints

Stephens criticised that the RBW Study's recommendation neglects the constructivist wisdom that human actions are based on self-identity. Yet, the precise nature of this "self-identity" has not been made clear in this debate. This sub-section analyses two possible understandings of the term to assess the practical feasibility of Stephens' agentially oriented approach.

12.3.1a "Self-identity" as a professional identity

Stephens at times spoke of "identity that comes from internalizing the values underpinning IHL"[29] while at other times considered "self-identity" as emerging from "identification with legal norms that are internalized through various processes of social agency" entailing "an attitude towards international legal

25 Ibid, p. 756.
26 Ibid, p. 755.
27 Ibid, p. 757.
28 Ibid, p. 765.
29 Ibid, p. 768.

concepts that is motivated by a 'logic of appropriateness' which induces a particular legally compliant behaviour and set of choices in any given instance."[30]

In the latter conception, "identification" is no longer with the values underlying the legal norms but with the legal norms themselves, compliance with which is motivated by the "logic of appropriateness" rather than a moral commitment. This less profound form of self-identity is in fact compatible with the RBW Study's reliance on legal normativity to generate restraint for "if [combatants] perceive IHL from a normative point of view, they are less tolerant of violations,"[31] thereby keeping combatants out of the spiral of violence "in which violations may become not only more and more serious but also more and more acceptable in the eyes of those who commit them."[32] Without adopting constructivist terminology and without discussing the issue of identity at all, the RBW Study in fact envisaged a very similar mental process on the part of the individuals engaged in warfare.

In constructivist terms, it is quite conceivable that an identity constructed by IHL norms is not an authentically "moral" identity, but one with which individuals engaged in armed conflicts as circumstances not of their own choosing, can identify. It is a "professional" identity in the sense that it is not necessarily moral in advancing the just cause under *jus ad bellum* or in sparing humanity as a whole by not harming its part, but that it is what a professional, "given the circumstances" with their limited enablement and dire constraints, can do as a compromise. This "professional" identity, similar to "role-taking," is pragmatic, contextual and resonant with a minimum but persistent sentiment of individuals' humanity in that force is restrained from at least a certain category of human persons, that is, civilians not directly participating in hostilities, which "minimal demands that we make on one another are, when denied, repeated with passionate insistence . . . thinness and intensity go together."[33]

The development of this professional identity in ameliorating violence in war could be complemented by other factors also inculcated by the emphasis on legal normativity. IHL norms, particularly when dispersed and enforced in the military hierarchy, generate secondary, desirable social norms that change behaviour through creating motivational pressure to conform,[34] without necessarily compelling change in moral values or attitudes. As "social norms are part of a larger motivational system … of complementary and competing pressures on behaviour,"[35] if atrocious behaviour in war is induced by social norms prevalent within a particular military setting, law can also "play a significant role in changing undesirable social norms, which are very often the problem, not the solution."[36]

30 Ibid, p. 768.
31 Muñoz-Rojas and Frésard, p. 203 (n. 7).
32 Ibid, p. 204.
33 Walzer, 1994, p. 5.
34 Prentice, 2012, p. 34–35.
35 Ibid.
36 Ibid, p. 36.

Law is particularly important in the military context because a key method to weaken or reverse an undesirable social norm (e.g. serious abuse of prisoners of war and civilian internees as seen during the Anglo-American invasion of Iraq in the early 2000s) is to afford members of the social group the opportunity to air their dissent to destroy the illusion of universality of the undesirable social norm, which method is difficult to implement in conformist settings[37] such as the military. In this kind of setting, legal normativity can usefully serve as an external "liberating voice" from an oppressive social norm prevalent within a group to which at least some of its members do not authentically subscribe.[38]

12.3.1b 'Self-identity' as a moral identity

However, Stephens' frequent emphasis on moral inquiry also indicates another vision of a much deeper kind of self-identity, in which the individuals engaged in warfare can identify their actions as authentically "moral," going beyond "role-taking" and approximating "role-making." The practical difficulty with the authentic, "moral" identification with the values underlying IHL norms is that it is doubtful as to whether these values are genuinely "moral" as ordinarily understood given that the "morality" of IHL norms themselves is subject to significant controversy. Since IHL is separate from *jus ad bellum*, there is no necessary alignment between IHL norms regulating a military action and the justice of the cause of that military action. The volumes of debate on the morality of IHL norms in just war theory literature attest to the moral ambivalence of IHL norms.[39] The "moral neutrality" of IHL is therefore quite real. In addition, and leaving aside IHL's separation from *jus ad bellum*, any kind of killing, even if routine in the battlefield, is repugnant to most human beings' innate moral sense, as attested to in much empirical literature.[40] Indeed, Stephens himself was at pains to stress that "[t]he law does rightly condemn violations of its rules and standards, but it also allows much violence to be undertaken in its name,"[41] "complying with the 'law', then, is the routine dispensation of violence to achieve political goals"[42] and "[e]normous death and destruction are manifested through an entirely lawful application of force."[43] Thus, unless it can somehow be demonstrated that the values underlying IHL are clearly moral despite the morally contentious nature of the IHL norms themselves, the deeper, "moral" identification with their underlying values could be difficult in practice.

37 Ibid, p. 36–37.
38 Ibid, p. 37.
39 For a small sample, see McMahan, 2006, p. 34; Walzer, 2006, p. 34; McMahan, 2009; Rodin and Shue, 2008.
40 Marshall, 2000, p. 54 (n. 4); Jesse Glenn Gray, 1970, p. 8; Holmes, 1989, p. 393; Grossman, 2014, p. 13, 23.
41 Stephens, 2014, p. 753 (n. 22).
42 Ibid, p. 758.
43 Ibid.

The purported construction of a deep, moral self-identity "that comes from internalizing the values underpinning IHL"[44] meets not only the obstacles in the moral doubt about these values, but also, perhaps even more significantly, the individuals' pre-existing, fully developed value and identity that are group-based, for example, their national group, ethnic group or armed group, whose demands may conflict with those of the values underpinning IHL. People are not cultural dopes whose deeply held worldview and "moral" identity can be kaleidoscopically changed from day to day at the dictates of external norms, be they legal or moral.[45] The RBW Study's insight on the limited impact of moral persuasion in changing the attitudes of individuals who act without a sense of autonomy in warfare[46] precisely seizes on this distinction between the recalcitrant nature of personal identity and the more transient nature of social or professional identity. If the individuals are not acting in their "real selves" in warfare to begin with, efforts to modify those "real selves" are in vain.

12.3.2 Principled merits of emphasising human agency at the expense of structural constraints in warfare

Whether emphasising the human capacity of passion, emotion and moral self-identity or structural constraints in law and military organisational commands is more effective in ameliorating violence in warfare is a question that ultimately needs to be studied and tested empirically, otherwise it remains a matter of theoretical speculation. Stephens criticised the RBW Study's "emphasis on 'the law' as the singular means of ensuring compliance … with an express avoidance of incorporating underpinning values" as "a particularly risky approach" without offering any empirical evidence. However, recent prominent cases such as Alexander Blackman in the UK[47] and Elor Azaria in Israel[48] fully demonstrate the potential of individuals engaged in warfare acting on their passion and emotion to commit atrocities against their demonised and de-humanised enemy. The complete lack of expression of remorse in their defences and the enormous

44 Ibid, p. 752.
45 Garfinkel, 1967, p. 68.
46 Frésard and Muñoz-Rojas, 2004, p. 204 (n. 7).
47 See Blackman, [2017], p. 190, and contrast Blackman, [2014], p. 1029 and R v Blackman, Case Reference: 2012CM00442, Sentencing Remarks by HHJ Jeff Blackett, Judge Advocate General.
48 See File 182/16 Military Prosecutor v. Sergeant Elor Azaria (Feb. 21, 2017), available at the Nevo Legal Database, www.nevo.co.il (in Hebrew, by subscription), as reported in Israel: Sentencing of Soldier Convicted of Killing Neutralized Palestinian Assailant, Ruth Levush, Senior Foreign Law Specialist, available at: www.loc.gov/law/help/military-court-decision/israel-sentencing.pdf (accessed 11 April 2018). See also File 182/16, Military Prosecutor v. Sergeant Elor Azaria (January 4, 2017), available at the Nevo Legal Database, www.nevo.co.il (in Hebrew, by subscription), as reported in Israel: Military Court Decision on Killing Neutralized Palestinian Assailant, Ruth Levush, Senior Foreign Law Specialist, available on www.loc.gov/law/help/military-court-decision/israel.php.

public, self-righteous support they each garnered[49] for their killing of wounded, defenceless enemy militants cast significant doubt on the moral reflexivity of individuals engaged in warfare. Where Stephens did discuss empirics, it was in making the extraordinary claim that "external reports that are available point (in contrast to the views expressed in the RBW Study) to a high level of compliance with IHL norms in the field, particularly in relation to avoiding injury to non-combatants," citing only one article about America's conduct of war in Iraq written by an American author on an American magazine (Colin H. Kahl, "How We Fight," *Foreign Affairs*).[50] This dubious claim seemed to deliberately brush aside the numerous reports of IHL violations that fill our daily news headlines[51] to fit IHL within the "33% ratification tipping point"[52] constructivist formula to build the case that "[g]iven that the 1949 Geneva Conventions have received universal world ratification/ accession, there is a greater likelihood that their underpinning norms have been internalized to a greater degree." It uncritically equates the "internalisation" process for states to that for individuals and obscures the point of advocating for the internalisation of values underlying IHL norms if these norms "have been internalised to a greater degree" already.

On this optimistic view of IHL compliance, it is unsurprising that to Stephens, "the issue isn't so much avoidance of the possibility of violations of IHL (i.e. 'compliance'), but the consequences of a routine dispensation of legally articulate but morally agnostic decisions that mete out considerable violence."[53] He

49 For Blackman, see e.g. "Evidence that could win justice for Marine: Mail uncovers bombshell report censored by MoD that says Marines were pushed to be too aggressive and senior officers failed to spot mental strain and fatigue", *Daily Mail*, 16 September 2015, www.dailymail.co.uk/news/article-3237600/Evidence-win-justice-Alexander-Blackman.html#ixzz4p4PansK0___(accessed 22 April 2018) and Marine A, who killed wounded Taliban fighter, released from prison, *The Guardian*, 28 April 2017, www.theguardian.com/uk-news/2017/apr/28/marine-a-alexander-blackman-released-from-prison (accessed 22 April 2018). In Azaria's case, see e.g. Israeli judges placed under guard amid death threats after convicting young soldier of manslaughter, *The Telegraph*, 5 January 2017, www.telegraph.co.uk/news/2017/01/05/israeli-judges-placed-guard-amid-death-threats-convicting-young/ and Please all, please none, *Israel Hayom*, 22 February 2017, www.israelhayom.com/site/newsletter_opinion.php?id=18461 (both accessed 22 April 2018).

50 Stephens, 2014, p. 769 (n. 22).

51 See e.g. Saudi Human Rights Delegation Chief: Houthis Violated International Humanitarian Law, Human Rights, *Asharq Al-Awsat*, 28 September 2017, https://english.aawsat.com/asharq-al-awsat-english/news-middle-east/saudi-human-rights-delegation-chief-arab-coalition-operations-aim-restoring-internationally-recognized-governemnt-power; Human Rights Watch says Saudi-led air strikes in Yemen are war crimes, *CNBC*, 12 September 2017, www.cnbc.com/2017/09/12/saudi-led-air-strikes-in-yemen-are-war-crimes-says-human-rights-watch.html; No more safe hospitals in Syria's Idlib, *Gulf News* 2 October 2017, http://gulfnews.com/news/mena/syria/no-more-safe-hospitals-in-syria-s-idlib-1.2098754 (all accessed 22 April 2018).

52 "Commentators point to the premise that once a treaty receives ratification by about 33% of States, there is typically an exponential increase in further ratifications/accessions, with a concomitant accelerated norm internalization process", see Stephens, 2014, p. 769 (n. 22).

53 Ibid, p. 763.

envisaged the consequence of the RBW Study's conclusion to be that "[e]normous death and destruction are manifested through an entirely lawful application of force in which individuals are all neatly allocated into categories and the formulas and maxims of law operate to dispassionately permit the application of force" and "elaborated reason and unalloyed positivism lead to outcomes that permit the routine application of violence in a very generic manner."[54] The suggestion that emphasising IHL norms are legitimating violence is based on a particular, wrong understanding of IHL that ignores substantial amount of authority[55] that IHL is a prohibitive law, not a permissive one. It also reflects a tunnel vision of the law that excludes all other bodies of international law than IHL to restrict this seeming misogyny of the law in permitting killing in armed conflicts. As Greenwood pointed out, ***jus ad bellum*** always provides an outer layer of constraint on the use of force.[56] Similarly, international human rights law could impose requirements other than those under IHL.[57] The portrayal of IHL as an unlimited license to kill simply draws a strawman of the law for denigration. The attempt to instrumentalise IHL to cause "enormous death and destruction" is a fault of the people, not of the law. If one keeps on blaming the hammer for a bent nail, the carpenter would never bear any responsibility.[58] If the structure always takes the blame, agents can act in a completely freewheeling, unpredictable and irresponsible manner, creating the dark sides of the dark sides as will be explored in the next section.

12.4 The dark sides of the dark sides – sociological super-individualism

Stephens' contempt for the RBW Study's structurally oriented approach stems from his opposition to the notion of "legal neutrality,"[59] which he re-described variously as "legal hegemony,"[60] "legal colonisation"[61] or "some kind of

54 Ibid.

55 "It needs to be remembered that the application of IHL confers not only protective rules, but also the entitlement to use force against fighters or, to be more accurate, recognition that such use of force *would not be a violation of IHL*", see Doswald-Beck, 2012. Emphasis added. For numerous writings by Baxter, see e.g. Baxter, 2013; Baxter, 1951, pp. 323–324. It was also reported to the Hague Conference of 1899 that 'no member of the subcommission [that dealt with the laws and usages of war] had any idea that the legal authority in an invaded country should in advance give anything like sanction to force employed by an invading and occupying army. On the contrary, the adoption of precise rules tending to limit the exercise of this power appeared to be an obvious necessity in the real interests of all peoples whom the fortune of war might in turn betray', see Scott, 1917, p. 140. This is resonated by Sassòli, "IHL cannot be seen as providing rights to states, but rather as setting forth objective rules of behaviour binding them for the benefit of individuals affected by war", see Sassòli, 2007, p. 245. See also Roberts, 2008, p. 935; Greenwood, 1983, p. 228; Bugnion, 2002, p. 535 (n. 17); Jinks, 2014, p. 666.

56 Greenwood, 1989, p. 279.

57 See in general Jinks, 2014, p. 666 (n. 57).

58 Kennedy, 2006, p. 135.

59 Stephens, 2014, p. 753 (n. 22).

60 Ibid, p. 754.

61 Ibid.

self-contained authority that compels neutrally predictable outcomes"[62] through providing supposedly objective standard of behaviour.[63] Stephens associated the "juridification of battlespace" with "political liberalism, which emphasizes the virtues of reasoned elaboration of the law … in the process of achieving outcomes on core political principles through mechanisms of rationalized reasoning and consensus"[64] leading to a blind faith in "more law"[65] when much of it is indeterminate.[66] For Stephens, this indeterminacy of the law counsels for the alternative of relying on our humanity to make good judgement.[67]

This section demonstrates that the wholesale denigration of the law in ameliorating the violence in war due to the former's association with political liberalism, itself underpinned by political individualism, ends up converting to a sociological form of super-individualism that inflates the power of the individuals and deflates the social process that puts some individuals but not others in power. This sociological super-individualism and its implications will be examined below at two levels.

Firstly, at the level of the law, this super-individualism, in singularly focusing on the indeterminacy of the law, ironically intensifies that indeterminacy[68] in a self-fulfilling prophecy through severing all possible links between the black-lettered law and the social reality that has shaped its mischief. In the context of IHL, it overlooks the sociological roots of the military establishment's preference for "rules-talk" in the highly structured environment of warfare that impairs the ability of the individuals to make judgement on killing under "epistemically forced choice situations,"[69] in the heat of the moment and amid existential threats. The law is favoured precisely by these individuals with limited agency to improvise authentically in the circumstances and is designed precisely to be technical and insulated from emotion[70] to prevent the ugly expressions of short-term human emotions in such improvisation. When the law is viewed against this sociological background, the content of IHL, by suppressing such short-term emotions, also gives expression to the long-term human emotions based on social and ethical commitment to refrain from doing in the short term what would be regretted in the long term. The law as an expression of long-term human emotions can be evidenced by the expectation that a strong record of IHL compliance would facilitate later peace reconciliation between the conflicting parties.[71] In this sense, law is the meeting point between logic and passion, albeit in the longer term.

62 Ibid, p. 757.
63 Ibid, p. 756.
64 Ibid, p. 755.
65 Ibid.
66 Ibid, p. 758–760.
67 Ibid, p. 764–765.
68 Indeed, Stephens' citation of and commentary on the case of Kupreškić seems rather to re-affirm the relative determinacy of the law in practice. See ibid, p. 762.
69 Dill, 2013, p. 26.
70 Stephens, 2014, p. 761 (n. 22).
71 Hoffmann, 2012, p. 19; Bangerter, 2011, p. 93.

Secondly, at the level of battlefield behaviour, this super-individualism provides an unjustifiably optimistic, sometimes even heroic, narrative of the individuals engaged in warfare. Stephens dismissed as "alarming"[72] and "obsolete"[73] the RBW Study's claim that the violation of the distinction principle was "more often the result of a deliberate intention to attack the civilian population rather than any objective difficulty in distinguishing the one from the other."[74] He argued that the RBW Study "has been overtaken" by developments such as the counterinsurgency (COIN) doctrine that "consciously seek to avoid civilian loss and increased risk to one's own military forces … to deliver greater humanitarian outcomes … albeit for instrumental reasons."[75] While the presence of initiatives such as COIN obviously does not prove the absence of deliberate targeting of civilians, flagging it as if it does betrays a certain presumption that the supposedly heroic acts of individuals practising COIN doctrine could "overtake" the much more generic claim that civilians killed in war are often deliberately targeted, by rendering it irrelevant and therefore unnecessary to be disproved.

Branding COIN as "an inversion of conventional interpretive approaches to the law … by excising the anonymity of potential targets and according them an accessible identity"[76] and associating it with "[q]ualities such as patience, self-reflection on ethical commitments and tolerance of military casualties from one's own military force,"[77] this narrative stresses, approvingly, the human agency of the individuals in determining their own conduct. While IHL certainly does not "mandate" killing, nor does it regulate any forbearance beyond the restraints it imposes, casting COIN as if it affects IHL interpretation or application so that it is applied in a "less formal or doctrinal manner"[78] suggests, wrongly, that these individual acts somehow liberate people living in war from the shackles of IHL when IHL does not regulate these acts to begin with.

But the most serious problem with this super-individualism is the brazen, unapologetic concentration of power to the individuals to decide who to kill based on "individual identity and broader socio-political considerations relating to the individual and the sectarian/tribal/regional connections he/she may be entwined within."[79] No doubt, the individuals positioned to give or take life based on these highly personal and idiosyncratic judgements would feel like supermen, if not actually God. Although Stephens stated upfront that COIN "is not about being 'nice' – it is about being effective,"[80] the judgement over who count as political "reconcilables" and political "irreconcilables" was ultimately

72 Stephens, p. 765 (n. 22).
73 Ibid.
74 Frésard and Muñoz-Rojas, 2000, p. 202 (n. 7).
75 Stephens, 2000, p. 765 (n. 22).
76 Ibid, pp. 765–766.
77 Ibid, p. 766.
78 Ibid, p. 767.
79 Ibid.
80 Ibid, p. 766.

described by him as an "ethical" commitment,[81] thereby completing the conflation between one's political agenda and one's moral agenda. As a troubling consequence of this super-individualism, the mundane image of large, opposing groups of people caught in political circumstances not of their own choosing gets transformed into one that glorifies one particular group of "warriors" and their Herculean efforts to "win hearts and minds," masking the structural violence inflicted upon local lives by the morally contestable transformative occupation. IHL might offer no more than minimum protection and treatment, the emphasis on its normativity at least serves as an important reminder of the brutal reality that to kill or not to kill in war is not merely a personal question as portrayed in this kind of super-individualism but also a social one in reality.

12.5 Conclusion

A realistic assessment of the freedom and constraints of those caught up in warfare helps shed light on the appropriate strategies for moulding behaviour in war. This chapter has demonstrated the inadequacies of an agentially oriented approach in the highly structured circumstances of war and has warned against the perils of abandoning legal normativity in favour of personal morality. Leff was correct to note that "whenever we do set out to find 'the law' we are able to locate nothing more attractive, or more final than ourselves,"[82] and the very same applies to morality. The difference between them is that the search for the location of the law takes place in relatively porous physical, discursive and intellectual spaces while the search for the location of morality takes place usually in the dark corners of the private minds of the people not chosen by those to be judged.

References

Louis Althusser and Etienne Balibar, *Reading Capital*, (Ben Brewster transl. 1979), Verso, London, 1965.

Margaret Scotford Archer, "Morphogenesis versus Structuration: On Combining Structure and Action", *British Journal of Sociology*, vol. 33, no. 4, 1982, pp. 455–483.

Olivier Bangerter, "Reasons Why Armed Groups Choose to Respect International Humanitarian Law or Not", *International Review of the Red Cross*, vol. 93, no. 882, 2011, pp. 353–384.

Richard Baxter, "The Municipal and International Law Basis of Jurisdiction Over War Crimes*", in Detlev F. Vagts et al. (Eds.), *Humanizing the Laws of War*, Oxford University Press, Oxford, 2013, pp. 59–72.

Richard Baxter, "So-Called Unprivileged Belligerency: Spies, Guerrillas, and Saboteurs", (1951), in Detlev F. Vagts et al. (Eds.), *Humanizing the Laws of War*, Oxford University Press, Oxford, 2013, pp. 37–57.

81 Ibid, p. 767.

82 Quoted in Stephens, 2000, p. 773 (n. 24).

Pierre Bourdieu, *Outline of a Theory of Practice*, Cambridge University Press, Cambridge, 1977.

François Bugnion, "Just wars, wars of aggression and international humanitarian law", *International Review of the Red Cross*, vol. 84, no. 847, pp. 523–546.

Carl von Clausewitz, *On War (1832)*, (James John Graham), Lea & Co, Wertheimer, 1873.

Janina Dill, "Should International Law Ensure the Moral Acceptability of War?", *Leiden Journal of International Law*, vol. 26, no. 2, 2013, pp. 253–270.

Louise Doswald-Beck, "Unexpected Challenges: The Increasingly Evident Disadvantage of Considering International Humanitarian Law in Isolation", *Santa Clara Journal of International Law*, vol. 11, no. 1, 2012, pp. 11–38.

Jean-Jacques Frésard and Daniel Muñoz-Rojas, *The Roots of Behaviour in War: Understanding and Preventing IHL Violations*, ICRC, Geneva, 2004, available at: www.icrc.org/en/publication/0853-roots-behaviour-war-understanding-and-preventing-ihl-violations (accessed 11 April 2018).

Harold Garfinkel, *Studies in Ethnomethodology*, Prentice-Hall, New Jersey, 1967.

Anthony Giddens, *Central Problems in Social Theory: Action, Structure, and Contradiction in Social Analysis*, University of California Press, Berkeley, 1979.

Jesse Glenn Gray, *On Understanding Violence Philosophically: And Other Essays*, Harper & Row, New York, 1970.

Christopher Greenwood, "The Relationship between Ius Ad Bellum and Ius in Bello", *Review of International Studies*, vol. 9, no. 4, 1983, pp. 221–223.

Christopher Greenwood, "Self-Defence and the Conduct of International Armed Conflict", in Yoram Dinstein and Mala Tabory (Eds.), *International Law at a Time of Perplexity: Essays in Honour of Shabtai Rosenne*, Martinus Nijhoff Publishers, Leiden, 1989.

Dave Grossman, *On Killing*, Open Road Media, New York, 2014.

Martin Heidegger, *Being and Time (1927)*, SUNY Press, New York, 2010.

Claudia Hoffmann, *Reasoning with Rebels International NGOs* (Research Paper Approaches to Engaging Armed Groups 11), Stiftung Wissenschaft und Politik German Institute for International and Security Affairs, Berlin, 2012.

Richard Holmes, *Acts of War: A Novel of Police Terror*, Simon and Schuster, New York, 1989.

Derek Jinks, "International Human Rights Law in Time of Armed Conflict", in Andrew Clapham and Paola Gaeta (Eds.), *The Oxford Handbook of International Law in Armed Conflict*, Oxford University Press, Oxford, 2014, pp. 656–674.

David W. Kennedy, "A New World Order: Yesterday, Today, and Tomorrow Symposium: Preferred Futures for the United Nations: Part I", *Transnational Law & Contemporary Problems*, vol. 4, 1994, pp. 329–375.

David Kennedy, "Reassessing International Humanitarianism: The Dark Side", in Anne Orford (Ed.), *International Law and its Others*, Cambridge University Press, Cambridge, 2006.

Samuel Lyman Atwood Marshall, *Men against Fire: The Problem of Battle Command*, University of Oklahoma Press, Norman OK, 2000.

Karl Marx and Friedrich Engels, *Selected Works in One Volume*, International Publishers, Moscow, 1968.

Jeff McMahan, "The Ethics of Killing in War", *Philosophia*, vol. 34, no. 1, 2006, pp. 23–41.

Jeff McMahan, *Killing in War*, Oxford University Press, Oxford, 2009.

Stanley Milgram, *Obedience to Authority: An Experimental View*, HarperCollins, New York, 2009.

Jean-Jacques Frésard and Daniel Muñoz-Rojas, "The Roots of Behavior in War: Understanding and Preventing IHL Violations", *International Review of the Red Cross*, vol. 86, no. 853, 2004, pp. 189–206.

Deborah A. Prentice, "The Psychology of Social Norms and the Promotion of Human Rights", in Ryan Goodman, Derek Jinks and Andrew K. Woods (Eds.), *Understanding Social Action, Promoting Human Rights*, Oxford University Press USA, New York, 2012, pp. 22–46.

Adam Roberts, "The Principle of Equal Application of the Laws of War", in David Rodin and Henry Shue (Eds.), *Just and Unjust Warriors : The Moral and Legal Status of Soldiers*, Oxford University Press, Oxford, 2008, pp. 226–254.

David Rodin and Henry Shue, *Just and Unjust Warriors : The Moral and Legal Status of Soldiers: The Moral and Legal Status of Soldiers*, Oxford University Press, Oxford, 2008.

Marco Sassòli, "The Separation between the Legality of the Use of Force and Humanitarian Rules to be respected in Warfare: Crucial or Outdated", in Michael N. Schmitt and Jelena Pejic (Eds.), *International Law And Armed Conflict, Exploring the Faultlines: Essays in Honour of Yoram Dinstein*, Martinus Nijhoff Publishers, Leiden, 2007, pp. 509–541.

James Brown Scott, *The Reports to the Hague Conferences of 1899 and 1907: Being the Official Explanatory and Interpretative Commentary Accompanying the Draft Conventions and Declarations Submitted to the Conferences by the Several Commissions Charged with Preparing Them Together with the Texts of the Final Acts, Conventions and Declarations as Signed, and of the Principal Proposals Offered by the Delegations of the Various Powers as Well as of Other Documents Laid Before the Commissions*, Clarendon Press, Oxford, 1917.

Dale Stephens, "Behaviour in War: The Place of Law, Moral Inquiry and Self-Identity", *International Review of the Red Cross*, vol. 96, no. 895/896, 2014, pp. 751–773.

Michael Walzer, *Thick and Thin: Moral Argument at Home and Abroad*, University of Notre Dame Press, Notre Dame IN, 1994.

Michael Walzer, "Response to McMahan's Paper", *Philosophia*, vol. 34, no. 1, 2006, pp. 43–45.

Alexander Wendt, *Social Theory of International Politics*, Cambridge University Press, Cambridge, 1999.

Colin Wight, *Agents, Structures and International Relations: Politics as Ontology*, Cambridge University Press, Cambridge, 2006.

13 War of Wor(l)ds – clashing narratives and interpretations of I(H)L in the intractable Israeli-Palestinian conflict

Alexandra Hofer[1]

13.1 Introduction

The Israeli-Palestinian conflict is often described as intractable. This does not mean that it is impossible to solve, but that it is deeply embedded within a socio-psychological infrastructure that strongly influences Israeli and Palestinian societies and policies and that contributes to its perpetuation.[2] This chapter focuses on the *collective memory* of Israelis and Palestinians and their *collective identities* as expressed by State representatives.[3] I am interested in how these social concepts influence the legal arguments that the two Nations express before international fora.

The overarching issue explored by this chapter is how parties in an intractable conflict appropriate and interpret international law where existential issues are at stake. This enquiry is highly relevant for the dispute regarding the legal nature of the occupied Palestinian territories and is illustrated in the proceedings surrounding the United Nations General Assembly's (GA) request to the International Court of Justice (ICJ) for an advisory opinion on the "Legal Consequences of the Construction of a Wall in the Occupied Palestinian Territory."[4] The question asked to the Court is regarding the legal consequences arising from the construction of the wall by Israel in the occupied Palestinian territories. This disagreement can be understood through the prism of collective memories and identities within which both groups operate (section 13.3), which, in turn, explain their response to the ICJ's findings (section 13.4).[5] I discuss the

1 Special thanks are owed to Mats Deland for his helpful comments during the drafting of this chapter. My thanks are also extended to Professor Emiliano Buis for allowing me to take part in the discussions in Uppsala in October 2016. Unless otherwise indicated, all websites were last accessed on 12 September 2017.

2 Bar-Tal, 2007, pp. 1430–1453.

3 Although these are of course not the only variables that could be used, we could have approached the issue through the notions of shared beliefs or ethos of conflict.

4 UNGA Resolution ES-10/14, 8 December 2003, UN Doc A/RES/ES-10/14.

5 This chapter therefore excludes the consequences of the ICJ's advisory opinion on Israeli and Palestinian policies and societies. It also sets aside the question of compliance and the effectiveness of international law.

implications for international law in the conclusion (section 13.5). First, however, some theoretical clarifications are required.

13.2 The collective memories and identities in intractable conflict

The conflict's causes and history have dominated speech acts since at least the Arab-Israeli war of 1948 and are frequently repeated.[6] On one side of the coin, 1948 is the year of Al-Nakba, the catastrophe that impeded Palestinian statehood. Since then, Palestinians have been fighting for their right to an independent State against the occupying power. On the other side of the coin, 1948 is the year that Israeli independence was finally fulfilled and recognized by the international community. However, ever since Israel's right to exist has been threatened by acts of aggression and terror committed by its neighbours.

These historical narratives are part of Israel and Palestine's *collective memories*: "social representations (or shared knowledge about the past) that are collectively constructed through interpersonal and institutional communications."[7] Collective memories are "the shared narrative[s] about the past of the given community – its origin and the main events that supposedly shaped the collective identity."[8] Indeed, collective history is central to a group's identity,[9] a key concept in social sciences. To put it in very simple terms, identity tells actors who they are and enables them to position themselves towards others.[10] Although individuals possess both personal and collective, or social, identities, in this chapter I focus on the latter, which constitutes an in-group's definition of itself in relation to an out-group.[11] Identity is therefore relational; in order for the Self to know who it is, it needs to be able to interact with an Other.

Importantly, in intractable conflicts, historical narratives are irreconcilable and contain storylines that justify why their own party is victimized by the other, the perpetrator.[12] Collective understandings of the past inform both groups of who they are and who the Other is. This scheme's influence is perceptible in both parties' arguments on the applicable law in the context of the wall advisory

6 This is perceptible in Israeli and Palestinian speech-acts. To give but one illustration, see statements by Mahmoud Abbas and Benjamin Netanyahu in UNGA Verbatim Records of the 71st session, 14th plenary meeting, 22 September 2016, UN Doc A/71/PV.14.

7 Smeekes, McKeown, and Psaltis, 2017, p. 283. Emphasis added. See also Hammack and Pilecki, 2012, p. 76 and Hammack, 2008, p. 222–223.

8 Reykowski, 2015, p. 8.

9 Smeekes, McKeown, and Psaltis, 2017, p. 283; See also Bar-Tal, 2007, p. 1443: the "narratives of collective memory and ethos fulfil the unique role of contributing to the formation, maintenance, and strengthening of a social identity that reflects the lasting conditions and experiences of intractable conflict." See further Hirsch, 2015, pp. 47, p. 51 and 97; Liu and Hilton, 2005, pp. 537–556; Weedon and Jordan, 2012, p. 146.

10 This chapter draws on constructivist understandings of identity, mainly Hirsch, 2015, pp. 93–95; Hopf, 1998, p. 174, footnote 10 and p. 175.

11 Bar-Tal, 2007, p. 1443.

12 Reykowski, 2015, p. 8; Bar-Tal, 2007, pp. 1436–1438.

opinion before the ICJ. A social approach to the issue explains not only the legal arguments formulated by Israel and Palestine (section 13.3) but also their response to the World Court's findings (section 13.4). Collective memories and identities can be channelled and expressed by diverse agents within a nation. In this chapter, my reference point is State institutions, and in particular officials and representatives. Their respective understandings of their groups' history and identity are most relevant as they are responsible for interpreting international law and articulating legal arguments before international institutions.

13.3 Situating legal arguments within collective memories and identities

The summary of arguments provided below comes from publicly available material and content submitted to the United Nations, in particular the General Assembly (GA) and the ICJ. I also rely upon documents provided by third parties, such as the Secretary-General and the International Committee of the Red Cross. I will demonstrate that the disagreement on the (legal) nature of the wall, the applicable law and the interpretation of the Other's policies are informed by both parties' collective memories and identities.

13.3.1 Palestine: an expansionist wall built by the occupying power

Palestine frequently referred to the wall as an "expansionist wall" and a "land grab." In Palestine's written statement to the ICJ, the wall was presented as a furtherance of Israel's colonial and expansionist aims: "the Wall is not just a fence; it is a regime, a regime of isolation, discrimination and the denial of rights which does not tally with its ostensible motive, security."[13] To demonstrate this, the background of Israel's policies to unilaterally change the legal nature of the territory and annex it, as well as its practices as an occupying power, were addressed:

> The Wall that is now being built by Israel in the Occupied Palestinian Territory is the culmination of [Israeli] policies and practices, leading to the de facto annexation of large areas of territory [...]. *The Wall cannot be understood except in the context of such longstanding, unlawful Israeli policies and practices.*[14]

Evidently, the causes and history of the conflict as understood by Palestine determine the applicable law and legal consequences of the wall's construction.[15]

13 Written Statement submitted by Palestine to the ICJ, 29 January 2004, p. 4, para. 11. Available at: www.icj-cij.org/en/case/131/written-proceedings (accessed 22 April 2018). Hereafter "Palestine Written Statement."

14 *Ibid.*, para. 196. Emphasis added.

15 *Ibid.*, Chapter 3. UNGA Emergency Special Session 23rd Meeting, 8 December 2003, UN Doc A/ES-10/PV.23, p. 4.

In its written memorial, Palestine explained that from 1948 to 1967, its territory was split into three. A large part was controlled by Israel, the West Bank and Eastern Jerusalem were under Jordanian control, and the Gaza Strip came under Egyptian control.[16] After the international armed conflict of 1967,

> Israeli armed forces invaded and occupied, inter alia, the West Bank and the Gaza Strip, which represented about one-half of the territory that had been allocated to the Arab State under the partition plan in General Assembly Resolution 181(II) of 1947.[17]

When seeing the territories as occupied, the applicable law to the territories is the international law of occupation – in particular, the Hague Convention IV of 1907 on the Laws and Customs of War on Land and Geneva Convention IV of 1949 – and Israel has obligations as an occupier;[18] "an Occupying Power does not have sovereignty over the territory subject to its occupation. It merely exercises authority over the territory on a temporary basis."[19] However, according to Palestine, "[s]uccessive Israeli Governments have been pursuing since 1968 the illegal policy of colonizing the Occupied Palestinian Territory, including East Jerusalem, through the transfer of parts of Israel's own civilian population to the territory."[20] Under international law, occupied territory cannot be unilaterally annexed and such attempts could amount to war crimes.[21] The Palestinian representative therefore submitted that the construction of the wall is a war crime so grave that it amounts to a crime against humanity.[22]

Israel's claim that the wall is a security measure[23] was rejected by Palestine as "not only ludicrous and illogical, it is a repetition of the same lie and pretext that has been used by Israel over the years to commit all its crimes against the Palestinian people, particularly its expansionist campaign of settler colonialism."[24] Palestine argued that it is not carrying out acts of terrorism but acts of resistance against occupation,[25] to which Israel responds with an "iron fist policy."[26] In its view,

16 Palestine Written Statement, para. 85.
17 *Ibid.*, para. 345.
18 *Ibid.*, Chapters 7 and 8.
19 *Ibid.*, para. 346.
20 *Ibid.*, para. 121. The settlement activities are described from paras. 122–156.
21 See also UNGA Emergency Special Session 21st Meeting, 20 October 2003, UN Doc A/ES-10/PV.21, p.3, where the Palestinian representative lists the international norms violated by the wall.
22 *Ibid.*, p. 3.
23 Section 13.3.2.
24 UNGA Emergency Special Session 21st Meeting, p. 4. See also UNGA Emergency Special Session 23rd Meeting, p. 4.
25 Palestine Written Statement, para. 217.
26 *Ibid.*, para. 207.

> Israeli policies and practices have created the conditions underlying the current instability, turmoil and "security issues", including the suicide bombings, in response to which Israel claims it must build the Wall in the Occupied Palestinian Territory to protect its citizens.[27]

Contrary to Israel's assertions, Palestine contended that the wall did not respect the principle of military necessity and violates the principles of proportionality; it also contributed to the dire humanitarian situation in the occupied territories.[28] Instead of guaranteeing security and stability, the wall aggravated the tense situation between the Palestinians and the Israelis.

13.3.2 Israel: a security fence as a proportionate and necessary defence against terrorism

It should be noted at the outset that Israel rejected the Court's jurisdiction over the proceedings.[29] Israel further contested the Palestinian narrative that the wall, which it calls "security fence," is the continuation of an expansionist policy. Instead, it emphasized that

> The security fence is a temporary, proven, necessary and non-violent measure adopted in accordance with international and local law to defend the people of Israel from a continuing and vicious campaign of terrorism. [...] As soon as the terror ends, the fence will no longer be necessary. The fence is not a border and has no political significance. It does not change the legal status of the territory in any way.[30]

This measure, they argued, was consistent with the principle of proportionality[31] and with

> [the] right of States to self-defence enshrined in Article 51 of the Charter. International law and Security Council resolutions, including resolutions 1368 (2001) and 1373 (2001), have clearly recognized the right of States to use force in self-defence against terrorist attacks, and therefore surely recognize the right to use non-forcible measures to that end.[32]

27 *Ibid.*, para. 198. See also para. 226.

28 Palestine Written Statement, paras. 225 and 227. Chapter 6 of the statement elaborates on the wall's effects on the civilian population.

29 The reasons for this are outlined in Letter dated 29 January 2004 from the Deputy Director General and Legal Advisor of the Ministry of Foreign Affairs, together with the Written Statement of the Government of Israel, Part Two. Available at: www.icj-cij.org/en/case/131/written-proceedings (accessed 22 April 2018). Hereafter, "Israel Written Statement."

30 UNGA Emergency Special Session 23rd Meeting, p. 6. See also Israel Written Statement para. 1.8.

31 UNGA Emergency Special Session 23rd Meeting, p. 7.

32 UNGA Emergency Special Session 21st Meeting, p. 5.

Israel argued that by seeking the adoption of a GA resolution requesting an ICJ advisory opinion, Palestine was attempting to divert attention from the issues raised by Palestinian terrorism, which is the main obstacle to the settlement of the Israeli-Palestinian dispute.[33] The real issue was Palestine's refusal to cut off ties with terrorism and to implement its counter-terrorism obligations.[34] Israel was critical of the GA's silence on this fact: "the request for an opinion [says] nothing – not a single word – about Palestinian terrorism directed against Israeli civilians and the ongoing reality of such attacks."[35]

Unlike Palestine, Israel's written statement to the ICJ did not contain its account of the conflict's historical background nor did it make submissions on the wall's legal nature or the applicable law. Instead, Israel elaborates upon the security issues Israelis face on a regular basis,[36] therefore contextualizing the need for the security fence and demonstrating that Palestine is responsible for the reasons behind its construction. Israel also refers to the importance of the conflict's historical background, especially with regard to the occupied Palestinian territories and applicable law.

The Israel MFA stresses that the settlements should be understood within their specific historical context: "attempts to present Jewish settlement in West Bank territory (ancient Judea and Samaria) as illegal and 'colonial' in nature ignores the complexity of this issue, the history of the land, and the unique legal circumstances of this case."[37] According to Israel, the Fourth Geneva Convention does not apply to situations where a people, such as the Jews, voluntarily return to their ancient homeland. In Israel's words,

> The prohibition against the forcible transfer of civilians to territory of an occupied state under the Fourth Geneva Convention was not intended to relate to the circumstances of voluntary Jewish settlement in the West Bank on legitimately acquired land which did not belong to a previous lawful sovereign and which was designated as part of the Jewish State under the League of Nations Mandate.[38]

33 *Ibid.*, p. 5. In fact, Israel considered that the adoption of the GA Resolution ES-10/14 was *ultra vires* and an abuse of the General Assembly's powers under the Charter, see UNGA Emergency Special Session 23rd Meeting, p. 6. This argument was also made in Israel Written Statement, para. 0.6 and more generally Chapter 4, section D.

34 UNGA Emergency Special Session 21st Meeting, p. 5. See also Israel Written Statement, Chapter 3, section D.

35 Israel Written Statement, para. 0.2.

36 *Ibid.*, para. 0.1, and Chapter 3, section D.

37 Extracts retrieved from the Israel MFA, "Israeli Settlements and International Law", 30 November 2015, available at: www.mfa.gov.il/mfa/foreignpolicy/peace/guide/pages/israeli%20settlements%20and%20international%20law.aspx (accessed 22 April 2018); Secretary-General Report prepared pursuant to General Assembly resolution ES-10/13, 24 November 2003, UN Doc A/ES-10/248.

38 Extracts retrieved from the Israel MFA, "Israeli Settlements and International Law."

Whereas Palestine argues that the territories were previously under Jordanian and Egyptian control and came under Israeli occupation in 1967, Israel asserts that,

> Occupied territories are territories captured in war from an established and recognized sovereign. As the West Bank and Gaza Strip were not under the legitimate and recognized sovereignty of any state prior to the Six Day War, they should not be considered occupied territories.[39]

Israel thus rejects that it is an occupying power. It further claims that

> the attempt to portray Jewish communities in the West Bank as a new form of "colonial" settlement in the land of a foreign sovereign is as disingenuous as it is politically motivated. At no point in history were Jerusalem and the West Bank subject to Palestinian Arab sovereignty. At issue is the right of Jews to reside in their ancient homeland, alongside Palestinian Arab communities, in an expression of the connection of both peoples to this land.[40]

It follows that, contrary to Palestine's assertions, it is not a question of ***occupied*** territories, but of ***disputed*** lands, meaning a "territory over which there are competing claims which should be resolved in peace process negotiations."[41]

Based on the above, through their legal submissions, both parties were battling for their respective narratives' validation as fundamental issues pertaining to both groups' history and identity were at stake. Their reactions to the Court's advisory opinion further demonstrate the existential nature of the underlying issues surrounding the legal consequences of the wall's construction.

13.4 Responses to the advisory opinion

Groups tend to resist threats to their identity, which can be triggered by the risk of historical discontinuity.[42] This perception of risk can emerge from narratives that contradict their collective memory and threaten the founding beliefs that cause a group to define itself in a particular manner. This is especially the

39 Israel MFA, "Disputed Territories – Forgotten Facts about the West Strip and Gaza", 1 February 2003, available at: http://mfa.gov.il/MFA/MFA-Archive/2003/Pages/DISPUTED%-20TERRITORIES-%20Forgotten%20Facts%20About%20the%20We.aspx (accessed 22 April 2018).

40 Israel MFA, "Israeli Settlements and International Law." They further specify that "Jewish communities in [the West Bank] have existed from time immemorial and express the deep connection of the Jewish people to land which is the cradle of their civilization, as affirmed by the League of Nations Mandate for Palestine, and from which they, or their ancestors, were ousted."

41 Israel MFA, "Israeli Settlements and International Law"; Israeli MFA, "Disputed Territories…".

42 Smeekes, McKeown, and Psaltis, 2017, pp. 282–283 and p. 292. Roth et al. 2017, pp. 322–323. Jetten and Hutchison, 2011; Jetten and Wohl, 2012; Smeekes and Verkuyten, 2015.

case in an intractable conflict, where identity insecurity is an important feature and where both groups seek to trump the other's narrative.[43] In the case of the Israeli-Palestinian conflict, the threat originates from the mere existence of the other group, let alone their counter-narrative. Inasmuch as the advisory opinion was to touch upon key aspects of the conflict such as the territories' status,[44] its findings were crucial to both parties and would have significant implications for Israel and Palestine's understandings of their history, themselves and each other.

The advisory opinion on the *Legal Consequences of the Construction of a Wall in the Occupied Palestinian Territory* was issued on 9 July 2004 and was subsequently endorsed by the UN General Assembly.[45] For present purposes, the most significant findings were that the territories are occupied and that Israel has the status of an occupying power.[46] The Court asserted that the Palestinian people has the right to self-determination.[47] It also found that the Hague Regulation has reached the status of customary international law and is applicable to the territories.[48] Furthermore, despite Israel's claims to the contrary, the ICJ considered that the Fourth Geneva Convention also applied.[49] The Israeli settlements in the occupied territories were found to breach, *inter alia*, the Palestinian people's right to self-determination[50] and the law of occupation.[51] The breaches of international humanitarian law could not "be justified by military exigencies or by the requirements of national security or public order."[52]

With regard to Israel's security concerns, the advisory opinion dismissed Article 51 UN Charter's applicability to the wall,[53] a view which was criticized by Judge Higgins, Judge Kooijmans and Judge Buergenthal.[54] Although recognizing Israel's right and duty to ensure the security of its population, this needed to be done in conformity with the applicable law.[55] The advisory opinion concluded, "Israel cannot rely on a right of self-defence or on a state of necessity in order to preclude the wrongfulness of the construction of the wall."[56]

43 Hammack, 2008, pp. 225 and 233.
44 *Legal Consequences of the Construction of a Wall in the Occupied Palestinian Territory*, ICJ, Advisory Opinion, 9 July 2004, para. 69ff.
45 Resolution ES-10/15, 20 July 2004, UN Doc A/RES/ES-10/15.
46 ICJ, Advisory Opinion, 9 July 2004, para. 78.
47 *Ibid.*, para. 118.
48 *Ibid.*, para. 89.
49 *Ibid.*, para. 101, see also paras. 125–126.
50 *Ibid.*, para. 122.
51 *Ibid.*, paras. 132–135 and 137.
52 *Ibid.*, para. 137.
53 *Ibid.*, para. 139.
54 See Separate Opinion of Judge Higgins para.33; Separate Opinion of Judge Kooijmans, para.35; Declaration of Judge Buergenthal, paras 5–6.
55 ICJ, Advisory Opinion, 9 July 2004, para. 141
56 *Ibid.*, para. 142.

13.4.1 Palestine's endorsement following international recognition

From the Palestinian perspective, the ICJ's opinion was a victory not only for the Palestinian people but also for all the people in the region and all those who believe in the rule of law and the authority and integrity of the UN.[57] It would have the effect of "developing and ingraining a culture of respect for the law" in Palestinian society. The Palestinian representative expressed "deep gratitude to the Court" and wished to honour "the judges who met the challenge before them with wisdom, courage and trueness to their responsibility to uphold the rules and principles of international law." The advisory opinion was described as "strong, clear and comprehensive" as well as an "important and authoritative" determination of the applicable law concerning this case, which included international humanitarian law. It was considered as

> a momentous and pivotal development. It has brought international law – which for too many years has been sidelined and undermined – back to the forefront of the dialogue concerning the question of Palestine and the Israeli-Palestinian conflict. [...] It is a watershed event that has the potential to elevate the situation in the Middle East to a new level – one that is based on international law and the ideals of peace and reconciliation.

The Court's determination represented the final and conclusive word on the matter:

> There can be no further question or doubt as to the illegal status of the wall – or the settlements, for that matter – that Israel has been building – and continues to build – in the occupied Palestinian territory, including East Jerusalem.

These findings were therefore "non-negotiable." According to Palestine, Israel's rejection of the advisory opinion was an attitude of non-compliance, disrespect and "blatant contempt for the rule of law in international relations." Ultimately, "Israel will have to choose whether to declare itself officially, morally and legally an outlaw State, or to reconcile itself with a new reality and comply with the Court's advisory opinion."

13.4.2 Israel's defensive response to the threat of discontinuity[58]

Whereas Palestine called upon Israel to reconcile with the reality that was confirmed by the advisory opinion, the Israeli representative found that Palestine

57 All quoted statements are taken from UNGA Emergency Special Session 24th Meeting, morning session, 9 July 2004, UN Doc A/ES-10/PV.24, pp. 5–10.

58 This brief commentary only focuses on Israel's immediate reaction to the Court's determinations and only the government's response was taken into account, whereas the advisory opinion had an

had dragged the ICJ into its "virtual reality"; a "comic-strip narrative of victim and villain that they have laboured so intensively to create."[59] In actual reality, Israel was "burdened with the heavy responsibility of saving the lives of its citizens from the most brutal and evil terrorist campaign." Israel expressed itself as shocked and appalled

> that in all 60-plus pages of the opinion the court fail[ed] to address the essence of the problem and the very reason for building the fence. [...] The real barrier between Israelis and Palestinians is not the fence, but the terrorism that made it necessary.

Israel's rights to live securely had not been recognized. The Court had ignored the "suffering of innocent Israelis from terrorism and the obligations of the Palestinian side to prevent it." It had also ignored the League of Nations' "express recognition of the Jewish people's right to self-determination in their ancient homeland"; it addressed "the wars between Israel and its neighbours as if they materialized out of thin air, rather than as a result of deliberate acts of aggression designed to wipe Israel off the map."[60]

Concerning the procedure, the Court had been asked a "grotesquely distorted question" and the process had been perverted. This had had the effect of discrediting the United Nations and creating an illegitimate and counterproductive outcome to the peace process. Thus, the judicial organ had become the victim of Palestine's political campaign and international law had been thwarted. Whereas Palestine's statement focused on the Court's authoritative and determinative findings, Israel's statement highlighted the dissenting opinions and concerns of individual judges. Israel also emphasized that the ICJ's advisory opinion was not-binding, contrary to the decisions of the Israeli Supreme Court. The latter was depicted as more legitimate than the World Court as it was "fiercely independent" and had carried out a thorough and vigorous judgement regarding the security fence, which the ICJ had failed to do.[61]

13.4.3 Concluding remarks

During the ICJ's proceedings, the struggle for recognition of both parties' narratives was outsourced to international law as they fought for historical

---

impact on different fractions of Israeli society. In addition, since the opinion, Israel took steps in 2005 to reduce the wall's incursion on the West Bank, as mentioned in Hirsch, 2005.

59 All quoted statements are taken from UNGA Emergency Special Session 24th Meeting, morning session, pp. 12–17. PM Ariel Sharon's statement is also insightful, see Israel MFA, "Cabinet Communiqué", 11 June 2004, available at: http://mfa.gov.il/MFA/PressRoom/2004/Pages/Cabinet%20Communique%2011-July-2004.aspx (accessed 22 April 2018).

60 On this issue, see also Hirsch, 2005, pp. 341–342.

61 See also Israel MFA, "Israel's High Court of Justice Ruling on the Anti-Terrorist Fence", 30 June 2004, available at: http://mfa.gov.il/MFA/PressRoom/2004/Pages/Statement%20on%20Fence%20Ruling%2030-June-2004.aspx (accessed 22 April 2018).

continuity and affirmation of their identity through legal arguments. As the advisory opinion confirmed Palestine's narrative, it comes as no surprise that Palestine endorsed and upheld the Court. On the other hand, Israeli identity and collective memory were threatened by the opinion, placing Israel in a defensive position as it resisted and delegitimized the procedure and its outcome. If the Israelis were to accept that they are occupying Palestinian territory, this would not only undermine their claims to the land but also run counter how they define themselves as a people. "Occupation" implies they are in possession of a territory that does not belong to them and that they are legally bound to withdraw. To be the occupier would therefore imply that Israelis are not in their rightful and ancient homeland.[62] On the other side of the spectrum, for the Palestinians, it is important that the international community recognizes that the territories are occupied as this not only renders legitimacy to their right to self-determination but also justifies and gives purpose to their resistance as they strive for independence.

13.5 Conclusion: international law as a means to an end

This chapter chose to focus on the collective memories and identities of Israel and Palestine to understand how they influence the legal claims invoked by opposing groups in intractable conflict. It should be noted that our focus was limited as these concepts do not explain everything; one should keep in mind that they are but one feature of a psychosociological structure within which Israelis and Palestinians interact. Importantly though, it has been argued that this setting is conducive to furthering the conflict.[63]

Though Israelis and Palestinians are arguably in opposition, it is interesting to observe that – like two sides of the same coin – their respective narratives complement each other, as they appear to be entangled and to mirror the Other's storyline. The Israelis and Palestinians both recall the history of suffering and exile, the intense bond with the land and how the Other is responsible for the continuation of the conflict. In fact, the narratives of both groups come across as interdependent, meaning they are mutually constitutive and reinforce each other.[64] If the Israelis are able to pursue their narrative of survival in the face of

62 This issue was perceptible in the Israeli government's response to the adoption of UNSC Resolution 2334, 23 December 2016, UN Doc S/RES/2335(2016). See UNSC 7853rd Meeting, 23 December 2016, UN Doc S/PV.7853; PM Netanyahu's remarks at the Chanukah candle lighting at the Western Wall, 25 December 2016, Available at http://mfa.gov.il/MFA/PressRoom/2016/Pages/PM-Netanyahu's-remarks-at-the-Chanukah-candle-lighting-at-the-Western-Wall.aspx

63 Bar-Tal, 2007, pp. 1446–1447.

64 Our definition of interdependence differs from that proposed by, e.g. Herbert Kelman, who speaks of negative independence: "the assertion of the group's own identity requires the negation of the other group's identity", in Kelman, 1999, p. 589. Here, we suggest that the interdependence between Israeli and Palestinian identity means that in order for a group's identity to exist they depend on the other group's existence.

annihilation attempts, this is because they face Palestinian acts of violence. On the other hand, if the Palestinians are able to fulfil the narrative of resistance despite insurmountable odds, this is because of Israel's security measures and pursuit of settlement policies. It follows that their understanding of the Other's motives justifies their own behaviour. Intense security measures are to be understood as a necessary response to senseless acts of terrorism; desperate acts of resistance are justified by ruthless colonial expansion. Palestinians would not be resistors if they would not have to resist Israeli occupation; and Israelis would not be implementing security measures if they would not have to defend themselves from Palestinian terrorism. Although these narratives strengthen both groups' identities in the conflict, they also help perpetuate it. Indeed, in order for their identity to exist, it is necessary for the Other to be the enemy. Peace therefore comes at a huge personal cost; the cost of accepting that the Other is not only a human being but also quite similar to who you are. This is threatening since it requires confronting one's identity and personal narrative.

It follows that in intractable conflicts where existential issues are at stake for both parties, law can help channel and frame the dispute but it cannot impose peace upon either party, especially if the proposed outcome threatens the foundations of either group's identity. As conflict is created in the mind of humans, it is only within these minds that it can be solved. Law is appropriated and integrated into group narratives, enabling them to extend their conflict-based policies by other means. Similarly, when both groups are ready to move away from conflict, international law will provide them with a framework through which they can cooperate. Law is therefore instrumental at achieving peace or pursuing war, whether it is used for the former or the latter depends on the mind applying it.

References

Daniel Bar-Tal, "Sociopsychological Foundations of Intractable Conflicts", *American Behavioral Scientist*, vol. 50, no. 11, 2007, pp. 1430–1453.

Phillip L. Hammack and Andrew Pilecki, "Narrative as a Root Metaphor for Political Psychology", *Political Psychology*, vol. 33, no. 1, 2012, pp. 73–103.

Phillip L. Hammack, "Narrative and the Cultural Psychology of Identity", *Personality and Social Psychology Review*, vol. 12, no. 3, 2008, pp. 222–247.

Moche Hirsch, "The Impact of the Advisory Opinion on Israel's Future Policy: International Relations Perspective", *Journal of International Law and International Relations*, vol. 1, 2005, pp. 319–344.

Moshe Hirsch, *An Invitation to the Sociology of International Law*, OUP, Oxford, 2015.

Ted Hopf, "The Promise of Constructivism", *International Security*, vol. 23, no. 1, 1998, pp. 171–200.

Jolanda Jetten and Paul Hutchison, "When groups Have a Lot to Lose: Historical Continuity Enhances Resistance to a Merger", *European Journal of Social Psychology*, vol. 41, 2011, pp. 335–343.

Joanda Jetten and Michael J. A. Wohl, "The Past as a Determinant of the Present: Historical Continuity, Collective Angst, and Opposition to Immigration", *European Journal of Social Psychology*, vol. 42, no. 4, 2012, pp. 442–450.

Herbert Kelman, "Interdependence of Israeli and Palestinian National Identities: The Role of the Other in Existential Conflict", *Journal of Social Issues*, vol. 55, no. 3, 1999, pp. 581–600.

James H. Liu and Denis J. Hilton, "How the Past Weighs on the Present: Social Representations of History and Their Role in Identity Politics", *British Journal of Social Psychology*, vol. 44, no. 4, 2005, pp. 537–556.

Janusz Reykowski, "Intractable Conflicts—How Can They be Solved? The Theory of Daniel Bar-Tal", in Eran Halperin and Keren Sharvit (Eds.), *The Social Psychology of Intractable Conflicts Celebrating the Legacy of Daniel Bar-Tal, Volume I*, Springer, Switzerland, 2015, pp. 3–16.

Jenny Roth, Michaela Huber, Annkatrin Juenger and James H. Liu, "It's About Valence: Historical Continuity or Historical Discontinuity as a Threat to Social Identity", *Journal of Social and Political Psychology*, vol. 5, no. 2, 2017, pp. 320–341.

Anouk Smeekes and Maykel Verkuyten, "The Presence of the Past: Identity Continuity and Group Dynamics", *European Review of Social Psychology*, vol. 26, no. 1, 2015, pp. 162–202.

Anouk Smeekes, Shelley McKeown, and Charis Psaltis, "Endorsing Narratives Under Threat: Maintaining Perceived Collective Continuity Through the Protective Power of Ingroup Narratives in Northern Ireland and Cyprus", *Journal of Social and Political Psychology*, vol. 5, no. 2, 2017, pp. 282–300.

Chris Weedon and Glenn Jordan, "Collective Memory: Theory and Politics", *Social Semiotics*, vol. 25, no. 6, 2012, pp. 143–153.

Part IV

14 The lawyer as an actor in history and society

Daniel Marc Segesser and Mats Deland

14.1 Introduction

Legal and general history are two neighbouring academic fields, the first one being a rather small part within more general legal studies, while the other deals with law as just one part of a much larger field, which includes for instance political, social, cultural, environmental and military aspects. Legal historians therefore often take more notice of general history than general historians take account of legal history.[1] Friedrich Carl von Savigny, who is often acknowledged to have been the founder of the *Historische Rechtsschule*, considered jurisprudence to be a historical science, whose job was to capture the substance of law as it had historically grown, to make it expedient for the law that was or is in force.[2] Structural aspects rather than the role of actors have therefore for a long time been at the centre of attention of legal historians while individuals only mattered as creative minds within a larger development of legal doctrine. Their individual ideas were in general only possible to develop within the given framework of the dominating era. This seems to be, for instance, how Wilhelm Grewe understands the troubling fact that although the 16th and early 17th centuries were a period when international law was dominated by Spanish expansionism, the most well-known lawyers at the time were Dutch or English (e.g. Grotius); they were, as he puts it, "in einer polemischen Abhängigkeit von den Spanischen Ideen und Begriffen verfangen."[3] Or take Martti Koskenniemi's *The Gentle Civilizer on Nations* that seems to argue that the reason why the first generation of professional international lawyers in the classical period (second half of the 19th century) never agreed to a common ideological understanding of society was that they were already united through the inner sensibility that was a result from their (bourgeois) upbringing.[4] This theory of sensibility also surfaces in for instance David Kennedy's theories of contemporary relations of legal relations.[5] However,

1 Dipper, 2005, pp. 57–58.
2 Savigny, 1815, p. 6; Klippel, 2002, p. 127.
3 Grewe, 1943, p. 40. Cf. Grewe, 1984, Grewe, 2000 or Ziegler, 1994 on the dominating legal doctrines within the epochs of international law.
4 Koskenniemi, 2001, p. 88.
5 Kennedy, 2016, p. 18.

in all these cases, what we see is a causal structure superimposed on the actions of individuals. It is not clear whether the intention is to explain the actions, or merely to give them a meaning through absorbing them into a greater whole.

On the other hand, history – as a consequence of historicism, which confined itself more and more to an analysis of the political dimension and dominated the field for much of the 19th century and partially well into the 20th century – generally focused much more on the actions of dominating (mainly political and male) actors. This kind of history is generally called hero history. In 1840, the Scottish philosopher Thomas Carlyle argued in his book *On Heroes, Hero-Worship and the Heroic in History*, that a small number of important persons, through their decisions, had a distinct influence on history.[6] It is probably a good guess that the figures of Napoleon Bonaparte and Wellington a few decades earlier had inspired him, but this belief in extraordinary personalities also signifies how secularization still lingered. The Russian Marxist Georgi Plechanov challenged Carlyle's understanding and discussed its limits in the famous article *The Role of the Individual in History* (1898, originally in Russian):

> Carlyle, in his well-known book on heroes and hero-worship, calls great men *beginners*. This is a very apt description. A great man is precisely a beginner because he sees *further* than others, and desires things *more strongly* than others. He solves the scientific problems brought up by the preceding process of intellectual development of society; he points to the new social needs created by the preceding development of social relationships; he takes the initiative in satisfying these needs. He is a hero. But he is not a hero in the sense that he can stop, or change, the natural course of things, but in the sense that his activities are the conscious and free expression of this inevitable and unconscious course.[7]

Understood this way, the individual actor seemed more like the carrier of impersonal tendencies than someone who autonomously influences the sequence of events. This perspective began to gain ground in general history at the beginning of the 20th century not least as a consequence of the Annales school in France, which showed a larger interest in structures and mentalities.[8] As a consequence, in the 20th century the fields of legal and general history moved closer towards each other, as the former began to take a greater interest in the role of individuals beyond their specific influence on the development of legal doctrine while general history moved in the opposite direction. The individual actor did, however, not play an essential role in this context. This began to change with the upsurge of cultural history – sometimes also linked to the idea of a more general cultural turn[9] – when the perspective of individuals and their motivations finally

6 Carlyle, 1840.
7 Plechanov, 1961, p. 32.
8 Burke, 2015, pp. 13–14.
9 Bachmann-Medick, 2006, who stresses the diversity of cultural turns; Landwehr, 2013.

began to be more and more influential in both legal and general history.[10] In contrast to the earlier "hero history," agency is now clearly understood within an existing structural framework. On the other hand, the contingency of epochs is challenged[11] while a concept of co-existing "layers of time" or *Zeitschichten* as Reinhard Koselleck calls them[12] forms the basic framework, in which individual actors operate.

14.2 Actors and structures

Looking at actors in international law, as this section of the book is going to do, we generally talk about someone who influences the shape of the law, either by drafting it or through adjudication. In this context, anyone trying to influence international law has to grapple with two kinds of structures. On one hand, there is the social and historical context where and when the intervention takes place. On the other hand, law is itself a structure with a certain kind of inertia (or rather, in Fernand Braudel's terms, a conjuncture).[13] To the extent that the latter also binds the former through institutional arrangements, there is a dialectical connection between the two. The space for individual action seems very limited. Yet, histories of international law are full of individual authors, who were mostly, but not exclusively lawyers, and historical development is often described as a sequence of works of individual legal scholars, each giving their contribution.[14]

Interpolation – showing how a development in international law was introduced – is one of the ways, in which international law is historicized or of the way the history of international law is used by present-day international legal specialists.[15] In these contexts, the primary relevance of history is to explain, how present-day law – be it national or international – came into being and/or, as in the case of Christopher Keith Hall, to point to the visionary character of past proposals, to strengthen the hands of those that go into a similar direction in the present.[16] This can be called a legal history approach to the historization of law, in which history has mainly a serving role to current-day legal processes. Of course, it would be too easy to say that this is the only way that legal historians, most of the time affiliated with legal departments, look at the history of law, but the fact that at least in German-speaking countries many legal historians at the same time teach at least one branch of present-day law in their universities, drives many of them into such a direction. This has also lead to an intensive debate on the use and the significance of legal history within the legal curriculum.[17] It is

10 Mommsen, 2004, pp. 34–37, Tallgren and Mégret, forthcoming.
11 Osterhammel, 2006.
12 Koselleck, 2003.
13 Braudel, 1980, p. 27.
14 Cf. for instance, the section on personalities in Fassbender et al., 2012.
15 Cf. for example Bergsmo et al. (Eds.), 2014–2015 and Kesmati, 2015, pp. 649–682.
16 Hall, 1998, pp. 59–78. Cf. Segesser's contribution to this section of the book.
17 Klippel, 2002, pp. 126 and 131–133.

in this context that legal historians like Pio Caroni, Diethelm Klippel or Thomas Vormbaum have stressed the importance of the fact that in its methodology legal history should follow a more historical approach based on a closer co-operation between historians and legal specialists.[18] In this connection, law should and could be understood much more than so far as a social and cultural category that needs to be analysed accordingly, including a broader contextualization of the development of legal norms in its political, social, cultural and economic context.[19] This is what Diethelm Klippel has called a "holistic legal history," which looks at legal norms in their relationship to ideas as well as human behaviour.[20]

14.3 Law and its makers

When we invite living people into history as actual actors, we also open the space for chance events, for idiosyncratic thoughts, for decisions taken with insufficient information and with particularistic motives – for passions, misunderstandings, ideologies and religion.[21] We also invite power and struggle, and a certain dialectic between actor and structure. As Karl Marx put it in his third Feuerbach thesis,

> The materialist doctrine that men are products of circumstances and upbringing, and that, therefore, changed men are products of changed circumstances and changed upbringing, forgets that it is men who change circumstances and that the educator must himself be educated.[22]

Law, on the other hand, does not just happen. Lawyers are not only the products of their historical circumstances; they also have to navigate within legal structures that are the result of struggles engaged in by their predecessors.[23] This is what gives legal doctrine a certain inertia, which many of those involved see as necessary for law to fulfil one of its essential functions, which is to guarantee peace as well as the social, political and economic stability and integrity of a certain society or of the international community.[24] While philosophers and novelists and for that matter economists can write new books, legal entrepreneurs generally have to engage with existing texts (law) in a piecemeal way. There seems to be a homology with how urban planners and architects rarely get to work in uncharted territories but have to work on the margins of historically

18 Caroni, 2005, pp. 27–29; Klippel, 2002, pp. 133–135; Vormbaum, 2007, p. 1.

19 Examples for such an approach are Holquist, forthcoming; Lewis, 2014, p. 7, Segesser, 2010 and Segesser, 2013, pp. 103–105.

20 Klippel, 2002, pp. 140–141.

21 Lovejoy, 1936, p. 22.

22 Marx, 2002.

23 Kennedy, 2016.

24 On the functions of law cf. Zippelius, 2012, pp. 80–98, on the interdependency of inertia and change in international law cf. Kimminich and Hobe, 2000, pp. 25–28.

constituted *built environment*. Legal work generally takes place within the confines of what we might call a *written* (or maybe more correct, codified) environment, with contextual prudence.

To understand how this may be done, and to escape the aporias that result from just binding actors to structural tendencies, one would need to specify more clearly, what is at stake when a human being decides anything. In other words, we need to talk about what an intentional explanation, in contrast to a causal explanation, would mean. Intentional explanations take the form of rationalities, and especially the idea of rational choice, as in liberal ideology and economic theory. To give humans the power to make autonomous and informed choices – which is what we do when we give them the ability to change the course of history – we need to fulfil a number of conditions. The Norwegian philosopher Jon Elster has helpfully divided the preconditions of these choices into two parts: the optimality part and the causal part. To fulfil the optimality part, we need to be sure that the human being follows a unique set of desires (i.e., really does what she wants), and furthermore bases her actions on beliefs that are in their turn based on the best evidence that is possible to gather at the moment (i.e., she knows what she is doing). The causal part in its turn needs to show that the beliefs were actually based on the evidence and the action actually based on the beliefs and the desires (leaving aside the basis of desire), and that is of course the trickier part to prove (although historians have many times tried).[25] This way of reasoning could be simplified through ideal-type rationalities such as those Max Weber created, but it is also question of emphasis, on how much we want to emphasize the individual and how much the context.

14.4 This section

In this last part of the book, we present three ways of dealing with the individuals' influence on legal history. Mark Klamberg shows in his chapter, how the Polish-American lawyer Raphaël Lemkin initially wanted to give his conception of Genocide a broader meaning, including also the protection of cultural artefacts. However, this was not only an attempt to broaden the scope to the convention – and the national laws that would be its result – but also a way to redefine the object of its protection and to give it a not only wider but perhaps also a deeper and more collective meaning. While the genocide convention in the end became merely a protection against mass killing of the human beings belonging to a certain group, protection for cultural artefacts would keep also the symbolic values of the group and for longer time spans than any individual life would last. In the end however, the protection of cultural artefacts continued to form a separate area of international law, without connections to the genocide concept.

25 Elster, 1988.

Daniel Marc Segesser sheds light on the little-known predecessor of the International Criminal Court that was formulated in 1872 by the president of what was to become the International Committee of the Red Cross, Gustave Moynier. His proposal was caused by the criticism directed against the still new Geneva Convention after numerous infractions during the war between Germany and France 1870–1871. It was modelled on rules for arbitrations that Moynier could observe first-hand in his native Geneva, where a settlement was negotiated between representatives of the US and UK after the conflictual sea blockade of the confederate states during the American Civil War. Just like Lemkin, Moynier had to accept that his proposal met little enthusiasm, and together with the rest of the committee he had to negotiate its surrender as part of the ultimately successful campaign to save the Geneva Convention. As Segesser points out, however, the fact that most states focused on the development of their national penal law during this period further diminished the chances for experiments with a transnational court.

The last chapter also deals with the Red Cross. Mats Deland discusses the background of the forming of the national branch in Sweden and finds it less in military needs than in a feminist campaign to broaden the access to higher education for women – where education of nurses became an important station on the course to the ultimate aim, academic medical training. However, contemporary gender ideas, largely derived from Lutheran theology, forced women to work in the background, with sympathetic men as vehicles for their aims, which has made their efforts almost invisible into our days.

Altogether, these chapters show that to grasp the influence of individuals of social and legal structures, it is mandatory to take into account the whole range of human motivations through detailed investigations. Structural history can only be an approximation, but still needs to be considered as the essential context, in which individuals were able to present their ideas and struggle for their implementation.

References

Doris Bachmann-Medick, *Cultural Turns. Neuorientierungen in den Kulturwissenschaften*, Rowohlt-Verlag, Reinbeck bei Hamburg, 2006.

Morten Bergsmo, Wui Ling Cheah, Song Tianying, Yi Ping (Eds.), *Historical Origins of International Criminal Law*, vols. 4, TOAEP, Brussels, 2014–2015.

Fernand Braudel, *On History* (1969, transl. Sarah Matthews), University of Chicago Press, Chicago, 1980.

Peter Burke, *The French Historical Revolution: The Annales School 1929–2014*, Stanford University Press, Stanford, 2015.

Thomas Carlyle, *On Heroes, Hero-Worship and the Heroic in History*, James Fraser, London, 1840.

Pio Caroni, "Blicke über den Gartenzaun: Von den Beziehungen der Rechtsgeschichte zu ihren historischen Nachbarwissenschaften", in Louis Pahlow (Ed.), *Die zeitliche Dimension des Rechts: Historische Rechtsforschung und geschichtliche Rechtswissenschaft*, Ferdinand Schöningh Verlag, Paderborn, 2005, pp. 27–55.

Christof Dipper, "Geschichtswissenschaft und Rechtsgeschichte", in Louis Pahlow (Ed.), *Die zeitliche Dimension des Rechts: Historische Rechtsforschung und geschichtliche Rechtswissenschaft*, Ferdinand Schöningh Verlag, Paderborn, 2005, pp. 56–73.

Jon Elster, "The Nature and Scope of Rational-Choice Explanation", in Edna Ullmann-Margalit (Ed.), *Science in Reflection*, Kluwer Academic Publishers, Dordrecht, 1988.

Bardo Fassbender, Anne Peters, Simone Peter and Daniel Högger, *The Oxford Handbook of the History of International Law*, Oxford University Press, Oxford, 2012.

Wilhelm G. Grewe, "Die Epochen den modernen Völkerrechtsgeschichte, erster Teil", *Zeitschrift für die gesamte Staatswissenschaft*, vol. 103, no. 1, 1943, pp. 38–66.

Wilhelm G. Grewe, *Epochen der Völkerrechtsgeschichte*, Nomos Verlagsgesellschaft, Baden-Baden, 1984.

Wilhelm G. Grewe, *The Epochs of International Law*, Walter de Gruyter, Belin, 2000.

Christopher Keith Hall, "Première proposition de Création d'une Cour Criminelle Internationale Permanente", *Revue Internationale de la Croix-Rouge*, vol. 80, no. 829, 1998, pp. 59–78.

Peter Holquist, *By Right of War: Imperial Russia and the Making of the 'Laws of War' (1868–1917)*, forthcoming.

David Kennedy, *A World of Struggle, How Power, Law, and Expertise Shape Global Political Economy*, Princeton University Press, Princeton, 2016.

Zahra Kesmati, "The Evolution of Conspiracy as a Mode of Collective Criminal Liability since Nuremberg", in Morten Bergsmo, Wui Ling Cheah, Song Tianying, Yi Ping (Eds.), *Historical Origins of International Criminal Law*, 4 Vols., vol. 3, TOAEP, Brussels, 2015, pp. 649–682.

Otto Kimminich and Stephan Hobe, *Einführung in das Völkerrecht*, Francke, Tübingen, 2000.

Diethelm Klippel, "Rechtsgeschichte", in Joachim Eibach and Günther Lottes (Eds.), *Kompass der Geschichtswissenschaft: Ein Handbuch*, UTB, Göttingen, 2002, pp. 126–141.

Martti Koskenniemi, *The Gentle Civilizer of Nations, The Rise and Fall of International Law 1870–1960*, Cambridge University Press, Cambridge, 2001.

Achim Landwehr, "Kulturgeschichte, Version: 1.0", in Docupedia-Zeitgeschichte, 14 May 2013, available at: http://docupedia.de/zg/Kulturgeschichte?oldid=125506 (accessed 13 April 2018).

Mark Lewis, *The Birth of New Justice: The Internationalization of Crime and Punishment, 1919–1950*, Oxford University Press, Oxford, 2014.

Arthur O. Lovejoy, *The Great Chain of Being. A Study in the History of an Idea*, Harvard University Press, Cambridge MA, 1936.

Karl Marx, "Feuerbach Theses, 1845" (transl. Cyril Smith and Don Cuckson), 2002. Available at: www.marxists.org/archive/marx/works/1845/theses/ (accessed 13 April 2018).

Wolfgang J. Mommsen, "Die Geschichtswissenschaft am Ende des 20. Jahrhunderts", in Christoph Cornelissen (Ed.), *Geschichtswissenschaften: Eine Einführung* (3rd ed.), Fischer Taschenbuch Verlag, Frankfurt am Main, 2004, pp. 26–38.

Jürgen Osterhammel, "Über die Periodisierung der neueren Geschichte", in *Berichte und Abhandlungen der Berlin-Brandenburgischen Akademie der Wissenschaften*, vol. 10, 2006, pp. 45–64.

Georgi V. Plechanov, "On the Role of the Individual in History" (1898, transl. John Heckman). *Selected Works II*, Lawrence & Wishhart, Dagenham, 1961.

Friedrich Carl von Savigny, "Ueber den Zweck dieser Zeitschrift", *Zeitschrift für geschichtliche Rechtswissenschaft*, vol. 1, 1815, pp. 1–17.

Daniel Marc Segesser, *Recht statt Rache oder Rache durch Recht? Die Ahndung von Kriegsverbrechen in der internationalen wissenschaftlichen Debatte 1872–1945*, Ferdinand Schöning Verlag, Paderborn, 2010.

Daniel Marc Segesser, "'Integrale Rechtsgeschichte': Ein interdisziplinärer Einblick in die Forschung in der Schweiz", *traverse: Zeitschrift für Geschichte – Revue d'Histoire*, vol. 20, no. 1, 2013, pp. 103–121.

Immi Tallgren and Frédéric Mégret (Eds.), *The Dawn of a Discipline: International Criminal Justice and its Early Exponents*, forthcoming.

Thomas Vormbaum, "Zum Geleit", *Journal der Juristischen Zeitgeschichte: Zeitschrift für die Rechtsgeschichte des 19. bis 21. Jahrhunderts*, no. 1, 2007, p. 1.

Karl-Heinz Ziegler, *Völkerrechtsgeschichte: Ein Studienbuch*, C.H. Beck'sche Verlagsbuchhandlung, Munich, 1994.

Reinhold Zippelius, *Grundbegriffe der Rechts- und Staatssoziologie*, Mohr Siebeck, Tübingen, 2012.

15 Lemkin on vandalism and the protection of cultural works and historical monuments during armed conflict

Mark Klamberg

15.1 Introduction

The destruction of cultural property has been subject to different attempts of criminalization at the criminal level and international prosecution is only a recent phenomenon. The conflict in Syria has not only led to massive human casualties and suffering but also the destruction of cultural and historical monuments, maybe most well known is the demolition by the Islamic State (IS)/ DAESH of cultural works in Palmyra. There may be several reasons for such destruction: symbolic, part of erasing an ethnicity or part of breaking the moral resistance of an enemy.[1] The destruction of cultural property may be part of an armed conflict as the case of Palmyra illustrates. It may also occur in the absence or an armed conflict as the Taliban's destruction March 2001 of the Buddhas of Bamiyian in Afghanistan shows. Cultural property is not only vulnerable in terms of destruction; it may also be subject to other crimes such as theft and illicit transport, during armed conflict as well as during peace.[2] This study focuses on the destruction of cultural property with a starting point with the concept used by Raphaël Lemkin: vandalism and his attempt to include it into genocide convention. Was Lemkin's effort key to the present status of the protection of cultural works and historical monuments under international law or merely a sidetrack? I will start with a general discussion on the history of legal protection of cultural artefacts, and Lemkin's intervention in part 2. In the subsequent parts, 3–5, I will follow the development to the present.

15.2 Vandalism and the genocide convention

In antiquity, there was no legal protection for cultural property against plunder, pillage or destruction. Instead, it was considered a legitimate aim of war, spoils belonging to the conqueror.[3] There were some attempts during the renaissance

1 Ehlert, 2013, p. 1.
2 Ibid, p. 2.
3 Cunning, 2003, pp. 212–213; Ehlert, 2013, p. 15.

to protect cultural works.[4] The Lieber code of 1863 was the first modern ratification of the laws of war; it included protection of cultural property and contained the first attempt to include penal norms for the destruction of such property.[5] Article 17 of the 1874 Brussels Declaration repeated largely the principles of the Lieber Code.[6] The term "cultural property" is absent from the 1907 Hague Conventions and the 1907 Hague Regulations. Article 27 of the regulations does contain a reference to cultural property when it states that "[i]n sieges and bombardments all necessary steps must be taken to spare, as far as possible, buildings dedicated to religion, art, science, or charitable purposes, historic monuments."[7] Article 5 of the Hague Convention (IX) contains a similar provision.[8] Ehlert has commented "that in the 1907 Hague Regulations 'buildings dedicated to religion' do not only comprise Christian churches, as protected by former treaties, but also mosques, synagogues and other buildings which represent religious views."[9] In 1922, an international commission drafted The Hague Rules Concerning the Control of Radio in Time of War and Air Fare.[10] Although the 1922 Hague never entered into force and remained recommendations, Ehlert notes that the rules "exerted a great influence on future developments relating to the law of wars as well as the protection of cultural property."[11]

Raphaël Lemkin is known for coining the term "genocide" when he published his book *Axis Rule in Occupied Europe* (1944). By the 1930s, Lemkin was known internationally as a scholar in international criminal law, participating in and contributing to conferences across Europe, notably conferences in Paris (1931), Madrid (1933), Budapest, Copenhagen (1935), Hague (1937), Paris (1937), Amsterdam and Cairo.[12] For the 1933 Madrid conference, Lemkin prepared a draft report that suggested outlawing the acts of "barbarism" and "vandalism" by identifying them as international crimes. He later used this as a basis for his proposal to outlaw genocide, made in *Axis Rule in Occupied Europe.*[13]

4 Grotius, 1995, Book 3, Chapter 12, pp. 751–754, paras. 6–7; Vattel, 1995, Chapter IX, pp. 139–140, para. 168; Ehlert, 2013, pp. 17–19.
5 Instructions for the Government of Armies of the United States in the Field prepared by Francis Lieber and promulgated as General Orders No. 100 by President Lincoln on 24 April 1863, articles 35 and 44.
6 Project of an International Declaration concerning the Laws and Customs of War. Brussels, 27 August 1874.
7 Hague Convention (IV) respecting the Laws and Customs of War on Land and its annex: Regulations concerning the Laws and Customs of War on Land, The Hague, 18 October 1907, article 27, see also article 56.
8 Hague Convention (IX) on Bombardment by Naval Forces in Time of War, The Hague, 18 October 1907.
9 Ehlert, 2013, p. 28.
10 Hague Rules on Air Warfare, The Hague, December 1922–February 1923, reprinted in Schindler/Toman, pp. 315–328.
11 Ehlert, 2013, p. 24.
12 Frieze 2013, pp. 68, 106; Power, 2002, pp. 19, 21–23; Szawłowski, 2005, p. 113; Segesser and Gessler 2005, p. 458; Schabas, 2009, pp. 29–30; Sands, p. 177.
13 Frieze 2013, pp. 68 and 232; Segesser and Gessler, 2005, p. 457; Vrdoljak, 2009, pp. 1176–1177, 1183; Lewis, 2015, p. 643.

Lemkin had received information that, as a consequence of efforts of the anti-Semitic newspaper *Gazeta Warszawska*, the Polish Minister of Justice was opposed to him attending the Madrid conference.[14] From the official documents of the Madrid conference, it seems that Lemkin was not personally present at the conference, which may explain why his report was dropped.[15] The crime of barbarity consisted of "destroying a national or religious collectivity" and the crime of vandalism consisted of "destroying works of culture, which represented the specific genius of these national and religious groups." Lemkin wanted to preserve both the physical existence and the spiritual life of these collectivities.[16] The proposal on outlawing "barbarism" and "vandalism" was of relevance for genocide because of their focus on group protection.[17] The basic idea of the proposal, as Lemkin subsequently formulated, was that "an international treaty should be negotiated declaring that attacks upon national, religious and ethnic groups should be made international crimes, and that perpetrators of such crimes should not only be liable for trial in their own countries but, in the event of escape, could also be tried in the place of refuge, or else extradited to a the country where the crime was committed."[18] This proposal was developed further in *Axis Rule in Occupied Europe:* genocide should be prohibited in war and peace and universal repression of genocide should be included in an international multilateral treaty as well as in domestic criminal codes.[19] Lemkin described the cultural field as an area where techniques of genocide were used by the German authorities. This included prohibiting the local population from using its own language in schools and in printing; excluding the population from liberal arts studies; control over cultural activities with requirement for persons engaging in the cultural field to obtain a license; burning of books; censoring of plays and operas; destruction of national monuments and the removal of libraries, archives, museums and galleries of art.[20] Lemkin was as concerned with the loss of culture as with the loss of life. He argued that mass murder should not be confused with genocide, stating that, "mass-murder or extermination do not convey the elements of selection and do not indicate the losses in terms of culture represented by the nation's victims."[21]

Cultural techniques of the Nazi genocide were highlighted in some of the post-war trials. In the RuSHA trial, which concerned various SS organizations and their racial policies of genocide, the defendants were charged with "acts, conduct, plans, and enterprises … as part of a systematic program of genocide … in

14 Frieze 2013, pp. 22–23; Cooper, 2008, pp. 20–21; Sands, 2016, pp. 160–161.

15 Segesser and Gessler, 2005, p. 458.

16 Frieze 2013, p. 22; Lemkin, 2008, p. 91.

17 Dirk, 2010, pp. 30, 33.

18 Lemkin, 1944, p. xiii.

19 Ibid, pp. 90–94.

20 Ibid, pp. 84–85, 139.

21 Memorandum from Raphael Lemkin to R. Kempner, 5 June 1946. United States Holocaust Memorial Museum, R. Kempner Papers (RS 71.001) quoted in and discussed Moses, 2010, p. 28, 34.

part by murderous extermination, and in part by elimination and suppression of national characteristics."[22] As Lippman noted, "[t]he notion that the Nazi's destruction [...] of cultural property was a component of genocide was most fully articulated in the prosecution of Artur Greiser, former Governor and National Socialist leader in Poznan in the annexed Polish territories."[23] In the *Greiser* case, the Supreme National Tribunal of Poland found the defendant guilty of "genocidal attacks on Polish culture and learning."[24] In the *Goeth* case, the same tribunal found the defendant guilty of "[t]he wholesale extermination of Jews and also of Poles [which] had all the characteristics of genocide in the biological meaning of this term, and embraced in addition the destruction of the cultural life of these nations."[25]

The UN General Assembly affirmed 11 December 1946 in resolution 96(1) that genocide is a crime under international law and requested the Economic and Social Council (ECOSOC) to "undertake the necessary studies, with a view to drawing up a draft convention on the crime of genocide."[26] ECOSOC instructed 28 March 1947 the UN Secretary-General to "undertake with the assistance of experts in the field of international and criminal law, the necessary studies" and draft a convention on the crime of genocide.[27] The UN Secretariat's Legal Department and Human Rights Department selected three jurists from the International Association of Penal Law (Association Internationale de Droit Pénal, "AIDP"), Lemkin, Pella and Donnedieu de Vabres, to write the first draft of the Genocide Convention in 1947. While Lemkin had a Polish-Jewish refugee background, Pella had remained a Romanian diplomat under the Antonescu military dictatorship. However, Pella claimed that he played a mitigating role and tried to negotiate Romania's exit from the war. A Swiss diplomatic report from 1943 states that he opposed Romania's fascist party, the Iron Guard. Donnedieu de Vabres had been France's chief judge at Nuremberg.[28]

The 1947 draft of the Genocide convention contained three categories of genocide: physical, biological and cultural genocide. There were five subcategories in relation to cultural genocide: (a) forced transfer of children to another human group; (b) forced and systematic exile of individuals representing the culture of a group; (c) prohibition of the use of the national language even in private

22 Trials of War Criminals Before the Nuernberg Military Tribunals Under Countrol Council Law No. 10, published 1949, reprinted 1997 by William S. Hein & Co. Buffalo, New York (Trials of War Criminals Before the Nuernberg Military Tribunals Under Control Council Law No. 10), vol. IV, p. 15, 609–610.

23 Lippman, p. 59. See also Frulli, 2005, p. 211 and Ehlert, 2013, p. 34, n. 88.

24 *Poland v. Greiser*, 1948, Supreme National Tribunal of Poland, Law Reports of Trials of War Criminals (LRTWC), London: Published 1947–1949 for The United Nations War Crimes Commission by His Majesty's Stationery Office, vol. XIII, p. 112.

25 *Poland v. Goeth*, 1946, Supreme National Tribunal of Poland, ibid, vol. VII, p. 9. See comment by Schabas, 2009, p. 207.

26 General Assembly resolution 96 (I) of 11 December 1946 (The Crime of Genocide).

27 Economic and Social Council resolution 47 (IV) of 28 March 1947 (Crime of genocide) (E/437 (E/325)).

28 Lewis, 2015, p. 647, 652–653.

intercourse; (d) systematic destruction of books printed in the national language or of religious works, or prohibition of new publications and (e) systematic destruction of historical or religious monuments or their diversion to alien uses, destruction or dispersion of documents and objects of historical, artistic or religious value, and of objects used in religious worship.[29] This section gave rise to divergent views among the experts. Professor Donnedieu de Vabres and Professor Pella held "that cultural genocide represented an undue extension of the notion of genocide." Lemkin argued the following:

> a racial, national, or religious group cannot continue to exist unless it preserves its spirit and moral unity. Such a group's right to existence was justified not only from the moral point to view, but also from the point of view of the value of the contribution made by such a group to civilization generally. … cultural genocide was much more than just a policy of forced assimilation by moderate coercion – involving for example, prohibition of the opening of schools for teaching the language of the group concerned, of the publication of newspapers printed in that language, of the use of that language in the official documents and in court, and so on. It was a policy which by drastic methods, aimed at the rapid and complete disappearance of the cultural, moral and religious life of a group of human beings.[30]

Lemkin thus fused the concepts of "barbarism" – physical and biological destruction of a group – and "vandalism" – the destruction of cultural works – into genocide. Lemkin tried to get cultural genocide into the Genocide convention, it was in the 1947 Draft presented by the UN Secretariat[31] and was recognized in April 1948 by the Ad Hoc committee on Genocide.[32] Perez-Perozo (Venezuela), who was member of the Ad Hoc committee, expressed the rationale behind this idea and stated that

> [t]he cultural bond was one of the most important factors among those which united a national group, and that was so true that it was possible to wipe out a human group, as such, by destroying its cultural heritage, while allowing the individual members to survive.[33]

The drafters included

> 1. Prohibiting the use of the language of the groups in daily intercourse or in schools, or the printing and circulation of publications in the language

29 Draft Convention on the Crime of Genocide (E/447, 26 June 1947), pp. 26–28.
30 Ibid, p. 27, see comment by Lippman, 1998, p. 60 and Ehlert, 2013, p. 34.
31 Draft Convention on the Crime of Genocide (A/362, 25 August 1947), article 1(II)(3).
32 Ad Hoc Committee on Genocide: summary record of the 5th meeting, held at Lake Success, New York, Tuesday, 8 April 1948, p. 8.
33 Ibid, p. 2.

> of the group; 2. Destroying, or preventing the use of, libraries, museums, schools, historical monuments, places of worship and other cultural institutions and objects of the group.[34]

The Sixth Committee of the UN General Assembly decided to omit the provision on cultural genocide. During the General Assembly Debate in October 1948, Mr. Khomussko, delegate of the Byelorussian Soviet Socialist Republic, argued that the deletion of a provision on cultural genocide "would be tantamount to stating in advance that crimes against the culture, religion or language of a group would remain unpunished."[35] However, it did not get support by the states and was subsequently excluded from the 1948 Genocide convention.[36]

Since the negotiations of the Genocide Convention, the issue of cultural genocide has been less discussed. The issue resurfaced in the context of the conflict in former Yugoslavia. The ICTY Trial Chamber rejected in *Krstić* the idea of cultural genocide by stating the following:

> It therefore recognises that, despite recent developments, customary international law limits the definition of genocide to those acts seeking the physical or biological destruction of all or part of the group. Hence, an enterprise attacking only the cultural or sociological characteristics of a human group in order to annihilate these elements which give to that group its own identity distinct from the rest of the community would not fall under the definition of genocide.[37]

However, destruction of cultural and religious property and symbols could be still relevant as evidence whether genocide occurred. The Trial Chamber stated the following:

34 Report of the Ad Hoc Committee on Genocide and draft Convention drawn up by the Committee, 5 April–10 May 1948 (E/794), article III.

35 UN General Assembly, UNGAOR, 3rd Sess., Part I, 6th Committee, 83rd Meeting, 25 October 1948, p. 202.

36 Ibid, p. 205: "a number of delegations held the view that the protection of groups against acts of cultural genocide could very well be ensured by the declaration of human rights, and that the idea of cultural genocide was not yet sufficiently developed to warrant its inclusion in the convention." See comments by Lippman, 1998, pp. 61–62; Schabas, 2009, pp. 61, 207–221 and 646; Moses, 2010, pp. 33, 37–38. Compare with Lewis, 2015, p. 653 who observes "the trio disagreed about whether genocide could be construed to mean the destruction of a group's culture, such as its religious sites and educational institutions, not just the murder of the group. Lemkin believed that such cultural suppression could be used to eliminate a group, even if it was not physically destroyed, but Donnedieu de Vabres and Pella believed that this problem was a civil one, not a criminal one – an issue that the interwar Minorities Treaties covered."

37 *Prosecutor v Krstić,* (Case No IT-98-33), ICTY T Ch , Judgment, 2 August 2001, para. 580; *Prosecutor v. Krstić* (Case No. IT-98-33-A), ICTY A. Ch., Judgment 19 April 2004, paras. 25–26.

> The Trial Chamber however points out that where there is physical or biological destruction there are often simultaneous attacks on the cultural and religious property and symbols of the targeted group as well, attacks which may legitimately be considered as evidence of an intent to physically destroy the group. In this case, the Trial Chamber will thus take into account as evidence of intent to destroy the group the deliberate destruction of mosques and houses belonging to members of the group.[38]

The findings of the Trial Chamber in this regard were upheld by the majority of the Appeals Chamber. However, Judge Shahabuddeen issued a dissenting opinion where he argued the following:

> Counsel for the appellant understandably relies on views expressed by the International Law Commission in 1991. Referring to the standard formula concerning "intent to destroy", the Commission stated that "the word 'destruction' ... must be taken only in its material sense, its physical or biological sense." The focus there was on whether the term "genocide", as used in the Convention, included cultural genocide, the generally accepted answer being in the negative. If that does not account for the view expressed by the Commission, then, with respect, that view is not correct. The intent certainly has to be to destroy, but, except for the listed act, there is no reason why the destruction must always be physical or biological.[39]

The International Court of Justice (ICJ) endorsed the rejection of the concept of "cultural genocide" in the *Genocide* case. The ICJ made a reference to the preparatory works of the Genocide convention, the *Krstić* case and stated the following:

> in the Court's view, the destruction of historical, cultural and religious heritage cannot be considered to constitute the deliberate infliction of conditions of life calculated to bring about the physical destruction of the group. Although such destruction may be highly significant inasmuch as it is directed to the elimination of all traces of the cultural or religious presence of a group, and contrary to other legal norms, it does not fall within the categories of acts of genocide set out in Article II of the Convention.[40]

38 *Prosecutor v. Krstić,* ICTY T. Ch. I, 2 August 2001, para. 580; see comment by Schabas, 2009, pp. 216–221.

39 *Prosecutor v. Krstić*, ICTY A. Ch., 19 April 2004 dissenting opinion of Judge Shahabuddeen, paras. 51 and 53. For the majority view, see paras. 25–26 of the Appeal judgement.

40 *Application of The Convention on the Prevention and Punishment of the Crime of Genocide (Bosnia and Herzegovina v. Serbia and Montenegro)*, ICJ, Judgment of 26 February 2007 (ICJ), para. 344.

To summarize, while the current definition of genocide covers barbarism and as such physical and biological genocide, vandalism and protection of cultural property during armed conflict is instead part of the law of international humanitarian law (IHL) and may amount to a war crime.

15.3 Destruction of cultural property as a war crime

The offence of destruction of cultural property in its modern form has its starting point in articles 27 and 56 of the Hague Regulations.[41] Even though cultural genocide was excluded from the 1948 convention, destruction of cultural property was as noted above firmly established as a war crime after the Second World War.[42] The International Military Tribunal in Nuremberg confronted "the suggestion that the purpose of seizure of art treasures was protective and meant for their preservation."[43] The Tribunal found that the purpose was "to enrich Germany by the seizures rather than to protect the seized objects."[44] The Tribunal held the following in relation to the defendant Rosenberg under the charges of war crimes and crimes against humanity:

> Rosenberg is responsible for a system of organized plunder of both public and private property throughout the invaded countries of Europe ... [He] organized and directed the "Einsatzstab Rosenberg," which plundered museums and libraries, confiscated art treasures and collections, and pillaged private houses. His own reports show the extent of the confiscations. In "Aktion-M" (Mobel), instituted in December 1941 at Rosenberg's suggestion, 69,619 Jewish homes were plundered in the West, 38,000 of them in Paris alone, and it took 26,984 railroad cars to transport the confiscated furnishings to Germany. As of 14 July 1944, more than 21,903 art objects, including famous paintings and museum pieces, had been seized by the Einsatzstab in the West.[45]

The Tribunal found Rosenberg guilty on all counts and he was sentenced to death by hanging.[46]

In the aftermath of Second World War, the four Geneva Conventions of 1949 were adopted. The Fourth Geneva Convention of 1949 (GC IV) does not deal specifically with the protection of cultural property. Ehlert has noted that "[i]t solely refers to the protection of property in general."[47] Article 53 provides that

41 Hague Convention (IV), regulations 1907.
42 See comment by Lippman, 1998, pp. 62–63.
43 Trial of the Major War Criminals before the International Military Tribunal, Volumes 1–42, published at Nuremberg 1947 reprinted 1995 by William S. Hein & Co. Buffalo, New York (Trial of the Major War Criminals before the International Military Tribunal), vol. 22, p. 485.
44 Ibid, vol. 22, p. 486.
45 Ibid, vol. 22, p. 540.
46 Ibid, vol. 22, pp. 541 and 588. See comment by Lippman, 1998, p. 46.
47 Ehlert, 2013, p. 40.

> [a]ny destruction by the Occupying Power of real or personal property belonging individually or collectively to private persons, or to the State, or to other public authorities, or to social or cooperative organizations, is prohibited, except where such destruction is rendered absolutely necessary by military operations.[48]

In addition, article 27 provides that "[p]rotected persons are entitled, in all circumstances, to respect for their persons, their honour, their family rights, their religious convictions and practices, and their manners and customs." In his comment on article 27, Pictet writes that "[p]rotected persons in the territory of a Party to the conflict or in occupied territory must be able to practise their religion freely, without any restrictions other than those necessary for the maintenance of public law and morals."[49] Heijden also perceives article 27 as part of the protection of cultural heritage during armed conflict.[50]

Article 53(a) of Additional Protocol I (AP I) prohibits acts of hostility directed against the historic monuments, works of art or places of worship which constitute the cultural or spiritual heritage of peoples. Moreover, article 85(4 (d) of the same protocol provides that attacks that cause extensive destruction to historic monuments, works of art or places of worship constitute grave breaches of the Protocol, as long as the objects are not used in support of the military effort and are not located in the immediate proximity of military objectives. The 1954 Hague Convention provides additional protection as explained in the next section.

15.4 The 1954 Hague convention

In 1949, the general conference of the United Nations Educational, Scientific and Cultural Organisation (UNESCO) instructed the Director-General of the organization to report to the General Conference next year on "measures suitable for ensuring the co-operation of interested States in the protection, preservation and restoration of antiquities, monuments and historic sites, and on the possibility of establishing an international fund to subsidize such preservation and restoration" with particular attention "to arrangements for the protection of such monuments, as well as to the protection of all objects of cultural value, particularly those kept in museums, libraries and archives, against the probable consequences of armed conflict."[51] Consequently, the Director-General organized a meeting of experts in 1950, followed by two more in subsequent years, to

48 Geneva Convention Relative to the Protection of Civilian Persons in Time of War of 12 August 1949.

49 Pictet, Jean S., ***Commentary on the Geneva Convention Relative to the Protection of Civilian Persons in Time of War of 12 August 1949*** (1958), p. 203.

50 Heijden, Iris van der, 'Other Issues Relating to the Treatment of Civilians in Enemy Hands' in Clapham, 2015, pp. 1246–1247.

51 Records of The General Conference of the United Nations Educational, Scientific and Cultural Organization, Fourth Session, Paris, 1949, 4 C/Resolution 6.42.

draft a convention on the protection of cultural property in the event of armed conflict.[52]

This led to the 1954 Hague Convention, which was the first international convention to exclusively address the subject of cultural property.[53] Under the convention, States are not only under obligation to respect the protection of cultural property, they must also – pursuant to IHL – deter individuals from committing violations and punish those violations that do occur.[54] Article 18 of the convention provides that it is applicable "in the event of declared war or of any other armed conflict which may arise between two or more of the High Contracting Parties, even if the state of war is not recognized by, one or more of them." This is the same threshold for applicability as common article 2 of the 1949 Geneva Conventions. Furthermore, the convention is also applicable during belligerent occupation pursuant to article 18(2) and in non-international armed conflicts pursuant to article 19. The convention offers general protection (chapter I) as well as special protection (chapter II). Destruction of cultural property is also a violation under customary international law and a war crime under the Rome Statute of the International Criminal Court as explained next.[55]

15.5 The Rome Statute and the Mali case

The goal of the drafters of the Rome Statute was that the provision on war crimes would reflect customary law. There was an agreement that the norms in The Hague Conventions and the 1949 Geneva Conventions gave rise to individual criminal responsibility under customary international law.[56] Destruction of cultural property is defined under the Rome Statute as a war crime of attacking protected objects under Article 8(2)(b)(ix) in an international armed conflict and Article 8(2)(e)(iv) in a non-international armed conflict. These provisions reflect customary international law.[57]

Elements of Crime "shall assist the Court in the interpretation and application" of the crimes in Articles 6, 7, 8 and 8 *bis*.[58] The material element of Articles 8(2)(b)(ix) and 8(2)(e)(iv) does not require any specific damage to the protected buildings or objects but does not exclude it either. There was some debate on

52 O'Keefe, 2006, pp. 92–93.

53 Convention on the Protection of Cultural Property in the Event of Armed Conflict adopted 14 May 1954; Gerstenblith, pp. 677–708.

54 1954 Hague Convention, articles 4(3) and 28; Werle, 2009, pp. 355–356, paras. 951–955; Ehlert, 2013, p. 4.

55 *Prosecutor v. Strugar* (Case No. IT-01-42), ICTY T. Ch., Judgement, 31 January 2005, paras. 229–230, 303–306; Rome Statute of the International Criminal Court, 17 July 1998, 2187 U.N.T.S. 90, article 8(2)(b)(ix). See also O'Keefe, 2006, pp. 317–343; Ehlert, 2013, p. 44 and Ehlert, 2017, pp. 89–91, 129–131.

56 von Hebel, Herman and Robinsson, Darryl, 1999, pp. 104–106 and 122; Klamberg, 2009, p. 399.

57 Werle, 2009, pp. 434–345, paras. 1190 and 1194.

58 Rome Statute, article 9.

this matter during the negotiations of the elements of crime where the Japanese proposal had required extensive destruction. This proposal was rejected in favour of US and Swiss proposals.[59]

The Trial Chamber in *Al Mahdi* traced the special protection of cultural property in international law back to Articles 27 and 56 of the 1907 Hague Regulations[60] and to the 1919 Commission on Responsibility, which identified "wanton destruction of religious, charitable, educational, and historic buildings and monuments" as a war crime.[61] It also mentioned the special protection of objects (such as hospitals) in the Geneva Conventions,[62] enhanced protection of cultural property in APs I and II to the Geneva Conventions[63] and the Second Protocol to the Hague Convention of 1954.[64] The Trial Chamber noted the following.

> The Chamber considers that the element of 'direct[ing] an attack' encompasses any acts of violence against protected objects and will not make a distinction as to whether it was carried out in the conduct of hostilities or after the object had fallen under the control of an armed group. ... The [Rome] Statute protects persons and cultural objects differently. Persons are protected by many distinct clauses that apply during hostilities, after an armed group has taken control, and against various and specific kinds of harm. However, cultural objects in non-international armed conflicts are protected as such, not generically as civilian objects, only in Article 8(2)(e)(iv), which makes no distinction between attacks made in the conduct of hostilities or afterwards.[65]

Al Mahdi was convicted of between 30 June 2012 and 11 July 2012 attacking religion and historic monuments with the status of protected UNESCO World Heritage sites, more specifically mausoleums and mosques in Timbuktu.[66]

59 Pfirter, 2001, pp. 162–163.

60 Hague Convention IV - Respecting the Laws and Customs of War on Land and annexed regulations adopted 18 October 1907, Articles 27 and 56.

61 'Commission on the Responsibility of the Authors of the War and on Enforcement of Penalities', 14, 1 *The American Journal of International Law* 1920, 95–154, p. 115: "Wanton destruction of religious, charitable, educational, and historic buildings and monuments."

62 Geneva Convention for the Amelioration of the Condition of the Wounded and Sick in Armed Forces in the Field of 12 August 1949 (GC I), Articles 19–23; Geneva Convention for the Amelioration of the Condition of Wounded, Sick and Shipwrecked Members of Armed Forces at Sea of 12 August 1949 (GC II), Articles 22, 23, 34–35; GC IV, Articles 14, 18 and 19.

63 Protocol Additional to the Geneva Conventions of 12 August 1949 and Relating to the Protection of Victims of International Armed Conflicts (Protocol I) of 8 June 1977, Article 53; Protocol Additional to the Geneva Conventions of 12 August 1949, and relating to the Protection of Victims of Non-International Armed Conflicts (Protocol II), 8 June 1977, Article 16.

64 Second Protocol to the Hague Convention of 1954 for the Protection of Cultural Property in the Event of Armed Conflict adopted 26 March 1999, Article 15; *Prosecutor v. Ahmad Al Faqi Al Mahdi* (Case No. ICC-01/12-01/15), ICC T. Ch. VIII, Judgment, 27 September 2016, para. 14.

65 *Al Mahdi*, ICC T. Ch. VIII, 27 September 2016, paras. 15–16.

66 Ibid, paras. 38–39, 46, 52, 62–63.

15.6 Conclusion: the evolution of the protection of cultural works and historical monuments during armed conflict

This study shows how the protection of cultural works and historical monuments has developed in different parts of international law, a process that in parts can be described as cumulative but also as parallel. The evolution of the protection under IHL from the 1907 Hague Regulations, the four Geneva Conventions, 1954 Hague Convention, the APs to the four Geneva Conventions and the Rome Statute is cumulative, confirmation as well as a gradual strengthening of a system of sanctions.

The process has been parallel in the sense that Lemkin's attempt to include cultural genocide was partly separate and had a different perspective compared with the evolution in IHL. The evolution of the protection of cultural works and historical monuments during armed conflict is similar of the two parallel ways of describing mass killing of people, either as genocide – with Lemkin's initial concept of barbarism – or as extermination as a crime against humanity. While a crime against humanity or war crime has its basis in killing of individuals or destruction of discrete protected objects, genocide has a group- or community-based perspective. While Lemkin was successful in establishing the legal concept of genocide in relation to killing of people, he failed to include the destruction of cultural works and historical monuments in the concept of genocide. Thus, Lemkin's efforts appear to be a sidetrack to the present status of the protection of cultural works and historical monuments under international law. However, this omission should not be exaggerated since acts which would amount to cultural genocide according to Lemkin's original idea could constitute war crimes and occur in a context of crimes against humanity or genocide.

References

John Cooper, *Lemkin and the Struggle for the Genocide Convention*, Palgrave Macmillan, New York, 2008.

Andrea Cunning, "The Safeguarding of Cultural Property in Times of War & Peace", *Tulsa Journal of Comparative and International Law*, vol. 11, no. 1, 2003, pp. 211–238.

Caroline Ehlert, *Prosecuting the destruction of cultural property in international criminal law: with a case study on the Khmer Rouge's destruction of Cambodia's heritage*, Martinus Nijhoff Publishers, Leiden, 2013.

Caroline Ehlert, "Article 8(2)(b)(ix) and (e)(iv)", in Mark Klamberg (Ed.), *The Commentary on the Law of the International Criminal Court*, TOAEP, Brussels, 2017.

Donna-Lee Frieze, *Totally Unofficial: The Autobiography of Raphael Lemkin*, Yale University Press, New Haven & London, 2013.

Micaela Frulli, "Advancing the Protection of Cultural Property through the Implementation of Individual Criminal Responsibility: The Case-Law of the International

Criminal Tribunal for the Former Yugoslavia", *Italian Yearbook of International Law*, vol. 15, 2005, pp. 195–216.

Patty Gerstenblith, "Protecting Cultural Heritage in Armed Conflict: Looking Back, Looking Forward", *Cardozo Public Law, Policy, and Ethics Journal*, vol. 7, no. 3, 2009, pp. 677–708.

Hugo Grotius, "*De Jure Belli ac Pacis Libre Tres" (1646), The Classics of International Law*, Hein, Buffalo, New York, 1995.

Iris van der Heijden, "Other Issues Relating to the Treatment of Civilians in Enemy Hands", Andrew Clapham, Paola Gaeta and Marco Sassòli (Eds.), *The 1949 Geneva Conventions: A Commentary*, Oxford University Press, Oxford, 2015, pp. 1241–1270.

Mark Klamberg, "International Criminal Law in Swedish Courts: The Principle of Legality in the Arklöv Case", *International Criminal Law Review*, vol. 9, no. 2, 2009, pp. 395–409.

Raphaël Lemkin, *Axis Rule in Occupied Europe: Laws of Occupation, Analysis of Government, Proposals for Redress, Introduction by William A. Schabas (1944)* (2nd ed.), Lawbook Exchange Ltd, Clark NJ, 2008.

Mark Lewis, "The History of the International Association of Penal Law, 1924–1950: Liberal, Conservative, or Neither?", in Morten Bergsmo et al. (Eds.), *Historical Origins of International Criminal Law: Volume 4*, TOAEP, Brussels, 2015, pp. 599–660, available at: www.legal-tools.org/en/doc/740a53/ (accessed 22 April 2018).

Matthew Lippman, "Art and Ideology in the Third Reich: The Protection of Cultural Property and the Humanitarian Law of War", *Dickinson Journal of International Law*, vol. 17, no. 1, 1998, pp. 1–97.

A. Dirk Moses, "Raphael Lemkin, Culture, and the Concept of Genocide", in Donald Bloxham and A. Dirk Moses (Eds.), *The Oxford Handbook of Genocide Studies*, Oxford University Press, Oxford, 2010, pp. 19–41.

Roger O'Keefe, *The Protection of Cultural Property in Armed Conflict*, Cambridge University Press, Cambridge, 2006.

Didier Pfirter, "Attacking Protected Objects", in Roy S. Lee (Ed.), *The International Criminal Court – Elements of Crimes and Rules of Procedure and Evidence*, Transnational Publishers, Ardsley, 2001, pp. 162–163.

Jean S. Pictet, *Commentary on the Geneva Convention Relative to the Protection of Civilian Persons in Time of War of 12 August 1949*, ICRC, Geneva, 1958.

Samantha Power, *A Problem from Hell*, Perennial, New York, 2002.

Philippe Sands, *East West Street: On the Origins of "Genocide" and "Crimes Against Humanity"*, Alfred A. Knopf, New York, 2016.

William A. Schabas, *Genocide in International Law* (2nd ed.), Cambridge University Press, Cambridge, 2009.

Daniel Marc Segesser and Myriam Gessler, "Raphael Lemkin and the international debate on the punishment of war crimes (1919–1948)", *Journal of Genocide Research*, vol. 7, no. 4, 2005, pp. 453–468.

Ryszard Szawłowski, "The Polish Lawyer Who Created the Concept of 'Genocide'", *Polish Quarterly of International Affairs*, vol. 14, no. 2, 2005, pp. 98–133.

Emmerich de Vattel, *Le droit des gens ou principes de la loi naturelle – The Law of Nations or the Principles of Natural Law (1758)*, The Classics of International Law, Hein, Buffalo NY, 1995, available at: http://lonang.com/library/reference/vattel-law-of-nations/ (accessed 13 April 2018).

Gerhard Werle, *Principles of International Criminal Law* (2nd ed.), T.M.C. Asser Press, Hague, 2009.

Herman von Hebel and Darryl Robinsson, "Crimes within the Jurisdiction of the Court", in Roy S. Lee (Ed.), *The International Criminal Court: the Making of the Rome Statute: Issues, Negotiations and Results*, Kluwer Law International, Hague, 1999, pp. 79–126.

Ana Filipa Vrdoljak, "Human Rights and Genocide: The Work of Lauterpacht and Lemkin in Modern International Law", *European Journal of International Law*, vol. 20, no. 4, 2009, pp. 1163–1194.

16 Forgotten, but nevertheless relevant! Gustave Moynier's attempts to punish violations of the laws of war 1870–1916

Daniel Marc Segesser

16.1 Introduction

On 15 June 1998, a diplomatic conference to establish an international criminal court opened in Rome. In this context, Christopher Keith Hall, legal adviser for Amnesty International at its International Secretariat in London, published an article on Moynier's proposal, which was almost unknown to most jurists involved in the process of setting up the International Criminal Court at the Rome Conference. Hall stressed the fact that it was difficult to judge the impact of this proposal, as it had been withdrawn quickly.[1] Giving a short overview – including Moynier's ten draft articles for a convention[2] – Hall looked at the strength and weaknesses of the proposal, and also pointed to the fact that, would it have been put into practice – especially in the context of the Hague Conventions of 1899 and 1907 – this would have had an enormous impact on world opinion and would certainly not have gone without consequences in regard to the conduct of war in the 20th century. At the end of his article, Hall pointed to the fact that some of the weaknesses detected already in Moynier's proposal were still under consideration in Rome and he expressed his hope that the many participants at the Conference there would be successful in elaborating a statute worthy of the visionary that Moynier had been.[3]

Basing myself on an approach that tries to understand law as a social and cultural category that needs to be analysed accordingly and that needs to undertake a broad contextualisation of the development of legal norms in its political, social and economic context,[4] this chapter will give an in-depth analysis of Gustave Moynier's attempts to get jurists as well as diplomats and their states to accept some sort of international obligation to punish violations of the laws of war and more specifically the Geneva Convention of 1864 on the basis of an international legal agreement. At first, I will look at Gustave Moynier and the Geneva Committee

1 Hall, 1998, pp. 61–67.

2 Ibid., 76–78. Cf. Moynier, 1872b, pp. 129–131.

3 Hall, 1998, p. 75.

4 In this I follow in the tracks of legal historians like Caroni, 2005, pp. 27–55, Klippel, 2002, pp. 133–135 or Vormbaum, 2007, p. 1 and general historians like Holquist, forthcoming or Lewis, 2014, p. 7. Cf. also Segesser, 2010 and 2013, pp. 103–105.

up to the Franco-Prussian War 1870–1871, before turning to the issue of the punishment of violations of the laws of war in the context of the Franco-Prussian War. The main part of the chapter will then deal with Moynier's activities in the context of proposals to revise the Geneva Convention between 1873 and 1906. Before concluding with some comments on the relevance of Moynier's proposals for the issue of historicising international law, a short section will deal with the repercussions of Moynier's proposals in the context of the First World War.

16.2 Gustave Moynier and the Geneva Committee up to the Franco-Prussian War 1870–1871

Gustave Moynier descended from a bourgeois family in Geneva, which did, however, not belong to the leading families of the city. Nevertheless, his father was elected to the Grand Conseil (and later even to the Conseil d'État) before losing all political power in the revolution of 1946.[5] This did not stop Gustave's career that benefited a lot from marrying well-off Fanny Paccard in 1851. Not least due to the fortune of his wife, Moynier could stop working for money and concentrate on what he was interested in most: pure jurisdictional reasoning and philanthropy, which he preferred much to the daily practice of law. It was in this economic and social context as well as with the vocation to improve society and to combat evil that as president of the Société Genevoise d'Utilité Publique that Moynier later met Henry Dunant, who was desperately looking for support for his idea to create voluntary societies to help the wounded in wartime.[6]

Together with Guillaume-Henri Dufour, Louis Appia, Théodore Maunoir and Henry Dunant, Moynier finally became a member of the committee of the five, the founding body of what was to become the International Committee of the Red Cross (ICRC).[7] While Dunant was the boisterous visionary, Moynier always remained the cool reasoner in the group, who was often – as in the case of the neutralisation of the wounded as well as of the medical service and the voluntary aid societies – much more reticent than Dunant. He would, however, be ready to fall in behind an idea, as soon as he would realise that there was a chance of getting it accepted. The result was the Geneva Convention of 1864, which, concentrating on the protection of the wounded, was the first international convention on land warfare. When Guillaume-Henri Dufour, the founding president, asked to be relieved of his duty as president already in 1864 Moynier succeeded him and became the leading figure of the movement until his death in 1910.[8]

5 Sennarclens, 2000, pp. 15–24.
6 Bugnion, 2012, pp. 12–23; Sennarclens 2000, pp. 56–59.
7 Up to 1875 the ICRC was known as the Geneva Committee. In this year it took the name of International Committee of the Red Cross (ICRC). Meeting of the Geneva Committee 20 December 1875, printed in Pitteloud (Ed.), 1999, p. 374. This article will use the terminology accordingly.
8 Bugnion, 2012, pp. 23–41; Harouel, 1999a, pp. 9–14; Riesenberger, 1992, pp. 20–32.

Moynier's views on international law before the beginning of the Franco-Prussian War are best recorded in his book *Étude sur la Convention de Genève pour l'Amélioration du Sort des Militaires Blessés dans les Armées en Campagne*, which he published in Paris in 1870. In his first words, he made it clear that in his view law (*droit*) formed the central basis of humanity's ascending road to a new social ideal. Moynier was very optimistic about the future of humanity's social fabric although he was at the same time aware of the fact that the final objective – a world without war – had not yet been achieved. The law of nature would, however, prevent the use of unlimited force in war and make sure that, should man nevertheless resort to it, this would not go unpunished.[9] War was only possible as a last resort, Moynier continued, making it clear that pillage, the poisoning of the enemy's army, the assassination of military leaders and massacres of prisoners of war as well as of innocent civilians were absolutely prohibited in any case,[10] as war was "inevitably an evil, which should not exceed the limits of strict necessity."[11]

To bolster his case, Moynier pointed to the work of different scholars from the enlightenment such as Emeric de Vattel or Jean-Etienne Potalis, jurists like Charles-Henri Vergé and also military leaders like Guillaume-Henri Dufour or Dmtri Alekseyevich Milyutin.[12] Moynier even gave a quote from the latter: "The belligerents shall only tolerate calamities in war that are imperatively necessary."[13] His aim was to show that not only scholars but also military leaders shared the same values whatever their reasons. Moynier also pointed to critics like Pierre Paul Leroy-Beaulieu, who believed that war had not changed. Although he did not agree with him, Moynier admitted that the French economist pointed to one important fact, that is, that apart from the Geneva Convention as well as the Declarations of Paris (1856) and St. Petersburg (1868), the governments had so far not signed any further written agreements on the laws of war.[14]

Although Moynier seems to have been aware of the fact that different people supported restrictions in war for different motives – a fact that Mark Lewis has rightly pointed to in his work on the post-First World War debates on "new justice"[15] – he seems nevertheless to have been convinced that all of them would do all they could in the position they were in to promote the acceptance of legal restraints in actual war. Pointing to the fact that the famous German jurist and diplomat Georg Friedrich von Martens had been sceptic that treaties on the laws of war would see the light of day, Moynier speculated that one day, even a complete code of the laws of war might come into existence.[16] In regard to the

9 Moynier, 1870, pp. 1–5.
10 Ibid., pp. 7–8.
11 Ibid., pp. 14–15. [Translation by the author].
12 Ibid., pp. 15–20.
13 Ibid., p. 17. [Translation by the author]. On Milyutin's role in the Russian debate on the development of the laws of war cf. Holquist forthcoming.
14 Moynier, 1870, pp. 19–28.
15 Lewis, 2014, pp. 3–6.
16 Moynier, 1870, pp. 28–36.

Geneva Convention, he was furthermore convinced that military leaders would do all they could to make sure that it would be observed. It was the duty of the signatories of the Geneva Convention to make sure that violations – should they nevertheless occur – would quickly be punished by military courts of the nations concerned.[17] Moynier was too optimistic on this point, as became clear shortly after the publication of his book during the Franco-Prussian War. Furthermore, he underestimated the fact that even those jurists that agreed with him on the fact that the rule of law needed to be strengthened on a national level, did not do so in regard to the expansion into the sphere of an international jurisdiction. The rule of law had been a national achievement and many of those, who had fought for it, were not (yet) ready to "sacrifice" that to a new universal and supranational legal system.[18] The Geneva Committee did not discuss Moynier's ideas but concentrated on its role of coordinating offers for help, collecting donations and serving as an intermediary between national Red Cross societies particularly of the belligerents.[19]

16.3 The Franco-Prussian War: the punishment of violations of the laws of war

Already during the Franco-Prussian War, it became clear that the norms of international law would not prevent the use of military violence beyond what Milyutin had called imperative necessity. Reports of such incidents reached the Geneva Committee in February and May 1871.[20] Moynier and his colleagues reacted quickly. The same year Gustave Rolin-Jaequemyns, with whom Moynier had been in close contact since the 1862 philanthropic congress in London,[21] in a long article in the *Revue de Droit International et de Législation Comparée* demanded clarifications in the Geneva Convention, especially in regard to the unjustified use of the Red Cross emblem as well as in regard to the training of soldier's knowledge about the convention. In this context, the Belgian jurist also wondered, whether it might be expedient to create an international tribunal or an international fact-finding committee to deal with violations of the Geneva Convention, to prevent national military courts from judging their own soldiers too leniently.[22]

Only a short time later, in January 1872 Moynier took up Rolin-Jaequemyns' ideas in a review of the article.[23] He also wrote another article, in which he claimed that, although the Geneva Convention had been respected most of the time during the Franco-Prussian War, it would be sensible to create an

17 Ibid., pp. 299–306.
18 Haouel, 1999a, pp. 15–17; Lewis, 2014, p. 26.
19 Minutes of the Geneva Committee between 18 July 1870 and 20 May 1871, in Pitteloud, 1999, pp. 97–238.
20 Minutes of the Geneva Committee 4 February and 10 May 1871, in Pitteloud, 1999, pp. 206 and 236.
21 Sennarclens, 2000, p. 223.
22 Rolin-Jaequemyns, 1871, pp. 327–331.
23 Moynier, 1872a, pp. 74–75.

international judicial body to try violations of the Geneva Convention. A purely moral sanction was not enough and states had not shown a large zeal to punish perpetrators from their own military forces.[24] Moynier, whose proposal was thoroughly approved by the committee at its meeting of 24 January 1872,[25] was aware that his proposal affected national sovereignty, but he believed that governments might be convinced, if such a proposal proved as advantageous to themselves as the recent and ongoing arbitration trial in regard to the ALABAMA case proved to be. Not least therefore, Moynier modelled his court on the ALABAMA arbitration court and left the execution of a sentence to the governments concerned. Furthermore, he was convinced that it made sense for the states involved to have a judge each and to be liable for financial compensation should one of their citizens be found guilty.[26]

In the same year, Gustave Rolin-Jaequemyns presented Moynier's proposal to a wider scholarly audience in his *Revue de Droit International et de Législation Comparée* together with some responses from other jurists. Amongst them was Francis Lieber, who agreed that violations of the laws of war needed to be punished. At the same time, he claimed that it would be wrong to restrict the autonomy of freedom-loving countries that were less well placed to use such a tribunal for their advantage than despotic leaders. For Lieber Moynier's proposal was just not practicable. He preferred national trials and suggested that eminent jurists should meet to discuss and decide upon undecided questions in regard to the laws of war.[27] Similarly, sceptical was British jurist John Westlake, who wondered, how witnesses should be brought to testify in such a court and how the court would seek to avoid false statements resulting from the passions of a war.[28] Even those more positive about Moynier's ideas, such as Rolin-Jaequemyns himself or Franz von Holtzendorff, were not sure, whether states would be ready to accept such a tribunal and claimed that it might be a better idea to create an international fact-finding committee as suggested by Rolin-Jaequemyns in 1871.[29]

The Geneva Committee discussed Moynier's proposal throughout the year 1872 but took no formal decision to drop it.[30] It seems, however, that Moynier and the committee silently did so in the context of the debate on the future of the Geneva Convention, which was severely challenged especially by a proposal of Jaromír Mundy, a Vienna physician. Supported by the French Red Cross Society, Mundy wanted to replace the Geneva Convention by inserting its content into the military regulations of the states. In this context, Mundy severely criticised the Geneva Committee and blamed not least Moynier's proposal for

24 Moynier, 1872b, pp. 122–123.
25 Minutes of the Geneva Committee 24 January 1872, in Pitteloud, 1999, p. 262.
26 Moynier, 1872b, pp. 124–127.
27 Rolin-Jaequemyns, 1872, pp. 330–332.
28 Ibid., pp. 334–335.
29 Ibid., pp. 332–334 and 339–341; Rolin-Jaequemyns, 1871, p. 328.
30 Cf. the minutes of the Geneva Committee for the year 1872 in Pitteloud, 1999, pp. 262–288.

the fact that the Geneva Convention had to be reworked completely.[31] Moynier and the committee therefore may have decided that although some had encouraged it to continue its work concerning the creation of an international criminal tribunal,[32] it was better to concentrate on maintaining the Geneva Convention as such rather than risking it for the sake of an ideal that did not seem possible to achieve. In this context, the criticism of Moynier's proposal by Prussian academics, made public only at a later stage,[33] might have played a decisive role. These critics should not be fended off on such an issue at a time when positive responses from their country as well as from Great Britain were so essential in the Committee's stand against Mundy's ideas for a revision of the Geneva Convention or even its abolishment.[34] These considerations indicate that Moynier was less, as Hall and Sennarclens suggest a premature visionary, whose ideas were taken up much later and most of the time without mentioning.[35] Rather, Moynier as well as the Geneva Committee were pragmatics, weighing their chances, trying to preserve what they had achieved and work towards other solutions in the time to come.

16.4 Moynier and proposals to revise the Geneva Convention between 1873 and 1906

In the years between the Franco-Prussian War and the turn of the century, the Geneva Committee was faced with further serious challenges to the Geneva Convention. Not least to forestall proposals from other parties the Committee itself, submitted five proposals for a revision of the convention, all of them finally turned down.[36] In this context, Moynier and the Geneva Committee only very rarely raised the issue of the punishment of violations of the Geneva Convention. It therefore comes as no surprise that when in 1879 in a publication on a possible revision of the Convention Luigi Olivi from Modena proposed to commit signatories to punish violations through their national penal military codes,[37] Moynier and the ICRC only presented the thoughts and did not give any comment.[38] They preferred to proceed carefully and Moynier only mentioned his 1872 proposal publicly once more. This was when in 1886 he congratulated the belligerents Serbia and Bulgaria on not making violations of the Geneva Convention a matter of public debate and propaganda. Instead, they had submitted their views to a group of impartial men, in which they trusted, that is, the ICRC

31 Minute of the Geneva Committee 1 October 1872, in Pitteloud, 1999, p. 277. Cf. Harouel, 1999a, p. 23.

32 Minutes of the Geneva Committee 15 May and 5 June 1872 in Pitteloud, 1999, pp. 266–269.

33 Lueder, 1876, pp. 431–433; Triepel, 1894, pp. 211–212.

34 Minutes of the Geneva Committee 22 December 1872, 15 January as well as 5 and 19 February 1873, in Pitteloud, 1999, pp. 286–291.

35 Hall, 1998, p.75; Sennarclens, 2000, p. 219.

36 ICRC-Archives: AF 26. Cf. Harouel, 1999b, pp. 365–386 and Segesser, 2010, pp. 111–122.

37 Olivi, 1879, pp. 120–129.

38 Moynier, 1879, pp. 125–127.

and an international fact-finding committee, which found that there had only been some rare instances of violations of the laws and customs of war.[39]

Moynier himself, however, concentrated on another track. In 1873, he had been one of the founding members of the Institute of International Law, within which he played an important role for a long time.[40] He believed that it was more important to find a "*uniformité de doctrine*" amongst jurists first. Only after this was achieved would it be possible to convince states to agree to an international convention.[41] At different levels, he continued to work for the development of international law. His major success in this context proved to be the Oxford Manual of 1880, which formed the final result of a thorough analysis of the national efforts to put into practice the results of the Declaration from the diplomatic conference in Brussels in 1874. In his report, Moynier criticised the governments for not doing enough to transform the laws of war into national legislation. He was convinced that it was the duty of the international legal community manifested in the Institute of International Law to remedy such a situation by presenting a model system of rules.[42] In this, he pursued ideas presented by his fellow citizen Joseph Hornung on the possibilities offered by national penal laws to punish violations of the laws of war. The latter was convinced that what diplomats had so far not achieved on an international level might finally be done by national legislation.[43] With some minor changes, the proposals made by Moynier and Hornung were accepted by the meeting of the Institute of International Law in Oxford in 1880. Moynier was convinced that at least some progress had been made in regard to the improvement of the state of the laws and customs of war although the governments received the new rules with large scepticism.[44]

Not least therefore, Moynier remained careful and preferred a step by step approach in regard to the further development of international law and to the issue of the punishment of violations of the Geneva Convention. Only in the 1890s did he try one more time to get his ideas of the early 1870s discussed again. In 1892, he wrote to an unknown colleague in the United States that he was still prepared to discuss and amend his 1872 proposal.[45] On the request of the then secretary-general of the Institute of International Law, Ernest Lehr, in 1893 – this time without consulting on the issue with other members of the ICRC[46] – Moynier finally published a booklet, in which he reformulated and adapted his ideas on penal sanctions for violations of the Geneva Conference. His main aim was to convince his colleagues

39 Moynier, 1886, pp. 554–557.

40 Sennarclens, 2000, pp. 221–232.

41 Moynier, 1890, p. 4.

42 Moynier, 1879-80, pp. 312–320.

43 Hornung, 1879-1880, pp. 320–325.

44 Moynier, 1882, pp. 149–174; Segesser, 2010, p. 111.

45 Library of the University of Michigan Law School, Ann Arbour: JX3 M9389n 1872: Note addressed by Gustave Moynier to an unknown colleague in the United States, dated Geneva 5 February 1892 and written into a copy of Moynier 1872c.

46 Pitteloud, 1999, pp. 568–580.

at the Institute of International Law to set up a committee, whose task should be to find a solution to the issue of penal sanctions for the Geneva Convention of 1864.[47] Moynier was aware that the issue of state sovereignty still posed a great obstacle to an international solution in regard to an agreement on penal sanctions for violations of the Geneva Convention.[48] However, he believed that at a time when communication and travel around the globe became possible, it would prove possible for jurists to overcome obstacles that had made an international solution impracticable so far. In what he saw as a globalised world, he believed that his idea had gained momentum. Moynier was still convinced that a national solution made it possible that persons responsible for violations of the Geneva Convention would not all be treated in a similar manner, but judged according to national conceptions and interests. In this context, it would be helpful for national judges to have access to an international fact-finding committee, which would arbitrate between a person accused of violations of the Geneva Convention and the national authorities of the country, in which this person was kept.[49]

Moynier's renewed proposal was submitted to the annual meeting of the Institute of International Law in Paris in 1894. A committee presided by Moynier himself and French diplomat Édouard Engelhardt was formed, which in turn presented its report at the following annual meeting at Cambridge in 1895. Although some of the committee members such as Gustav Roszkowski, Friedrich Geffcken and to some extent also Paul Pradier-Fodéré would have supported a solution on an international level, as Moynier had suggested, the majority of the committee preferred a solution with an obligation for states to punish violations of the Geneva Convention. Nevertheless, the idea of the creation of an international fact-finding committee was put up for discussion.[50] Neither Moynier nor Engelhardt were present at Cambridge and therefore it was almost only Gustave Rolin-Jaequemyns who defended Moynier's proposal. He even went as far as to propose that the ICRC should take over the functions of a fact-finding committee, but this proposal was not accepted by a large number of the members present at Cambridge. The main opponents were Fjodor Fjodorovitch Martens, Jacobus Catharinus Cornelis den Beer Poortugael and Emilio Brusa.[51] The latter was giving his own opinion in a separate publication, in which he stressed the fact that Moynier's proposal was an attack on the central principle of national sovereignty. If a state would not punish violations of the Geneva Convention, it would be more severely punished than any individual could be, namely by being proscribed by the family of nations.[52]

47 Moynier, 1893, p. 3.
48 For Moynier's ideas in regard to state sovereignty in the context of the issue of humanitarian intervention cf. Segesser, 2016, pp. 62–64.
49 Moynier, 1893, pp. 7–12 and 14–24.
50 Engelhardt and Moynier, 1895, pp. 17–31.
51 Ibid., pp. 179–187.
52 Brusa, 1895, pp. 326–345. This article was not well received by the ICRC, as a comment by the secretary of the committee, Gouttes, 1895, pp. 196–199, shows. On positions taken by jurists

Moynier was not discouraged by the failure of his proposal at Cambridge. In May 1898, the Geneva Committee decided to have a new publication printed, which dealt with the issue of a revision of the Geneva Convention.[53] Moynier decided to take up some of the criticism voiced against his proposal in Cambridge. Too much of a pragmatic and a diplomat, he stressed that penal law was at present very much a national issue. What would be necessary in any case, however, was that all states should be bound to have laws, making sure that violations of the Geneva Convention would be punished.[54]

Shortly afterwards, for medical reasons, Moynier had to leave the issue to others.[55] It was a like-minded person[56] that took up the torch. Louis Renault was a professor of international law at the University of Paris, who after 1890 also bore the title of a minister plenipotentiary and extraordinary ambassador of his country. This combination of an academic and a diplomat would finally open the road for a revision of the Geneva Convention. In 1901, one of Renault's students, Louis Gillot, presented his doctoral thesis on a possible revision of the 1864 Geneva Convention. He looked at all the different proposals made in regard to the punishment of violations of the Geneva Convention and concluded that an international tribunal to judge such violations was hardly practicable. Furthermore, the proponents of such a solution had so far not been able to agree amongst themselves as to its formation, organisation and functioning. Therefore, it was clear that the duty to punish violations of the Geneva Convention remained with the states, who should be called up to increase their publicity of the Convention amongst the troops and to rectify their penal laws where necessary.[57] At the end of his study, Gillot submitted a draft for a revised convention, in which article 28 stipulated that if necessary the signatories committed themselves to complement their penal legislation in regard to violations of the Geneva Convention within three years after the convention was signed and to communicate such changes via the Swiss government.[58]

It still took another five years, before a diplomatic conference to revise the 1864 conference finally took place in 1906. Moynier was still present, but due to his age and for health reasons he did not play a central role. His place was taken by Édouard Odier, a Swiss diplomat and member of the ICRC, as well as by the already mentioned Louis Renault, who succeeded to have the contracting parties agree to a renewed convention, which with small changes matched the proposal made by Gillot in 1901. Although a penal sanction for violations of the Geneva Convention was finally agreed, for Moynier and his

on the issue of national sovereignty in the context of "humanitarian intervention" cf. Segesser, 2016, pp. 56–72.

53 Meeting of the ICRC of 10 May 1898, in Pitteloud, 1999, pp. 601–602.

54 Moynier, 1898, p. 35.

55 Cf. Moynier's comment on his health at the meeting of the ICRC of 11 October 1898, in Pitteloud, 1999, p. 602.

56 Cf. Gouttes, 1899, pp. 155–156.

57 Gillot, 1901, pp. 300–328.

58 Ibid., p. 343.

fellow campaigners the success was but a moderate one, as no international solution was reached.[59] This was on one hand due to the fact that at a time of heightened tensions and high-running nationalist feelings the states would not agree to a limitation of their national sovereignty. On the other hand – as the meeting of the Institute of International Law in Cambridge in 1895 and Gillot's analysis had shown – jurists had not been able to agree amongst themselves to such a solution, a fact, which in 1890 Moynier himself had seen as a prerequisite for reaching an international agreement.[60] Nevertheless, for a long time, article 28 of the 1906 Geneva Convention remained the only article in an international convention in regard to the punishment of violations of the laws of war. French jurist Jacques Dumas was the only one who noticed this fact after the 1907 second Hague Peace Conference. He was, however, not too worried, as in his view many of the violations of the laws of war were crimes according to national law and could be punished accordingly, should the need arise.[61]

16.5 Beyond death: Moynier's proposals and the First World War

In 1910, Gustave Moynier died.[62] In the eulogy published by the ICRC in the *Bulletin des Sociétés de la Croix-Rouge*, his efforts to create an international body to deal with violations of the Geneva Convention were not mentioned, the only reference remaining that Moynier had "deployed all his abilities to put into practise the principles of justice, solidarity and humanitarianism, which he had favoured."[63] The punishment of violations of the laws of war in general and the Geneva Convention in particular had lost much of its importance already in the context of the two Hague Peace Conferences and the efforts of Moynier and others were quickly forgotten. Peaceful conflict resolution had become the main topic, on which many jurists focused in the decade before the beginning of the First World War. Timothy McCormack was probably not wrong, when he claimed in 1997 that the growing number of national trials for violations of the laws of war and the high acceptance of The Hague Rules of Land Warfare "resulted in a growing recognition and acceptance of a principle of individual culpability for violations of the international law of war crimes."[64] On the other hand, some issues remained as well. A unification of the national penal norms for the violations of the laws of war that Moynier had proposed in the Oxford Manual in 1880 had not taken place and the growing acceptance of international norms mentioned by McCormack only applied to the countries that were

59 Harouel, 1999a, pp. 27–29; Segesser, 2010, pp. 121–122.
60 Moynier, 1890, p. 4.
61 Dumas, 1908, pp. 569–579.
62 Sennarclens, 2000, pp. 292–293.
63 Comité International, 1910, pp. 171–207, quote p. 188 [Translation by the author].
64 McCormack, 1997, p. 43.

acknowledged to be members of a law abiding community of civilised states (but not their colonies).[65]

As soon as the opposing side was not seen as a member of this community of civilised states, things became more complicated. This was exactly the situation encountered in July 1914. On one hand, the Balkan Wars of 1912–1913 seemed to have shown – as an International Commission to Inquire into the Causes and Conduct of the Balkan Wars had found – "that there [was] no clause in international law applicable to land war and to the treatment of the wounded, which [had] not [been] violated, to a greater or less [sic!] extent, by all the belligerents."[66] On the other hand, especially the Austro-Hungarian political and military authorities wondered more and more, whether Serbia would keep to the laws of war in a potential military confrontation with the monarchy. The enemy was increasingly seen as a criminal, not least in the context of the murder of heir to the throne Franz-Ferdinand in Sarajevo on 28 June 1914.[67] Moynier's apprehension that the failure to adopt international rules or at least to unify existing national rules for the punishment of violations of the laws of war in general and the Geneva Convention in particular[68] would cause grave problems if a future war came true.[69] Some like Louis Renault raised their voices claiming that trials in national courts remained a viable option[70] and only Jacques Dumas in 1916 explicitly deplored that Moynier's proposals of 1872 and 1893, which he called "wise propositions," had been rejected.[71] It took some more time, before the issue was raised again at the Paris Peace Conference,[72] but by that time, Moynier's proposal seems to have been almost completely forgotten. Other people such as Hugh Bellot, Walter George Phillimore, Fernand Larnaude as well as later Vespasien Pella or Henri Donnedieu de Vabres took over.[73]

16.6 Conclusion: relevant for the present? Moynier's proposals and the issue of historicising international law

As we have seen, on one hand, Gustave Moynier was a man of principles and not so much a man dealing with the practicalities on the ground. On the other hand, he was a pragmatic, who adapted his proposals to the political, social and cultural environment of his time. Military men were not amongst the people he communicated with very often. Exceptions were Guillaume Henri Dufour or Dmtri Alekseyevich Milyutin, with whom he believed to share attitudes and values. Before

65 Segesser, 2010, pp. 140–142.
66 Carnegie Endowment, 1914, p. 208.
67 Segesser, 2014, p. 63; Segesser, 2018, pp. 76–77.
68 Moynier, 1872b, pp. 122–123; Moynier, 1893, pp. 15–16.
69 Cf. Segesser, 2010, pp. 170–176 for the alignment of most academics to their nation's position on the issue.
70 Bellot, 1916, pp. 636–660; Renault, 1915, pp. 406–493.
71 Dumas, 1916, pp. 63–65, quote p. 64.
72 Cf. Lewis, 2014, pp. 27–55; Segesser, 2010, pp. 212–225.
73 Lewis, 2014, pp. 78–149; Segesser, 2010, pp. 233–302. Tallgren and Mégret (Eds.), forthcoming.

the Franco-Prussian War, Moynier was very optimistic concerning the adherence of states and their armies to the laws of war and he trusted the competent authorities to deal with any violations that would occur. When the facts on the ground showed that this was not the case – and impressed by the ALABAMA arbitration – he looked for another ideal solution and did not at first pay too much attention to the issue of the practicability of his proposal. When faced with criticism by his colleagues especially as to such a practicability he would, however, follow a pragmatic line. The preservation of his achievement of the Geneva Convention was much too important for him to risk for the sake of introducing an international criminal tribunal for violations of this convention. He – and the ICRC – took a step by step approach, weighing their chances and working towards ideal solutions, when they thought the time had come to bring it up again.

In the 1890s, when no further challenges seemed to affect the Geneva Convention as such any more Moynier came back on his solution for punishing violations of the Geneva Convention on an international level. National sovereignty proved to be too strong an obstacle, however, and Moynier decided to fall back on a position, which he had already stood in for at the Institute of International Law in Oxford in 1880, that is, an obligation and a unification of national penal regulations for violations of international legal rules. Moynier only withdrew from the debate for medical reasons after one last proposal in 1898. Others, such as Louis Renault and Louis Gillot, then took up the torch and succeeded in introducing a minimal obligation into the revised Geneva Convention of 1906.

On one hand, this result can be traced back to the political, social and cultural circumstances that have not been part of this text in detail.[74] On the other hand – as Moynier had pointed out himself[75] – it would have been essential for a success of his proposals for an international solution that jurists would have agreed on it amongst themselves. This was not the case and was, in turn, due to the fact that their motives as well as their social backgrounds differed too much to make agreement possible. Dealing with another field Mark Lewis has rightly pointed to this fact.[76] Moynier and his colleagues failed to improve society through law because no such "one society" existed.

Another important aspect in this context is the assessment of the other. If he or she is not trusted or – at worst – even considered a criminal as in the case of the Serbian authorities in 1914, a solution is difficult, if not impossible. This is something to learn from Moynier's attempts to establish an international solution for the violations of the Geneva Convention even for present-day lawyers. What is absolutely essential in this context, however, is a transdisciplinary dialogue, a precise historical analysis and a contextualisation of process of the rules of international law, which can best be described as a very twisted road and not – as Moynier would have believed – a neat way from barbarism to civilisation.

74 Cf. Fisch, 2002.
75 Moynier, 1890, p. 4.
76 Lewis, 2014, pp. 3–6.

References

Hugh H. L. Bellot, "War Crimes: Their Punishment and Prevention", *Nineteenth Century and After*, vol. 80, 1916, pp. 636–660.

Emilio Brusa, "Di una sanzione penale alla convenzione ginevrina per i ferriti in guerra", *Atti della R. Accademia delle Scienze di Torino*, vol. 31, 1895, pp. 326–345.

François Bugnion, *Gustave Moynier 1826–1910* (2nd ed.), Éditions Slatkine, Geneva, 2012.

Carnegie Endowment of International Peace, *Report of the International Commission to Inquire into the Causes and Conduct of the Balkan Wars*, CEIP, Washington, DC 1914.

Pio Caroni, "Blicke über den Gartenzaun: Von den Beziehungen der Rechtsgeschichte zu ihren historischen Nachbarwissenschaften", in Louis Pahlow (Ed.), *Die zeitliche Dimension des Rechts: Historische Rechtsforschung und geschichtliche Rechtswissenschaft*, Ferdinand Schöningh Verlag, Paderborn, 2005, pp. 27–55.

Comité International, "Gustave Moynier", *Bulletin International des Sociétés de la Croix-Rouge*, vol. 41, no. 164, 1910, pp. 171–207.

Jacques Dumas, "Les Sanctions du Droit International d'après les Conventions de la Haye de 1899 et 1907", *Revue Générale de Droit International Public*, vol. 15, 1908, pp. 557–580.

Jacques Dumas, *Les Sanctions Pénales des Crimes Allemands*, Paris, 1916, pp. 63–65.

Edouard Engelhardt and Gustave Moynier, "Rapport sur la Sanction Pénale à donner à la Convention de Genève", *Annuaire de l'Institut de Droit International*, vol. 14, 1895, pp. 17–31 & pp. 170–189.

Jörg Fisch, *Europa zwischen Wachstum und Gleichheit 1850–1914* (Handbuch der Geschichte Europas, vol. 8), UTB, Stuttgart, 2002.

Louis Gillot, *La Révision de la Convention de Genève*, A. Rousseau, Paris, 1901.

Paul Des Gouttes, "Sanction Pénale de la Convention de Genève", *Bulletin International des Sociétés de la Croix-Rouge*, no. 104, 1895, pp. 196–199.

Paul Des Gouttes, "Conférence de M. Renault sur la Convention de Genève", *Bulletin International des Sociétés de la Croix-Rouge*, vol. 30, no. 119, 1899, pp. 155–156.

Christopher Keith Hall, "Première proposition de Création d'une Cour Criminelle Internationale Permanente", *Revue Internationale de la Croix-Rouge*, vol. 80, no. 829, 1998, pp. 59–78.

Véronique Harouel, *Histoire de la Croix-Rouge*, Presses universitaires de France, Paris, 1999a.

Véronique Harouel, "Les Projets Genevois de la Révision de la Convention de Genève du 22 Août 1864, 1868–1898", *Revue Internationale de la Croix-Rouge*, vol. 81, no. 834, 1999b, pp. 365–386.

Peter Holquist, *By Right of War: Imperial Russia and the Making of the 'Laws of War' (1868–1917)*, forthcoming.

Joseph Hornung, "Note sur la Répression des Délits contre le Droit des Gens et plus spécialement sur celle des Délits contre les Lois de la Guerre", *Annuaire de l'Institut de Droit International*, vol. 3/4, 1879–1880, pp. 320–325.

Diethelm Klippel, "Rechtsgeschichte", in Joachim Eibach and Günther Lottes (Eds.), *Kompass der Geschichtswissenschaft: Ein Handbuch*, UTB, Göttingen, 2002, pp. 126–141.

Mark Lewis, *The Birth of New Justice: The Internationalization of Crime and Punishment, 1919–1950*, Oxford University Press, Oxford, 2014.

Carl Lueder, *Die Genfer Konvention: Historisch und kritisch-dogmatisch mit Vorschlägen zu ihrer Verbesserung. unter Darlegung und Prüfung der mit ihr gemachten Erfahrungen und unter Benutzung der amtlichen, theilweise ungedruckten Quellen*, Verlag von Edoard Besold, Erlangen, 1876.
Timothy L. H. McCormack, "From Sun Tzu to the Sixth Committee: The Evolution of an International Criminal Law Regime", in Timothy L. H. McCormack and Gerry J. Simpson (Eds.), *The Law of War Crimes: National and International Approaches*, Kluwer, The Hague, 1997, pp. 31–63.
Gustave Moynier, *Étude sur la Convention de Genève pour l'Amélioration du Sort des militaires Blessés dans les Armées en Campagne (1864 et 1868)*, Librairie de Joël Cherbuliez, Geneva, 1870.
Gustave Moynier, "La Guerre Actuelle dans ses Rapports avec le Droit International par G. Rolin-Jaequemyns", *Bulletin International des Sociétés de Secours aux Militaires Blessés*, no. 11, 1872a, pp. 73–75.
Gustave Moynier, "Note sur la Création d'une Institution Judicaire Internationale propre à prévenir et à réprimer les Infractions à la Convention de Genève", *Bulletin International des Sociétés de Secours aux Militaires Blessés*, no. 11, 1872b, pp. 122–131.
Gustave Moynier, *Note sur la Création d'une Institution Judicaire Internationale propre à prévenir et à réprimer les Infractions à la Convention de Genève*, Imprimerie Soullier et Wirth, Geneva, 1872c.
Gustave Moynier, "La Convention de Genève étudiée par M le Prof Olivi", *Bulletin International des Sociétés de Secours aux Militaires Blessés*, no. 40, 1879, pp. 125–127.
Gustave Moynier, "Rapport sur la Réglementation des Lois et Coutumes de la Guerre", *Annuaire de l'Institut de Droit International*, no. 3–4, 1879–80, pp. 312–320 & pp. 326–328.
Gustave Moynier, "Rapport sur la Réglementation des Lois et Coutumes de la Guerre", *Annuaire de l'Institut de Droit International*, vol. 5, 1882, pp. 149–174.
Gustave Moynier, "De Quelques Faits Récents relatifs à la Convention de Genève", *Revue de Droit International et de Législation Comparée*, vol. 18, 1886, pp. 545–562.
Gustave Moynier, *L'Institut de Droit International*, A. Picard, Paris, 1890.
Gustave Moynier, *Considérations sur la Sanction Pénale à donner à la Convention de Genève*, Imprimerie F. Regamey, Lausanne, 1893.
Gustave Moynier, *La Révision de la Convention de Genève: Étude Historique et Critique suivi d'un Projet de Convention Révisée*, ICRC, Geneva, 1898.
Luigi Olivi, *Cenni storici e critici sulla Convenzione di Ginevra*, Paolo Toschi e C, Modena, 1879.
Jean-François Pitteloud (Ed.), *Procès-Verbaux des séances du comité international de la Croix-Rouge 1863–1914*, Societe Henry Dunant/Comite international de la Croix-Rouge, Geneva, 1999.
Louis Renault, "Dans quelle mesure le droit pénal peut-il s'appliquer à des faits de guerre contraires au droit des gens?", *Revue Pénitentiaire et de Droit Pénal*, vol. 39, 1915, pp. 406–493.
Dieter Riesenberger, *Für Humanität in Krieg und Frieden: Das Internationale Rote Kreuz 1863–1977*, Vandenhoeck & Ruprecht, Göttingen, 1992.
Gustave Rolin-Jaequemyns, "Essai Complémentaire sur la Guerre Franco-Allemande dans ses Rapports avec le Droit International", *Revue de Droit International et de Législation Comparée*, vol. 3, 1871, pp. 288–384.
Gustave Rolin-Jaequemyns, "Convention de Genève: Note sur le Projet de M. Moynier, relatif à l'Établissement d'une Institution Judiciaire Internationale, Protectrice de la

Convention", *Revue de Droit International et de Législation Comparée*, vol. 4, 1872, pp. 325–346.

Daniel Marc Segesser, *Recht statt Rache oder Rache durch Recht? Die Ahndung von Kriegsverbrechen in der internationalen wissenschaftlichen Debatte 1872–1945*, Ferdinand Schöning Verlag, Paderborn, 2010.

Daniel Marc Segesser, "'Integrale Rechtsgeschichte': Ein interdisziplinärer Einblick in die Forschung in der Schweiz", *traverse: Zeitschrift für Geschichte – Revue d'Histoire*, vol. 20, no. 1, 2013, pp. 103–121.

Daniel Marc Segesser, "Verrechtlichung des Krieges? Völkerrechtliche Konventionen und das Ius in Bello im Vorfeld und zu Beginn des Ersten Weltkrieges", in Jürgen Angelow and Johannes Grossmann (Eds.), *Wandel, Umbruch, Absturz: Perspektiven auf das Jahr 1914*, Frenz Steiner Verlag, Stuttgart, 2014, pp. 57–68.

Daniel Marc Segesser, "Humanitarian Intervention and the Issue of State Sovereignty in the Discourse of Legal Experts between the 1830s and the First World War", in Fabian Klose (Ed.), *The Emergence of Humanitarian Intervention: Ideas and Practice from the Nineteenth Century to the Present*, Cambridge University Press, Cambridge, 2016, pp. 56–72.

Daniel Marc Segesser, "Katastrophe der Wissenschaft?! Gewaltseskalation, Kriegsgräuel und Kriegsverbrechen als Instrumente der internationalen (Nicht-)Kooperation in der Rechtswissenschaft 1914–1919", *Zeitgeschichte*, vol. 45, no. 1, 2018, pp. 57–77.

Jean de Sennarclens, *Gustave Moynier: Le Bâtisseur*, Édition Slatkine, Geneva, 2000.

Immi Tallgren and Frédéric Mégret (Eds.), *The Dawn of a Discipline: International Criminal Justice and its Early Exponents*, forthcoming.

Heinrich Triepel, "Die neuesten Fortschritte auf dem Gebiete des Kriegsrechts", *Zeitschrift für Litteratur und Geschichte der Staatswissenschaft*, vol. 2, 1894, pp. 188–226 & pp. 289–303.

Thomas Vormbaum, "Zum Geleit", *Journal der Juristischen Zeitgeschichte: Zeitschrift für die Rechtsgeschichte des 19. bis 21. Jahrhunderts*, no. 1, 2007, p. 1.

17 The feminist origins of the Swedish Red Cross

Mats Deland

17.1 Introduction

During the first decades of the classical period, the second part of the 19th century, international law was created in close cooperation between states and social movements.[1] What was later to be known as the Red Cross movement was among the most important of these movements. The few men, that in the early 1860s, gathered in and around what was to become the Geneva-based International Committee of the Red Cross had a matchless influence on the shape of international humanitarian law. But there were women too. Florence Nightingale, almost a decade after her heroic episode in the Crimean war, was among the advisors to the British delegates for the first conference in 1863. Clara Barton, the hero from the North American Civil War, lobbied for the diplomatic conference in Brussels in 1874, whereas Amalie Fréderique Kattenbusch, the wife of Cristiaan Basting, in the small hours of a September night 1863 translated the unofficial appendix of the invitation to the Geneva conference that introduced its very core: the neutrality issue (written by her husband and Henry Dunant, but most probably with input also from her). In the first decades, it was also women who carried out the main part of the hands-on work of the Red Cross movement.[2] However, their role is little understood.

This chapter gives an overview of the developments that led to the formation of the Swedish branch of the Red Cross (or, as it was called at that time, "The voluntary society for the succour of wounded and sick on the battlefield") between the spring of 1864 and the summer of 1865. Over the years, a number of different theories have been presented as to who really was the founder of the Swedish Red Cross. In 1906, the secretary Axel Hultkrantz found the origins in a meeting between one of the members of the first board, the language teacher Carl Gustaf Pauli and Henry Dunant.[3] Pauli had met Dunant during a visit to his mother in Switzerland and in September 1864, he, 27 years at the time, talked to major general Edvard Ulrik Rudebeck (born 1803). Rudebeck

1 On the role of the social movements in this period, see Calhoun, 1993.
2 On the early history of the Red Cross movement, see Riesenberger, 1992; Moorehead, 1999.
3 Hultkrantz, 1945, pp. 11–14.

has confirmed this in a private memorandum probably written shortly before his death in 1898. After meeting Pauli, he had talked to his colleague, Johan August Hazelius, secretary of the Royal Martial Academy, who introduced him to the doctors Johan Magnus Lemchen and Carl Gustaf Grähs. There also exists a tape recording made in 1973, with Pauli's daughter Gunni Hermelin, who claims that Pauli first was excited by one of Dunant's lectures, before he received the assignment to bring the cause to Sweden.

Hultcrantz's version was questioned in 1965, in a book written for the centenary by the journalist Sten Söderberg. The origin of inspiration was still found in Switzerland, but rather through one of the delegates at the 1863 conference, Sven Eric Sköldberg.[4] He particularly pointed to a conflict that erupted in spring 1865, when Sköldberg backed up by Geneva secretary Gustave Moynier tried to convince the board to underline the international character of the organisation and particularly its independence from the state. This attempt was unsuccessful, and Sköldberg soon left the Red Cross.[5] That Pauli internally was considered as the main founder of the organisation and could thus be understood as a way to avoid mentioning this early, but serious conflict. Söderberg's version was followed by a text published at the university of Umeå by Olof Cronenberg in 1985 and a master thesis by Cecilia Österberg in 2001, both providing more empirical backing for this interpretation.[6]

However, there is also a third version, only mentioned by Cronenberg that emanated from Sigrid Leijonhufvud's biography about her aunt Sophie, a prominent early feminist, published in 1923. It was clear from this book that also Leijonhufvud and a friend of hers had met Rudebeck and Lemchen in September 1864 and had acted behind the scenes before the organisation was formally created.[7] However, in later interpretations, their role is downplayed as in best case inspirational. I will try to correct this.

In the following part of the chapter, I will give an overview over the Swedish relations to the international Red Cross, and the first generations of Swedish feminism. After that, I will explain how the founding of the Swedish Red Cross became part of feminist strategy before I proceed to investigate the limits that religious doctrine at the time put to feminist action. The rest of the paper will show how the feminists activists grappled with these difficulties in a way that made their contribution less well known than it would otherwise have been.

17.2 The inspiration from Geneva

Sweden was represented at the first Geneva conference, in October 1863, by two doctors, Sven Eric Sköldberg and Nils August Edling. Sköldberg had originally been sent out by the National Medical Board, and his visit in Geneva

4 Söderberg, 1965.
5 *Nordisk Familjebok*, 1890, p. 1391.
6 Cronenberg, 1985; Österberg, 2001.
7 Leijonhufvud, 1923, pp. 88–98.

was a departure from an inspection trip where he was studying the continental developments in military medicine. Edling was a young undergraduate military doctor on a scholarship trip to Vienna. By Government orders, he was redirected to Geneva to assist Sköldberg – with the research trip, not particularly the conference.[8]

When Sköldberg returned, his enthusiasm was caught up by a bureaucratic strife.[9] Instead, he tried to appeal to the general (middle-class liberal) public, by publishing a book that contained translated extracts both from Henry Dunant's book *A memory from Solferino* and from the conference minutes. The book also included updates particularly from the German side in the war raging between Denmark and a Prussian-Austrian coalition (February to October 1864), about the fate of the duchies in southern Jutland.[10] However, although well received, Sköldberg's book, which came out in early June 1864, failed to spur much interest.

17.3 The feminists

In 1859, two women in their mid-thirties (both born 1823) started the first feminist journal in Sweden, *Tidskrift för hemmet* (Journal for the Home). Rosalie Olivecrona, born Roos, lived in Uppsala, 70 kilometres north of Stockholm with her husband, the professor of Roman Law Knut Olivecrona and his four children from another marriage. Sophie Leijonhufvud, married Adlersparre in 1869 (and better known under that name), lived in Stockholm with her mother. They drew their mainly anglosaxon ideological inspiration from Olivecrona's long stay in the south of the United States in the mid-fifties, and a trip they had made together to the British Isles a couple of years later. They were both politically conservative and deeply religious, belonging to the theologically liberal strand of the Lutheran state church. Their journal was printed in Uppsala, but Leijonhufvud seems to have been the main editor. They have intentionally left a large collection of letters that lets us follow their editing work for several years.[11] Both authors were part of a fledgling feminist movement that tried to expand the fields of activity for women, and particularly women of the middle and upper classes that could be expected to afford getting an education advanced enough to keep them away from the labour market for some years.[12]

8 Two others, the military medical inspector Carl Gustaf Grähs and the Norwegian (Sweden was united with Norway until 1905) surgeon general Johan Fritzner Heiberg, had for different reasons cancelled their journeys but their greetings were read before the conference by Henry Dunant.

9 The conclusions from the Geneva conference were made part of general proposal to reform the military medical corps. Largely, Sköldberg's views were left without consideration in the decision process. There is scarcely any literature about this, but I will cover the issue in a forthcoming book.

10 Sköldberg, 1864.

11 On the letters, see Nordenstam, 2003.

12 Ambjörnsson, 1974, pp. 58–78.

In March 1863, Olivecrona presented the idea to write an article on the general state of medical care in Sweden.[13] She drew her inspiration from a booklet by a doctor, Gustaf Hjort, who presented an experiment with strict isolation of patients at the Sahlgrenska teaching hospital in Sweden's second city, Gothenburg. Hjort was the head of the midwifery department at the hospital and Bataillon doctor at the local artillery regiment. In his conclusion, he drew attention to the many nurses that had been sent by the US Sanitary Commission to the battlefields on the North American Civil War, and argued that a substantial enhancement of the schooling of nurses could both help improving the military medical preparations, and in the meanwhile provide the manpower needed to expand civilian hospital care along the indications that his study had given. He also suggested that education should be linked to the military organisation, meaning that those women that received the education, in return would enlist to serve as military attendants in war. The book was sold for the benefit of families affected by the war in Denmark.[14]

Olivecrona's initiative inspired Leijonhufvud to write an article of her own. There are interesting differences between the two articles. At first glance, it seems that Olivecrona's is the least radical of the two. She follows Hjort's book in connecting the need for reforms both in the military and the civilian medical organisations. However, the manuscript for the article still exists, and shows, together with the letters, that Olivecrona also had intended to have a substantial section requesting the acceptance of women into the education for medical doctors – that is, a university education – an issue that had been raised in the UK and the USA already in the 1850s. On Leijonhufvud's suggestion, she agreed to leave that part out of the article, and she would not take it up again until 1870.[15]

Leijonhufvud's article, on the other hand, drew its inspiration both from the ongoing war in Denmark and from the volunteer riflemen's movement (*skarpskytterörelsen*) that had quickly established itself in Sweden in the early 1860s. She explicitly mentioned both Sköldberg's book and the military reformer Peter Olof Liliewalch, who since the news from the Crimean war reached Sweden in 1854 had argued for radical reforms of military medicine.[16] In particular however, she argued for the formation of a medical corps of women, to tend not only for the wounded and sick of the regular army, if needed, but also for those of the new volunteer force. Who, she concluded, would be better placed to join such a corps than the relatives of the men who had already volunteered? Furthermore, why should, after all, women be any less patriotic than men? The conclusion, however, was the same in both articles: there was a demand for mass education of female medical attendants, desperately needed both in war and in peace.[17]

13 Rosie Olivecrona to Sophie Leijonhufvud ? March 1864, Olivecronska familjearkivet, Riksarkivet (Sweden's National Archives; forthwith RA).

14 Hjort, 1864.

15 Letter from Rosalie Olivecrona to Sophie Leijonhufvud 31 mars 1864, Olivecronska släktarkivet, RA.

16 Cf. Engberg and Liljevalch, 1854; Liljewalch, 1857.

17 Letter from Sophie Leijonhufvud to Rosalie Olivecrona without date, appr. 24–25 May 1864, Olivecronska släktarkivet, RA.

17.4 Evangelical feminism

The articles led to a conflict between the two editors about how the project should be presented. Olivecrona, who had come up with the idea, felt that she had been mimicked by Leijonhufvud.[18] Even worse, claiming editorial reasons, Leijonhufvud lifted her article out from their journal and chose instead to publish it in the liberal daily *Aftonbladet*, where it actually appeared just before Olivecrona's journal article.[19]

It might seem that this would be a small matter, considering that both women, keen about their anonymity, were publishing under several different aliases. They had no interest in launching themselves as authors. However, Olivecrona accused her co-editor not only of plagiarism but also of ambition and of a wish to put herself in the lead of the organisation that she wanted to launch.

To understand this kind of reasoning, we need to understand one of the basic conditions of mid-19th century feminism. At this point, there were still legal rules that were not only blocking women from full participation in society but also upholding a strong demarcation between the (male) public sphere and the (female) sphere of family and child rearing. This demarcation, however, did not only exist in institutions; it was also an important part of the mental constitution of the period. It is all too easy to forget that in those days most people were deeply religious.[20]

The Swedish historian Inger Hammar in her dissertation *Emancipation och religion* (1999), which deals with the work of among others Leijonhufvud/Adlersparre and Roos/Olivecrona, has argued that the frames of action that women had in this period must be looked upon in a religious context.[21] Religion in Sweden meant the works of Martin Luther, especially in their widely spread popular version in the so-called *Little book of Cathechism*. The gender contract proposed by Luther largely focused on the institution of marriage, as an arrangement both for joy and joint labour.[22] The woman belonged to *oeconomia*, the domestic order, whereas *ecclesia* and *politia*, church and government, belonged to the male sphere.[23] On the other hand, activity, to "earn our bread by the sweat of our brow," was a precondition for salvation and bliss – Luther had only contempt for both monastery contemplation and celibacy.[24] Considering the surplus of women in the 19th-century society, this meant that many women had to find work outside their families. Most of these women became house servants or factory workers, but for the social strata that Leijonhufvud and Olivecrona

18 Rosalie Olivecrona to Sophie Leijonhufvud 24 maj 1864, Olivecronska familjearkivet, RA.

19 Sophie Leijonhufvud to Rosalie Olivecrona without date, appr. 25–29 May 1864, Olivecronska familjearkivet, RA; "En fråga i menniskokärlekens namn. Till Redaktionen af Aftonbladet" (by S. L–d.), *Aftonbladet* 10 June 1864.

20 Haupt, 2008.

21 Hammar, 1999, pp. 67–78.

22 On the gender contract theory, see Hirdman, 2001.

23 Hammar, 1999, p. 24. Cf Westhelle, 2015, pp. 26–27.

24 Ibid, p. 85.

belonged to the situation was different. Women from the small middle class needed education to take up more advanced jobs.[25] These changes had to be made acceptable to Lutheran theology. The simplest solution was philanthropy, which didn't demand much education and could be defined as an expansion of *oeconomia*.[26] But Lutheran theology also strongly believed that humans had a responsibility to develop their talents, according to the often cited tale of the Lost Minas (Luke 19:16–27).[27] This could and would be interpreted as that all humans should have the chance to get an education.

Both editors made a tactical choice to avoid promoting doctor's education (i.e., permission for university studies for women) to be able to argue for medical attendant's education at the hospitals. They were convinced that doctor's education was the long-term goal and therefore Olivecrona had had to back down a bit.[28] They could have decided otherwise; it was a question of tactics, of making the right call. In this way, there was a modicum of flexibility built into liberal, Lutheran theology that could lend itself to different interpretations.

But there was also another, interrelated level, which was: who could argue for this kind of changes? For women in this period, there were basically two ways to influence society. One alternative was the exceptional way – in times of emergency also women could take the initiative. But when there was no emergency, things were different. Since the Red Cross issue was a basically military (and medical) concern, it was also male territory. That is, Gustaf Hjort, or for that matter, Sven Eric Sköldberg, could argue for such a reform, a woman could not, according to a strict interpretation of gender relations of the time. In normal times, and with the exception of issues that belonged to the private sphere (such as children or aesthetic issues), women only had recourse to the public sphere in an indirect way. That is, they could rear responsible boys, or, but with caution, support their male spouses or family members – or other men – in their activities in the public sphere.[29] But they had to stay out of sight.

17.5 Staying out of sight

We have already seen from Olivecrona's reaction that the general idea was that Leijonhufvud should not officially take the lead in forming the organisation they both wanted to see. Instead, she started a campaign to convince someone else to do that on her behalf:

> Exhorted from a number of directions, since these issues, following *Dunant*'s celebrated work and the congress in Geneva, during the winter have been *uppermost in everyone's mind*, I have steadfastly given a negative

25 Ibid, p. 25.
26 Ibid, p. 38.
27 Ibid, p. 85.
28 Cf. Hammar, 1999, pp. 82, 114.
29 Hammar, 1999, p. 98.

answer, and I would only with difficulty have let myself be talked into playing the role of interpreter in the service of the beautiful idea. I thought I had mentioned all this for you. I have also tried to convey to them, who have turned to me in this regard, my own conviction that the initiative for such an organisation should be taken not by a more or less unknown woman with limited influence, but by a man of public repute and the ability to make his views known. I have all the time kept for myself a role as passive as possible, explaining, truthfully, that I have already taken on more trouble for the public good than time and energy and my duties at home permit me in the way that I wish.[30]

It seems that, at first they thought that the articles that they had written anonymously would have that effect, that is, to convince some men to take action.[31] In July 1864, Leijonhufvud met Hjort in Gothenburg, and received his appreciation for her mentioning his book in the article. To her disappointment, though, he declined her suggestion that he should be the one taking the lead for the founding of the new organisation, and obviously, he also was not the first to turn her down:

> However, it seems to be with him as with the Stockholm doctors, that everybody wants the axe to swing, but nobody wants to hold the handle.[32]

Instead, she turned to a doctor she knew better. Johan Magnus Lemchen had been her acquaintance since a number of years back. He had visited her in her home two years earlier, when he asked her to use the journal for a petition for a school for children with impaired hearing, later known as the "Silent School" (*Tysta skolan*, opened in 1866 and named so after a suggestion from the author Fredrika Bremer). In other words, she had favours to claim. In September 1864, as mentioned, Lemchen was invited together with general Rudebeck to a meeting in Leijonhufvud's apartment. Olivecrona was also present.[33] This is when the two women's initiative was transferred to men.

The results of the diplomatic conference in Geneva were also published in the Swedish papers in September 1864, and at the occasion of the definitive peace treaty between Denmark and the Prussian-Austrian alliance in October, the Swedish doctors who had been active during the conflict talked about their experiences at a meeting with the Association of Swedish Doctors (***Svenska läkaresällskapet***). Professor Carl Gustaf Santesson, Head Surgeon at the Serafimer Hospital in Stockholm, who had served at the Danish war hospital at Augustenborg castle,

30 Sophie Leijonhufvud to Rosalie Olivecrona, without date, appr. 24–29 May 1864, Olivecronska familjearkivet, RA. English in italics in original.

31 Sophie Leijonhufvud to Rosalie Olivecrona without date, appr. 24–25 May 1864, Olivecronska familjearkivet, RA.

32 Sophie Leijonhufvud to Rosalie Olivecrona (from Marstrand, summer residence) 23 July 1864, Olivecronska familjearkivet, RA.

33 Leijonhufvud, 1923, p. 93.

gave witness about the great services done by female Danish and Swedish medical attendants (sent by the welfare departments of the respective state churches). Different from the male attendants, that had been taken from the military reserve, the women had been motivated and well educated.[34]

In the end of November 1864, Lemchen reported that it was time to start advertising in papers for women with an interest for the education that they were going to offer.[35] On 5 December 1864, a group of men gathered in the home of Rudebeck on Riddargatan in central Stockholm. This was the first official (i.e., with minutes) meeting of the Swedish Red Cross. Officially, this has also been considered as the foundational meeting of the Swedish Red Cross.[36]

Leijonhufvud does not seem to have been directly involved in convening this first meeting of the interim executive committee – she was informed a couple of days later – but she supported the meeting with a long article in the next issue of the journal. The article had been discussed with the interim executive committee members before it was written (in great haste). It gave Leijonhufvud an occasion to further underline what had been her major interest all the time.[37]

Leijonhufvud's article was much more than just the advertising discussed with Lemchen in November. It contained some strange masquerading, where she talked about herself in third person, even as a "he," when she went through the differences in opinion that had crystallised around the organisation issue during the past year.[38] She also conceded that the issue had caused a difference of opinion within the journal's editing staff. At the same time, she signed the article with her most well-known signature Esselde, which was practically the same at the one she had used in *Aftonbladet*, six months earlier (S. L-d, which of course was short for her real name). However, the ideological position was now spelled out more clearly. First, she argued, against Sköldberg (and the Geneva Committee), that the organisation must be restricted only to Sweden.[39] Secondly, she underlined the connection to the voluntary defence movement.[40] She still lamented about the lack of "a forceful personality." Instead, she hoped that enough women would follow the call she did by sending notes of interest to the journal under the label "L. R.," which Cecilia Österberg helpfully has interpreted as likely to mean Lemchen and Rudebeck.[41] Although "the initiative should be taken by men," she argued, "the women however

34 "En fråga i menniskokärlekens namn. Till Redaktionen af Aftonbladet" (by S. L–d.), *Aftonbladet* 10 June 1864.

35 Sophie Leijonhufvud to Rosalie Olivecrona 29 November 1864, Olivecronska familjearkivet, RA.

36 See the official history in Söderberg, 1965, pp. 57–59.

37 Sophie Leijonhufvud to Rosalie Olivecrona 28 December 1864, Olivecronska familjearkivet, RA.

38 "Sjukvårds-föreningens första sammanträde d. 24 maj 1865", *Tidskrift för Hemmet* No 3, 1865, p. 324.

39 Ibid, pp. 332–333.

40 Ibid, p. 333.

41 Österberg, 2001, pp. 48–64.

should not refrain from contributing, from the beginning, as *participants*." It was also obvious that she believed that this view was shared by the men who now had started the work.[42]

17.6 The existential dimension

In spite of the sympathies she received from the executive committee, however, the article was obviously written under some duress, visible in her letters:

> Only my *conviction of what is right and my sense of duty to work for this*, could conquer my inherent chicken-heartedness. Mum can testify that I was half sick out of fear, when the general's visit was announced the day after.[43]

This tone of writing conforms to a pattern often found in the letters of this age. Researchers have discussed whether what we see in these letters is real anxiety or just a stylistic manier.[44] Leijonhufvud's – and Olivecrona's – descriptions of the anxiety, or *Angst*, that they felt during politically active periods are nevertheless so concrete (lack of sleep, somatic symptoms, chronic fatigue) that I would argue that (in most cases) they describe actual fear. I would also argue that this fear relates to the limitations set by Lutheran theology concerning the place that women were to occupy in the governing of society. These issues were further emphasised a couple of years later, in a conflict that led to the decisive breakup between the two editors. The discussion was brought on by the different positions that they took to (rather than in) the debate about the pending change from an estate to a chamber parliament in 1865–1866. Under the direction of Leijonhufvud, the journal took a position that was clearly for the change. Olivecrona, who was against, protested not so much about this, but against that the journal by doing this was meddling into spheres of the polity that, she maintained, did not belong to women, that is, that could not be linked to the domestic sphere. As Olivecrona saw it, this was unnatural (meaning against the intention of the Creator):

> A manly woman, and this is what the woman will turn into, who wants to interfere with the activities that belong to men, who sees herself as capable to assess the great social issues and entitled to give her view about them, will in all times be an abnormity, just as unnatural, just as exposed to ridicule as a female man. The instinct, if not also the discretion, tells most of us, that both are deviations within their species. My own reaction to this is to shrink from the contact with external impulses, with public life, and when I nonetheless felt the urge to, although only insignificantly, play a rôle in it, I have

42 "Sjukvårds-föreningens första sammanträde d. 24 maj 1865", *Tidskrift för Hemmet* 3, 1865, p. 336.

43 Sophie Leijonhufvud to Rosalie Olivecrona, 19 juni 1865, Olivecronska familjearkivet, RA.

44 For example, Ulvros, 2010, pp. 13–14; Meyer Spacks, 1988.

> always had to force myself and I have also, as soon as I have had the chance to, retired to the home, the property of the woman, the sacred pond, where she finds refuge from the storms of external life.

If we believe that this should be understood more or less literally, and that this general view, at least up to this point, was shared also by Leijonhufvud, this explains the ambiguity and masquerade-like anonymity that characterised how the journal handled their activities before the formation of the Red Cross branch. The ideological limitations became fears because they were existential. In this particular Lutheran shape, they were, on the other hand, also linked to a strong ethical duty which meant that the ascribed role could be breached on particular occasions ("times of rebellion, of foreign invasion"), but as she formulated it, reproaching Leijonhufvud, "which noble woman would wish for such times only to get an opportunity to distinguish herself?"[45] Normally, female influence should be indistinguishable:

> It is exactly in the woman's work in concealment, in the calm, indistinguished home life, that the secret of her influence lies, while on the other hand it [the influence] only looses by being trumpeted with great, ringing words and phrases.[46]

17.7 Correcting the gender imbalance

Already at one of the preparatory meetings, on 27 January 1865, the board decided that the organisation should also be open for women.[47] Education of female attendants was discussed on the following meeting. This and the fact that a formal cooperation with the journal was introduced with the decision that Dr Grähs would be responsible for spreading the articles that had been published on the subject in *Tidskrift för Hemmet* in wider circles suggest that Leijonhufvud was continuously influencing in the background. Lemchen also proposed that she would be assigned to contact Florence Nightingale, to send some women to be educated at one of the London hospitals.[48] However, neither of these events are commented on in the letters between Leijonhufvud and Olivecrona.

The Swedish Red Cross Branch had its constitutional meeting on 24th May 1865. The report in *Dagens Nyheter* emphasised the strong female attendance.[49] *Tidskrift för Hemmet* had published a short article about the upcoming meeting in its spring issue and both editors were present.[50] The meeting conceded that educating medical attendants should be its main task in peacetime, it confirmed

45 Rosalie Olivecrona to Sophie Leijonhufvud 4 January 1866, Olivecronska familjearkivet, RA.

46 Rosalie Olivecrona to Sophie Leijonhufvud 4 January 1866, Olivecronska familjearkivet, RA.

47 Red Cross (forthwith RK) Minutes 27 January 1865, §4 #2, RA.

48 RK Minutes 24 March 1865, §4, #6.

49 RK Minutes Annual meeting 24 May 1865. *Dagens Nyheter* 26 May 1865. Original italics.

50 "Föreningen för frivillig vård af sårade och sjuke i fält", *Tidskrift för Hemmet* No. 3 1865. The article was signed L-d, that is, Leijonhufvud.

the decisions to turn to Florence Nightingale and also send out a letter to the Swedish county hospitals to investigate the possibility to educate female attendants also in Sweden.[51] But on one, decisive, count the executive committee had discarded the view taken by Leijonhufvud and Olivecrona: it had kept for itself the discretion of who should be given support and permission for the education (in particular the so-called proof of good repute (*vandelsintyg*)).[52] At this point, it was finally necessary for the two editors to make way for women's direct participation in the board, "as in their territory leading, directing, educating." Direct intervention now was possible since the question was limited to something definitely belonging to *oeconomia* (women's repute). Leijonhufvud proposed that the board should appoint a committee, consisting of as many women as men, for the process of choosing among the applicants.[53]

The exchange of letters shows that Leijonhufvud's reaction was no secret for the members of the board. The description that she gives in a letter to Olivecrona was much more outspoken than the one she had published: "this total neglect of the woman's share of the work, except what concerns '*the drudgery*', that indeed was put on her shoulders."[54] After speaking to Lemchen, she had sent a draft of her article to Rudebeck before it was published.[55] When the article was published a couple of weeks later she could, in a footnote, explain that a committee of the form that Leijonhufvud had asked for had already been appointed by the executive committee.

17.8 Conclusion: how to appreciate women on their own terms

As demonstrated in this paper, the contribution of Leijonhufvud and Olivecrona, and thus, post-Bremer Swedish feminism, in the formation of the Swedish Red Cross has so far not been understood. There is no reason to downplay the influence of Sven Eric Sköldberg, who brought the results of the Geneva conference of 1863 to the Swedish public sphere and the military bureaucracy. There is also no reason to forget general Rudebeck, whose actual main contribution was to recruit the crown prince Oscar as the first chair, and of doctor Lemchen, or even young Pauli. However, the project started as a feminist enterprise, before any of these men had taken the first steps in the organisational work. The feminists also influenced and supported the project during the whole initial effort, and they made sure that the end result would have the design purpose that they had anticipated the whole time. Many persons participated, but if in the end we should

51 RK Minutes 27 January 1865, RA.

52 "Sjukvårds-föreningens första sammanträde d. 24 maj 1865", *Tidskrift för Hemmet* 3, 1865, p. 213.

53 "Sjukvårds-föreningens första sammanträde d. 24 maj 1865", *Tidskrift för Hemmet* 3, 1865, pp. 213–4. Emphasis in original.

54 Sophie Leijonhufvud to Rosalie Olivecrona 19 juni 1865, Olivecronska familjearkivet, RA.

55 Sophie Leijonhufvud to Rosalie Olivecrona 7 juni 1865, Olivecronska familjearkivet, RA.

talk about the most important founders of the Swedish Red Cross branch, it should be Leijonhufvud and Olivecrona.

We have also seen that the reason why neither the organisation's own historians nor subsequent critical historians have understood their part in the event is that they had on purpose hidden from public eye. They did not want to be seen (or for that matter, remembered). We can add to this that history is still often written out of an unconsciously male perspective that does not take into account the complexities of the public sphere.[56] Let's remember this when we investigate the history of international law.

References

Ronny Ambjörnsson, *Samhällsmodern, Ellen Keys kvinnouppfattning till och med 1896*, Institutionen för idé- och lärdomshistoria, Göteborgs universitet, Gothenburg, 1974.

Craig Calhoun, "'New Social Movements' of the Early Nineteenth Century", *Social Science History*, vol. 17, no. 3, 1993, pp. 385–427.

Olof Cronenberg, *Röda korset 1863–1915*, Institutionen för idéhistoria, Umeå universitet, Umeå, 1985.

Erland Gabriel Engberg and Peter Olof Liljewalch, *Upplysningar om sjukligheten inom en armée på fältfot, med särskildt afseende på behofvet af läkare för svenska arméen och dess beväring*, P. A. Norstedt & söner, Stockholm, 1854.

Inger Hammar, *Emancipation och religion, Den svenska kvinnorörelsens pionjärer i debatt om kvinnans kallelse ca 1860–1900*, Carlsson, Stockholm, 1999.

Heinz-Gerhard Haupt, "Religion and nation in Europe in the 19th century: Some comparative notes", *Estudos Avançados*, vol. 22, no. 62, 2008, pp. 77–94.

Yvonne Hirdman, *Genus- om det stabilas föränderliga former*, Liber, Stockholm, 2001.

Gustaf Hjort, *Sjukvården i Krig och Fred, Uppmaning och Uppmuntran till Sveriges Qvinnor att bidraga till dess fullkomnande. Föredrag hållet vid nedläggandet af Ordförandeskapet i Göteborgs Vetenskaps- och Vitterhets-Samhälle d. 24 Jan. 1864 af Professor G. Hjort*, Bonnier, Göteborg, 1864.

Axel Hultkrantz, *Under Prins Carls ledning, Minnesanteckningar från fyra decennier i Röda Korsets överstyrelse*, Iduns tryckeri Esselte, Stockholm, 1945.

Sigrid Leijonhufvud, *Sophie Adlersparre (Esselde), Ett liv och en livsgärning I*, Norstedts, Stockholm, 1923.

Peter Olof Liljewalch, *Krigshistoriska intyg om behofvet af läkarvård för svenska arméen: högloft. Stats-utskottet vördsamt meddelade*, P. A Norstedt, Stockholm, 1857.

Caroline Moorehead, *Dunant's Dream: War, Switzerland and the History of the Red Cross*, Carroll & Graf Pub., New York, 1999.

Anna Nordenstam, "'Min älskade vän!' Sophie Adlersparres och Rosalies Olivecronas brevväxling", in Paulina Helgeson and Anna Nordenstam (Eds.), *Brevkonst*, Brutus Östlings bokförlag/Symposion, Stockholm/Stehag, 2003.

Nordisk Familjebok Konversationslexikon och realencyklopedi (1st ed.), Bd 14, Expeditionen av Nordisk familjebok, Gernandts boktryckeri-aktiebolag, Stockholm, 1890.

Cecilia Österberg, *Den internationella humanitära rättens introduktion i Sverige, Ett stycke rödakorshistoria*, Juridiska institutionen, Stockholm, 2001.

56 Hammar, 1999, passim. Cf Hirdman, 198, passim; Smitley, 2009.

Dieter Riesenberger, *Das Internationale Rote Kreuz 1863–1977. Für Humanität in Krieg und Frieden*, Sammlung Van den Hoeck, Göttingen, 1992.

Sven Eric Sköldberg, *Sårades vård I fält: Den internationella konferensen i Genève oktober 1863 och dess resultater*, L. J. Hierta, Stockholm, 1864.

Megan Smitley, *The Feminine Public Sphere. Middle-Class Women and Civic Life in Scotland, c. 1870–1914*, Manchester University Press, Manchester, 2009.

Sten Söderberg, *Svenska röda korset 1865–1965 – de första 100 åren*, AB Svensk Litteratur, Stockholm, 1965.

Patricia Meyer Spacks, "Female Rethorics", in Shari Benstock (Ed.), *The Private Self, Theory and Practice of Women's Autobiographical Writings*, University of North Carolina Press, Chapel Hill and London, 1988.

Eva Helen Ulvros, *I skuggan av män – kvinnliga röster i Tegnérs tid*, Tegnérsamfundet, Lund, 2010.

Vítor Westhelle, "Planet Luther, Challenges and Promises for a Lutheran Global Identity", in Carl-Henric Grenholm and Gören Gunner (Eds.), *Lutheran Identity and Political Theology*, Pickwick publications, Eugene, 2015.

Index

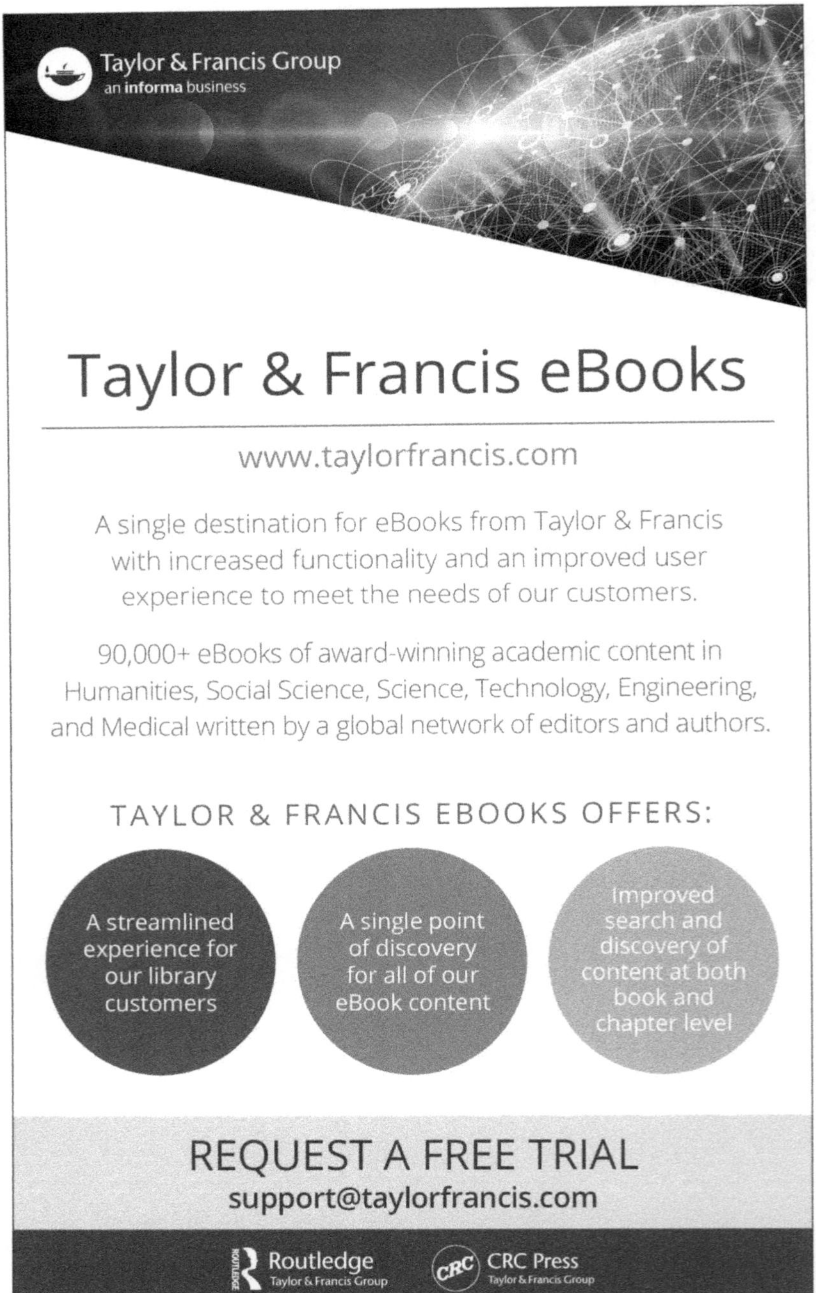

Taylor & Francis Group
an informa business
Taylor & Francis eBooks
www.taylorfrancis.com
A single destination for eBooks from Taylor & Francis with increased functionality and an improved user experience to meet the needs of our customers.
90,000+ eBooks of award-winning academic content in Humanities, Social Science, Science, Technology, Engineering, and Medical written by a global network of editors and authors.
TAYLOR & FRANCIS EBOOKS OFFERS:
A streamlined experience for our library customers
A single point of discovery for all of our eBook content
Improved search and discovery of content at both book and chapter level
REQUEST A FREE TRIAL
support@taylorfrancis.com
Routledge
Taylor & Francis Group
CRC Press
Taylor & Francis Group

For Product Safety Concerns and Information please contact our EU
representative GPSR@taylorandfrancis.com
Taylor & Francis Verlag GmbH, Kaufingerstraße 24, 80331 München, Germany

www.ingramcontent.com/pod-product-compliance
Ingram Content Group UK Ltd.
Pitfield, Milton Keynes, MK11 3LW, UK
UKHW022132190926
475702UK00013B/1761
9780367498566